BIBB

Management control systems

the proceedings

of a symposium

held at

System Development

Corporation,

Santa Monica,

California,

July 29-31, 1959

MANAGEMENT CONTROL SYSTEMS

edited by:

DONALD G. MALCOLM

*Operations Research Incorporated,
formerly with System
Development Corporation*

and

ALAN J. ROWE

System Development Corporation

general editor:

LORIMER F. McCONNELL

System Development Corporation

John Wiley & Sons, Inc.

New York · London

SECOND PRINTING, APRIL, 1961

Library of Congress Catalog Card Number: 60-14714

Printed in the United States of America

*F*oreword

To an ever-increasing degree, the executive is being pushed further
and further away from the actual job of managing the enterprise. The
major impelling forces have been the continuing increase in the size of
the business unit, the geographical decentralization of operations, the
combination of businesses through mergers and acquisitions, the development of multiple product lines with varying managerial requirements,
and an increasing specialization sired by competition and the push for
enhanced business effectiveness.

As an outgrowth of these business trends, the executive is often-
times faced with a complex organizational structure which promises
continually to become even more proliferated. Partially as a result of
this, the executive has to contend with extended communication lines
that lack clear transmitting abilities, with maximum delegation neces-
sities which invert the leadership of the enterprise, and with new and
unfamiliar functions which challenge his composure and incite frustra-
tions. There is small doubt that the managerial requirements of modern business have mounted almost geometrically with the increasing
complexity and specialization of the enterprise.

The executive thus finds increasingly that he is being removed from
a firsthand and intimate knowledge of the business and therefore is remote from information on which to base his decisions. To compensate,
he surrounds himself with added staff functions and interposes additional layers of management. He usually finds this a moderately

v

successful move but one with diminishing returns. Thus, he seeks a permanent answer to his problem by another means.

The lasting answer can only be in improved management methods and processes. Within this context, management may mean several things, but its basic constituent is control. Controls, as we have known them in the past, fail to meet fully the challenge of modern business complexity and size. A strong creative effort must thus ensue to yield modern business controls.

The required attributes of such controls may be envisioned as follows. Modern controls should be so constituted as to be passive when operations are within expectations but instantly active to signal the exception. A major accent is the "immediate signal," for lags spawn historical data unsuited to the dynamics present in today's business world. Modern controls should also be automated and largely automatic, for present-day management can tolerate neither the numbers of people nor their inherent limitations to administer controls if business is to be run with economy and effectiveness. Finally, controls should be simple enough to permit uniform interpretation of results; else an undirected diversity of effort will prevail. These, then, are the basic characteristics that must be creatively blended to form modern control systems.

The development of such systems presents a challenge of great importance and it seems especially timely and valuable to gather within the confines of this volume the thinking of intelligent management representatives on the pervading problem of improved controls. To the serious minded, forward-thinking executive this book will be required reading—it is an important contribution to improved management in the vital area of effective controls.

C. Wilson Randle
Partner
Booz, Allen & Hamilton

Preface

A symposium on Management Information and Control Systems held at the System Development Corporation in Santa Monica, California, on July 29-31, 1959, was called to explore the present state of the art, likely future developments, and the need for research in the field. This book includes the papers which were presented at that meeting and a summary of the discussions that were conducted.

A word of explanation as to System Development Corporation's interest in this area is in order. System Development Corporation is a non-profit corporation chartered to "receive and administer funds and property exclusively for scientific, educational and charitable purposes for the public welfare and security of the United States of America." Under this charter SDC has engaged in developing computerized control systems for the military.

The proper relationship of the management function and electronic computers is of vital concern in this work. In the designing and computer programming of large-scale control systems, a fundamental requirement is to obtain the best match of the human being and the control function. At System Development Corporation this task has been undertaken with the tools of systems analysis. Human factors specialists develop the most appropriate man-machine relationships; data-processing experts develop computer programs; and operations research and management specialists aid in the analysis and optimization of the systems. The approach SDC has taken in SAGE (Semi-

Automatic Ground Environment) and the other large-scale computer-based military control systems under development appears to be useful in solving management information and control problems. This appears to be especially true in the area of management controls. To explore this idea further, a symposium was planned to bring together a group of leading experts in the business and government management world—people who have had actual experience in management—to discuss a major problem of our times: the evolution of appropriate management controls in this electronic age. In exploring the various current approaches to management controls, our hope was to develop and generalize the structuring of effective control concepts.

There is a distinct opportunity for innovation in management controls—an opportunity to make a quantum jump in the field to a total integrated system. This is in distinct contrast to evolutionary change, i.e., succesive automation of the components of the business. The task of designing the management controls of a total system is a task heretofore untackled and one of tremendous scope. Recognizing this, System Development Corporation decided to explore the possibility of developing an example of such a total system by creating a research project dedicated to the public interest. As part of this research, a necessary first task has been to develop a good appraisal of the state of the art of management controls. Consequently, the articles in the book are directed to the following topics: present philosophy and practices in management and management controls, new approaches being undertaken, and a discussion of research in the area of management control systems design.

In the first section, concepts of management control and present practices in both business and the military departments are examined. Here, selected papers are organized to show the current management thinking that has led to the control philosophy extant in these areas. Some of the problems and the proper perspective required in developing management controls are explored.

In the second section, the impact of computers on the design of management controls is discussed. A brief discussion of some of the current computer applications highlights the need for improved systematic and effective control approaches. The impact of computers on an organization is also explored.

The third section presents examples of automated management controls, illustrating the approach and the kind of results achieved in well-thought-out and advanced programs in business.

The fourth section is concerned with new approaches, touching on the future possibilities in management control and information systems. In this section, the concept of "real-time control" as practiced in military command control systems is explored for its utility and guidance in the business management control system area. A prediction of the next step in management controls, as well as some of the implications of computer programming research and the treatment of human factors involved, is also included.

In the last section, the need for research in management control system design is discussed, and the program that is under way at the System Development Corporation is briefly described.

The papers in this book thus provide a basis for exploring the problems of total management controls properly interwoven with the concepts of modern business management and organizational theory. Effective utilization of information for the orderly and timely control of a purposeful organization is a problem of tremendous complexity, one whose surface is but scratched in the articles presented herein. Although the challenge is great, the rewards are commensurate to the successful.

We want to take this opportunity to express our gratitude for the fine contributions to the Symposium made by all of the participants, who are listed on page xi.

Also, we want to offer our thanks to Lorimer F. McConnell for his general editing and compiling of the manuscript for this book, to Ruth Keane for her unfailing assistance in producing the final manuscript, to John K. Herzog and his staff for their excellent help in arranging for the Symposium, to Eleanor Sisson for her cheerful assistance to visiting participants, and to William A. Johnston for his assistance in arranging press interviews.

Finally, we wish to thank the following guests of the Symposium: C. A. Alders, Assistant for Special Projects, SDC; R. C. Hopkins, member, Research Directorate, SDC; J. R. Goldstein, Vice President of the RAND Corporation (and Chairman of the Executive Committee of the SDC Board of Trustees); William Karush, Head, Center for System Science, Research Directorate, SDC; Thomas C. Rowan, Head, Special Development Department, SDC; and Ellis Scott, member, Information Processing Directorate, SDC.

Donald G. Malcolm
Alan J. Rowe

Santa Monica, California
August, 1960

List of participants in the symposium

xi

James D. Gallagher — Assistant Director, Systems Planning, Lockheed Aircraft Corporation, Burbank, California

Robert H. Gregory — Manager, Planning and Market Development, Data Systems Operations, Sylvania Electronic Systems, a division of Sylvania Electric Products, Inc., Needham, Massachusetts

Irving Kessler — Manager, Management Engineering, Defense Electronic Products, Radio Corporation of America, Camden, New Jersey

John F. Lubin — Assistant Professor of Industry, Wharton School of Finance and Commerce, University of Pennsylvania, Philadelphia, Pennsylvania

Alan O. Mann — Commercial Coordinator, Government and Industrial Division, Philco Corporation, Philadelphia, Pennsylvania

Gordon O. Pehrson — Director of Planning and Control Office, Special Products Office, Department of the Navy, Washington, D.C.

Alex W. Rathe — Professor of Management, School of Engineering, New York University, New York, New York

Norman Ream — Director, Systems Planning, Lockheed Aircraft Corporation, Burbank, California

Andrew Schultz, Jr. — Professor and Head of Department of Industrial and Engineering Administration, Cornell University, Ithaca, New York

Charles K. Simon — Technical Specialist, Polaris Development, Engineering Division, Aerojet-General Corporation, a subsidiary of the General Tire and Rubber Company, Solid Rocket Plant, Sacramento, California

Roger L. Sisson — Manager, Systems Department, Operations Central Project, Aeronutronic, a division of the Ford Motor Company, Newport Beach, California

R. Clay Sprowls — Associate Professor of Business Statistics, School of Business Administration, University of California, Los Angeles, California

SYSTEM DEVELOPMENT CORPORATION SPEAKERS AND PARTICIPANTS

M. O. Kappler — President

William C. Biel — Vice President

W. W. Parsons — Vice President

Donald G. Malcolm — Director, Operations and Management Research Directorate

Milton G. Holmen   Head, System Training Operations Department

Robert Bosak   Assistant Director for Techniques, Data Processing Directorate

Alan J. Rowe   Manager, Business Management Control Systems Research Project, Operations and Management Research Directorate

Joel M. Kibbee   Staff Member, Operations and Management Research Directorate

Contents

THE OPPORTUNITY
FOR INNOVATION IN
MANAGEMENT CONTROLS

SECTION *I*

*T*he opportunity for *innovation in management controls*

CHAPTER **A** by M. O. KAPPLER

In the application of computers to management control systems there is a real opportunity to make a big step forward in the next few years. A quick look at the history of data processing for business and management will help to show how significant a step forward it will be.

The early uses of record keeping machinery and simpler forms of data-processing equipment were in connection with accounting activities. These initial efforts were directed toward mechanization of jobs that had previously been done by manual methods. Although such activities as payroll preparation are fairly complicated, data-processing equipment was introduced simply to mechanize those accounting processes. New data-processing equipment then moved step by step into summary accounting records and similar areas. These advancements presented management with summaries of actions that had previously been taken, but these displays were still essentially the traditional accounting-type displays. The next step was the use of electronic data-processing machines for control purposes. An illustration is what was done at the Home Laundry Department of the General Electric Company at Louisville, Kentucky. They established in the factory headquarters the automatic transmission of data from outlying distributors and warehouses. On the basis of information which told the conditions existing one day, the next day's manufacturing of appliances was determined. This was a big step forward—this was actual management control in business, and this control was recurrent. The

3

process happened day after day, and the system solved essentially the same problem but reacted to different input information each day.

COMMAND CONTROL SYSTEMS IN THE MILITARY

While progress has been made with the use of data-processing equipment in business management control, the military has also been trying to achieve control, but in a different manner. They embarked on a project to establish an integrated command control system. And recently there have been rapid advances in the technology of "live" command (or management) control systems—probably more rapid than in any other technology. At present, the Air Force is considering the implementation of at least twenty-five or thirty control systems. Several of these will cost up to 100 million dollars to implement. All of these systems are based on large, high-speed computers, on automatic input of information, and on automatic displays and automatic communication of control action as outputs. All are world-wide in scale. This is a tremendous effort, and the understanding of these systems and how to implement them has grown explosively in the last few years.

The SAGE (Semi-Automatic Ground Environment) Air Defense System was the forerunner of all of the military control systems. Next came the SAC (Strategic Air Command) Control System, which is designed to provide information about SAC, and to control action to send it on its way. There are at least two types of military intelligence systems now under development that "control" only in the sense that they gather information, process it, and suggest new avenues for exploitation. Then there are two other typical control systems. One of these is intended for Headquarters North American Air Defense Command and the other for Headquarters USAF. Both of these will be based on very large computers and on world-wide communication systems with automatic data inputs.

All of these command control systems have the property of being recurrent in their operation. As a matter of fact, they will complete a cycle within a minute, perhaps in fifteen seconds or less. These systems are "on-line" in the sense that they are connected to and operate on automatic data inputs. They are also on-line in the sense that they affect the operation while it is in process, and do not simply collect historical information, tabulate it, and present it for someone to cogitate about for possible influence on future operations. They exert their influence before the operation is complete. The numerous functions to be performed require time sharing of computers. This last may not be a necessary property, but is common to all the command systems mentioned above.

Some of the functions that are performed in these systems are straightforward tabulations for the commander, informing him of the number of aircraft he has, and the number on alert status. There is no sophisticated mathematical analysis made; items are simply summed up and displayed. But these displays are updated during the operation, and this requires considerable computer capacity and sophistication.

Three Levels of Control Automation

A major class of operations performed by a control system is illustrated by the aircraft tracking operation in SAGE. Data automatically flow into and are processed by the computer. This results only in a display. The tracking crew doesn't necessarily take action, and no control action is taken automatically as a result of the tracking function itself. It is an "open loop" activity.

A variant of the tracking-type activity, and one which is a little more sophisticated, is the identification function in air defense. Here the tracking display is matched with known flight-plans (airplane pilots' predictions of where they would be) to distinguish a particular radar track from others and decide whether it is "known" (friendly) or "unknown" (possibly hostile). This is an example of a "semi-open loop" control.

There is a further variation of the tracking function that might be called "closed loop." This function controls the interceptor weapons in the air defense system. Radar information is processed in the same way as it is in any tracking operation; however, it is not displayed only for monitor action, but it is also used in a logical and mathematical operation in the machine to compute the desirable position of the interceptor aircraft at some later time. This information, when coupled with tracking data about the path of the target aircraft, is used to determine an optimum intersection point for the two tracks. On the basis of this computation, orders are issued to the interceptor aircraft to bring it to the previously calculated intersection point. (In terms of classical servo theory, this is a typical closed servo system; and, it has to have all of the properties of a stable servo system.) This is the most sophisticated control element in SAGE.

Command Control (or Top Management) System Pyramid

One way of thinking about the command control system is to consider it as a many-sided pyramid. This pyramid has sides that all

come up to a point at the top, and command (or management) is located at this top. On each facet, there is a control activity taking place;
there might even be a completely automated control loop on each
facet of the pyramid. Current military systems have automated each
facet to the greatest extent possible. Some control functions cannot
presently be formulated mathematically and some require human
judgment. People make decisions and put information based on their
decisions back into the computer, which either closes the command
loop or forwards the open ended type of information up toward the
command at the top. These decision makers on the facets are not the
command people themselves, but are people who are working in the
system as "mechanisms" because real decision-making mechanisms
cannot now be designed to perform certain functions. However, these
people need the same matching with the machine as do the people at
the top of the pyramid, who receive the displays and make the final
decisions. From a man-machine standpoint, some of the jobs that
they have to do may be extremely difficult. In the design of displays
for these jobs, the decisions as to just where to put the man and
how to present information to him may also be very difficult.

The Use of Simulation

In designing command control systems, simulation is a valuable
tool. At SDC we think of simulation as the simulated environment
with which we can surround a control system for test or training
purposes. A model of the control system is designed as we think it
will operate. Mechanized elements are provided where possible and
people are used in positions where it is not possible to mechanize.
Simulated input materials are then produced and made to flow in the
regular data channels. We examine the match between the people and
the system inputs and outputs. This, also, allows us to be sure that
the operation looks reasonable to experts who may have done the job
manually.

Simulation is used for three purposes at SDC. We use it for system design by bringing in experts to operate in the positions and to
give us their reactions to the adequacy of the operations. We also
use simulation for training. Finally, we use simulation to demonstrate feasibility. To enlarge on this last point: a new system is not
always readily acceptable to the people who operate within it because
they lack confidence in it. They can't immediately see and understand
the mathematical formulation that underlies the operation. And, before
the system is acceptable to them, they need to work with it and gain
some confidence by seeing it yield the proper results. As more
sophisticated systems are developed, this problem of acceptance will

become more difficult to overcome. When such systems go operational, neither the managers nor the people who are in the system as
linkages will be able to follow and confirm mentally the complex system calculation and logic which will have been formalized and ration-
alized in the design stage. An example from SDC's field experience
may serve to illustrate this point. The early version of SAGE fighter
control was not quite as completely automated as it is now. The
fighter interceptor controllers gave voice commands to the fighter
pilots on the basis of computer processed information that was displayed to the controllers on their consoles. These controllers had all
had experience in directing fighter interception from the radar control position on the ground. When they first sat down at the SAGE consoles they didn't believe the mathematics that were involved. They
had a great tendency to do as they had done before—estimate interception by eye and then override the computer. They gradually began
to discover that the mathematics, which weren't at all obvious, really
did work and they finally accepted the system. Now they are enthusiastic about it.

APPLICATION OF MILITARY EXPERIENCE TO BUSINESS

Some work that has been done in the management controls field in
industry is probably more advanced than that done in some specialized areas of the military control systems that are in use or under
development. On the other hand, those of us who have had experience
in developing integrated military control systems, have a knowledge
that does not exist anywhere in the business field. Now, these considerations have formed the basis of a proposed research project at
SDC. We want to attempt to capitalize on what has been learned from
the military systems and to call on others for advice on the work that
has been done in the business management control field. The over-all
technology of the military command control system is advanced beyond that of other management control systems. However, the opportunity exists to catch up. We want to explore the status of various
classes of control systems and work out what we think are the possibilities for combining them into an integrated control system for
business management

DISCUSSION   (Following Mr. Kappler's presentation of his paper)

H. F. DICKIE: You spoke of military control systems as being more
advanced than those of business. This may be true in certain respects,
such as the automaticity of controlling an aircraft. However, in terms

of complexity of information or the comprehensiveness of activities, they may not be more advanced than those in business.

M. O. KAPPLER: Referring to my analogy of the pyramid, I believe that less has been done in the business world toward putting the various facets of control together into an integrated control system. While there is considerable sophistication in business in many of the sides of the pyramid, less has been done in integrating the sides for top management control.

H. F. DICKIE: Do you find that military security restriction "hold up" information? It is my understanding that SAGE and related projects were secret, and that we could not expect to know about them for many years.

M. O. KAPPLER: Technical information concerning military systems can usually be released if specific military applications are not revealed. Now, we could not turn aside any amount of our military effort in order to communicate technical developments to the non-military. But, one of our objectives would be to effect an educational bridge between the military and the non-military.

R. L. SISSON: Would you say a few words about the long-range objective of the SDC research project? What do you hope to accomplish in the next ten years?

M. O. KAPPLER: First, we'd like to learn how to establish a management control system that would be as integrated and as automated as we can make it. To start out we will use rapid simulation on a computer and study these questions. Then, we'll need actual information about live industrial organizations to test some of their hypotheses about the controls. Next, we should concentrate on the interactions between these facets—for example, how inventory problems interact with capital control.

J. D. GALLAGHER: Rather than attempting to apply the military systems experience, maybe research on business systems should start at a much lower level. We might start by determining what factors affect the conduct of the business in a way to make decisions on the interactions.

M. O. KAPPLER: This basic research needs to be done both in business and in military systems.

A. R. BROWN: You gave an example of the problems of man-machine interaction and interceptor control. This problem still exists. Even though the computer does the right thing, the operator who doesn't understand the computer doesn't trust it. Instead of letting the computer do it's job, he is inclined to second-guess it. There appears to be a tremendous education problem here.

M. O. KAPPLER: It is in this area that our simulation training has had tremendous payoffs. One of the benefits of using simulated inputs is that you can design these all in the beginning. For example, in the case of SAGE you design all aspects of an attack. After the exercise is run, you know precisely what happened. You can then call the attention of the crew to the action that they took, and if they took an inappropriate action they will recognize it. It's this ability to give them knowledge about what they did in response to a simulated situation that strengthens their confidence.

Many people have said that because many military operations are sort of mechanical the problems are easier to formulate, that military systems do not have imponderables such as in business. Actually some of the most difficult command decisions have to be made on the basis of imponderables. In developing military systems we have learned to provide aids for decision making. The problems in business should be amenable to a similar approach.

M. G. HOLMEN: There's another aspect to the control problem. In military research and development, a lot of money can be spent to achieve only a little more performance. But the economics of industry are not "insurance" economics—they are "operating" economics. It is necessary to demonstrate that industry can do better and justify the amount of money it will cost to do it the new way.

A. RATHE: What has been proposed here sounds like a real research project in the sense of trying to find something new. It seems not merely a development project but an investigation that goes beyond what exits currently in people's minds.

R. L. SISSON: I'd like to say the same thing a different way. Assuming a reasonable level of intelligence in the research group, they will undoubtedly think of, stimulate, test, and publish a lot of ideas.

I. KESSLER: The suggestion that we should look for solution in future problems, in the integration of data, and also the timeliness of data for management decisions, seems to hold real promise. We should recognize that the computer is a tool and the output from the computer must be in a form to be used in a timely fashion by qualified men.

The problem in managerial decision making today is that adequate data upon which to base decisions is not always available when needed. A computer can be helpful in making all the data available with the purpose of aiding the executive in making a decision, and not for the purpose of making the decision for him.

M. O. KAPPLER: This approach has been used in SAGE. When tracking information flows to an operator, he still has to do the identification. Not everything can be automated; rather, for most business
activities the computer would be of assistance. In some instances this
involves both the data collection and the controls. It seems to depend
entirely on how well you describe the activity to obtain a mathematical solution. In certain cases, it's just a yes-no decision; in others
a very sophisticated optimization is required. In still other cases we
don't have any idea how to tackle the problem. The computer provides
the decision maker the kind of aid which permits him to adequately
design the business.

J. D. GALLAGHER: The emphasis in industry has been to use the
computer for data processing rather than for providing information
required to make meaningful decisions. Perhaps increased emphasis
should be on the use of data-processing equipment to demonstrate the
ability to provide timely information which is not merely a duplication of the system that we previously had.

J. R. GOLDSTEIN: There is a similarity in these discussions to ones
held at RAND when the study was initiated. We were confronted with
the problem of reducing the areas of uncertainty in military decisions.
Rather than use military judgment solely, we would provide data that
could be useful along with military judgment. In this way, the chances
were that better decisions could be made. This approach has been
difficult to sell; however, for many general problems, we have been
successful in aiding the military.

J. E. FLANAGAN: I have a general question on the organization at
SDC for research on management control. Could you say a few words
about the size of the group and the backgrounds and the general structuring of the organization as it exists today?

M. O. KAPPLER: In our Operations and Management Research Directorate we are doing research on mathematical technology that may
apply to all of our contracts. We also have our own self-sponsored
research funds and one of the directorates leads research of that kind.
The Management Control System Research, which we are talking about
here, is being led by our Research Directorate. Alan Rowe is in
charge of that particular project. We presently have a very small
number of people since we have been doing a preliminary investigation of where this project might go. However, if it seems to all of us
that this is really a worthwhile project, we could put in the order of
a million dollars over a period of a good many years. All of us are
personally very enthusiastic.

THE CONCEPTS OF
MANAGEMENT CONTROL–
PRESENT PRACTICE

SECTION **II**

*P*roper perspectives in developing management controls

CHAPTER **A** by WARREN E. ALBERTS

The term, "control" in management control systems is easy to use but hard to define. It has unfortunate reactions when transferred too literally from physical to human systems. A better term to use would be "information" in place of "control" so that we can concern ourselves in a positive fashion with the total communication interchange within a business organization.

[handwritten margin note: not control but information or Service]

Attitudes and concepts concerning control systems in business life are usually based on an individual's past experience in staff or line roles, plus the philosophy and size of the business organization to which he has been exposed. In some cases the growth of specialized staffs has led to control philosophies which are designed to perpetuate and enhance the staff's position rather than to serve the line organization.

This raises the question as to whether or not controls born of this philosophy may not be limiting in reaching goals of increased productivity and lower costs. We might also ask whether control systems developed in the past twenty years have been really geared to realization of the company's total potential or merely designed for making good on individual production, sales, and budget goals.

Measurement is the crux of control, but are we not frequently faced with situations where most of the elements of present-day control systems are based on ease of measurement rather than need? In this respect, it seems that in many areas, management is just beginning to realize that little is known concerning what is measurable,

13

what is controllable, and what information is needed to make the kind of decisions that will help shape and influence the future rather than to follow statistical projections of the past.

ENABLING VERSUS RESTRICTIVE APPROACHES

The foregoing observations can well lead to some rather basic questions about management information and control systems. For example:

• Are our present control systems based on a restrictive philosophy which assures adherence to an agreed upon plan?

• Or are they based on an enabling philosophy which provides the organization with the tools to meet and exceed the plan?

What are some of the basic differences between restrictive and enabling approaches in designing management control systems? The restrictive approach (the easiest to take) sets specific standards and goals for every group in the system with adherence assuring attainment of the plan. Under this concept, large deviations in quality, cost, or performance, whether they be up or down, are not well received. In addition, getting groups back on the track takes precedence over analysis of why some groups are doing better than others. Nevertheless, restrictive control systems have become so well developed today that they threaten to filter out the natural flow of information up and across the line which top management and the organization is dependent on; customers' needs are ignored (not according to plan); good ideas are discarded at too low a level (our budget won't permit it); and, interests become narrow and departmentalized.

Contrast this to an enabling approach which seeks to provide managers and workers with the tools and information which permit them to understand and audit their role in an organization—an approach that is more concerned with the answer to the question "How well are we doing compared with what we could do?" than with the answer to "What is our deviation from plan?"

ORGANIZATION IMPLICATIONS

It is my belief that control or information systems cannot be considered separately from the organizational environment and philosophy within which they are supposed to operate. All business organizations are in one sense, communication systems. Too often the greatest emphasis has been placed on the division of responsibilities and authorities rather than the flow of information and ideas.

The research on information and control systems which is now just gaining impetus is going to have quite an impact on company organizations. This is based on the simple fact that when the formal and informal communication systems within a company are plotted and the interaction between certain groups and their decisions understood, basic changes in the organization may well result. And it should be noted that such basic changes would apply not simply to the data or information processing groups, but to all parts of organizations to recognize the role of distribution, planning, management research, material control, and other functions. In the past, divisions such as sales, engineering, manufacturing, and accounting have served well; however, it is now important to recognize the need for relating those critical functions which are common to all departments. One of the most costly elements in any company today is the time lag which exists in its management information and control systems. In fact, many so-called controls are in reality crutches used in place of appropriate data which would permit scheduling and planning ahead.

Most employees, including managers, are often concerned about departmental curtains and the apparent lack of coordination which exists between functions who supposedly are working together. In fact, everyone below the president in most companies has a specialized responsibility or objective with the result that probably only the president sees the company as a whole.

Persons studying current management information and control systems may find some answers to the above problem. One can hardly expect a broad viewpoint from a manager—whether he be in production, sales, or engineering—when cost and performance controls are primarily designed to measure departmental efficiency rather than any impact the department's actions may have on enabling the whole company or other departments to achieve over-all objectives. When a company sends a man away for training, his mind and viewpoint are stretched to a new dimension and he comes back with a broader outlook. In making his first decisions, he may well ask himself: ''What will be the consequences of my decisions on Joe's department? Certainly the company will understand that even though I may have to go over my budget, it will reduce costs in Bill's area.'' Well, it's a sad but too often true story that, because there is no informational means for measuring the interaction between company functions, the comptroller and Bill are not at all enthusiastic about having him upset their production or budget goals. In fact, it takes an unusual man not to revert right back to playing the game according to the old rules.

DESIGNING TOOLS FOR MANAGEMENT

A management information or control system must be able to cope with poor as well as good situations in the company's economic condition. The system must also recognize, if the managers do, how far ahead the various levels of management should be looking. The ability to gather and process tremendous amounts of data or information must not hide the real need for organizing, analyzing, and translating information into a form which will be meaningful and helpful to the user in making decisions. Unfortunately, there appears to be far too much emphasis being placed on the rapid gathering and processing of information rather than the development of analytical and evaluative tools which can translate this data into a readily usable form. The designers of tools for management are sorely needed, and they must think in terms of combining quality, service, cost and other factors as the basis for decision making. These tools may range from complex simulations to a simple nomograph or chart.

The integration and display of information is an area which requires a lot of work. Means can be found to excite rather than deaden human responses. Information should be depersonalized so as to eliminate the fear and reduce the human bias when serious problems must be brought up and discussed.

THE NEW AWARENESS

There are several things which managers are becoming aware of and they relate directly to management information and control systems. To illustrate, we might compare a business to a missile. We can think of the thrust section as the operating organization, the programmed section as the plan to hit the target or goal, and the nose section as the control system. But now we run into some real differences. First, management is not sitting in any bombproof control station, but is riding with the missile; second, the thrust section, a man-machine organization, is extremely variable and dynamic. In addition, the real target is never seen, only sensed, and its position only guessed at. To further complicate matters, each missile team knows that other teams are competing in the same area. As a result, here are some factors that managements are just becoming aware of:

- They have very little knowledge of the inherent variation, potential, or interaction of the functions which make up their organization. Their traditional controls in the accounting, cost, and performance areas are still dealing in terms of historical average and treating the organization as a multitude of unrelated compartments.

- The target is moving and the control systems and plans must be flexible enough to acknowledge this and capitalize on the dynamic nature and potential of the thrust section.

- Management information and control systems thread through the entire company and must be identified, studied, and improved from an over-all company viewpoint. They represent the organization's total communication and nervous system.

- Means must be found to evaluate and test new policies, courses, and ideas. Our work since 1954 in developing management tools and models to simulate various phases of our operation and planning processes have convinced us that management can rightfully expect a corporate laboratory in which it can evaluate and compare ideas and better assess the risks and consequences in making decisions.

One doesn't abruptly change the course of a 10,000 man, 150 million dollars a year business without evaluating the consequences any more than would one who fires a 10 million dollar missile. This does not imply that managements generally make abrupt changes. The comparison, however, points out the need for providing management with the means to better evaluate the results of alternative courses of action.

Managements that have become aware of the above four points are immediately faced with the problem of what to do about it in their company. It would seem that the first step is to bring together either a task force or, on an organizational basis, the many specialists and technicians who are working on fragments of the problem in different areas of the company. They must be led by a generalist, a man who can see the company as a whole and who understands the system approach, one who is not awed by the language or apparent complexity of mathematical, social, or technical skills and who can differentiate between management tools, techniques, system concepts, and organizational philosophies.

UNITED AIR LINES' APPROACH

Mr. W. A. Patterson, our President, recognized the above need in 1940 and at that time set up a Work Analysis Group that could take an over-all view of the company and continually search for better ways of doing things. This group subsequently became a part of an Economic Controls Administration which was set up to provide a central research, planning, and control function serving the entire company. It reports to the President and is on an equal footing with the operating administrations but has no principal operating functions.

Today, the Economic Controls Administration consists of two head-quarter departments: Business Research and Industrial Engineering. Two field groups which represent these functions serve our operating base at Denver and our maintenance and engineering base in San Francisco. The Business Research Department includes an Economic and Market Forecasting Division, which seeks to measure and fore-cast consumer needs; an Airplane Schedules Division, which coordi-nates a company-wide plan of meeting them; and a Budget Division, which helps the company coordinate its economic life. The Industrial Engineering Department has an Organization Planning Division, which helps management find ways to meet the company's changing needs and realize the potential of its individual human resources, an Opera-tions Research Division, which seeks a better understanding and measurement of how we operate plus the development of new manage-ment tools; a Work Analysis Division, which develops and maintains manpower controls, quality and service level controls, and facility and equipment planning approaches and standards. Here is an example where we have drawn together those functions which we do not feel can be separated in real life. Job demands, manpower, quality, facil-ities, and equipment all interact in any work situation. Project lead-ers who are skilled in the systems approach and can head up a study group which may cut across all company lines are available. A Regulations and Forms Division provides a uniform communications medium for the company plus systems and procedures skills.

The philosophy of the entire administration is one of service to the president and the company. It keeps only those planning and con-trol functions which require an over-all view. The remaining func-tions, when developed, are turned over to the group best able to use and operate them. Much of our work is on a request and consulting-type basis with the volume of our project backlog representing the best criteria of acceptance and results. Many staff groups proclaim a service attitude and support the premise that their authority is the authority of ideas but in practice most of their time is spent on sell-ing pet ideas versus trying to understand just what the individual manager on the line needs.

A good example of the objective viewpoint which this type of serv-ice organization can bring to a company is illustrated in the develop-ment of the recently announced electronic reservations system. Instead of seeking to justify or apply existing hardware to the mod-ernization of our 12 million dollar reservations system, we managed to get an effort started which sought to step back and analyze the whole system, isolate the basic problems, and project requirements ten to fifteen years into the future. As a result of this "system approach," we developed a <u>functional specification</u> which when translated into a technical one (based on the state of the art) enabled us to obtain in open competition a real time information system. This electronic system will not only solve our speed and accuracy problems but make a substantial contribution to profits and increased productivity. It consists of a nation-wide communication system using low intelligence buffers and switching centers, to connect over seven hundred agent-operated sets throughout the country with two transistorized computers in Denver. Inquiries and transactions will be handled in seconds with a print-out to audit each transaction.

It was during the course of this work that we recognized the importance of information communication systems and their flow problems apart from any computer or data processor. Also, the fact that computers, large and small, plus input-output devices, could be tied into such a system like organizational blocks. This is in opposition to the theory that since we have giant computers, company information and control systems plus their organization counterparts must be centralized.

COMPUTERS AND CONTROL SYSTEMS

There appears to be a common fallacy of thinking that computers and information and control systems are synonymous; this kind of thinking can be dangerous. Probably the most significant advances in management information and control systems will be made by a study of them as such. The computer may help to analyze or simulate them and be used as a part of the system but only in the same way that any other tool or machine takes over part of a system when it can do the job faster, more accurately, or more economically.

This leads us to an important principle, that of first determining the functional requirements of a management information or control system in a given company before going all out on machine applications. No matter how theoretical or revolutionary a system concept may be, it still must be constructed and understood by a human designer and fit the human organization it is to serve. This is independent of whether a final analysis shows the ultimate application and operation to be manual, man-machine, or completely computerized.

If the computer is considered an extension to mental skills in the same way that machines extended physical skills, a better perspective of its ultimate role will result. Forecasts that computers will assume decision-making roles simply means that our definition of what constitutes decision making must be refined. The concept of one over-all business model appears to be a bit of blue sky at this point, but in my opinion there is no reason why we cannot focus our attention on developing models which can at some later date interact directly with one another. For example, we have our station model, which represents a primary part of our operation. On the other hand, we have models which simulate the flow of people at our airport terminals, the flow of information through our reservations system, and the flow of aircraft engines through our Maintenance Base.

A BLUEPRINT FOR MANAGEMENT SYSTEM DEVELOPMENT *

We are at a point in our work where it seems like many things are falling into place. Figure II-A-1 represents a blueprint or plan of what we consider a typical information system to look like. You will notice first of all a basic data-processing communications system with the traffic controlled automatically by what might be called data-control centers. These directly service input-output devices, which in our case may be in the flight dispatch offices, reservations offices, overhaul shops, storerooms, etc.

The basic processing of data would be done by a central information processor; however, we do and are recognizing the need for specialized processors which may or may not tie into the system. For example, our flight planning computer which will compute the best flight plan for our jets to fly is such a computer. Since the bulk of the central information processors' capacities will be tied up in real-time operation, it will have to spin off basic data which then can be processed and analyzed in the regular data-processing and analysis group. This is the area where most of the computer applications to date have been made and primarily involves recording or accounting functions.

On the other side, however, is what may be called the "corporate laboratory" which contains a staff and the models which are used to test and plan over-all company operations. For example, there may be a corporate finance model, a production model, a distribution system model, and in many cases, some of these models, when once developed, will become real-time operation devices for planners or schedulers in a particular department and should be given to them as a management tool. Tied in with this corporate laboratory is the staff

---

*Reprinted by the permission of the editors and publishers from Management Organization and the Computer, edited by George P. Schultz and Thomas H. Whisler, The Free Press, Glencoe, Illinois, 1960, copyright by the Graduate School of Business of the University of Chicago.

Blueprint of a Typical Information System

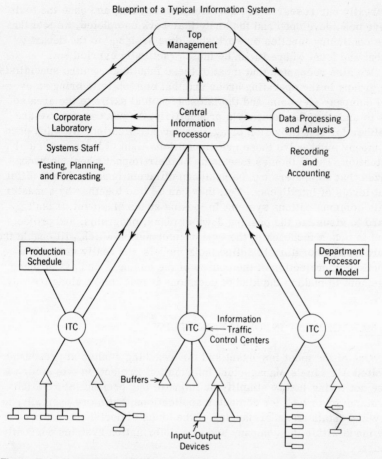

Figure II-A-1. (Reprinted by the permission of the editors and publishers from Management Organization and the Computer, edited by George P. Schultz and Thomas H. Whisler, The Free Press, Glencoe, Illinois, 1960, copyright by the Graduate School of Business of the University of Chicago.)

which is capable of analyzing company-wide system problems and developing concepts or models if necessary so that they can be better understood, necessary process changes made, or new concepts or policies evolved.

We in United feel that we are already a long way towards filling in this blueprint. First, the staff functions of work measurement, systems engineering, quality control, operations research, data processing, and organization planning are all integrated under one head and free to serve the entire company. This staff, it must be remembered,

is really our research and development function, and once the tools
have been developed and the analytical work completed, we feel that
the continuing function or work should be assigned to the department and level where it can be most practically carried out.

We also recognize that most of these functions require specialists
in groups in the operating areas and that our job is to bring an over-
all company viewpoint and the latest technical skills to the area so
as to maintain the company's productivity. As you can see, we are
neither for centralization or against decentralization. We think each
company must solve these questions in the light of their particular
situation. These themes lose some of their impact when one recog-
nizes that computers can be assigned different tasks and have different levels of intelligence. Yet, they can be tied together by a master
data communications system. In looking at the blueprint, it isn't
hard to visualize the passing down of plans, programs, and projects
and in turn a feedback of the type of information which will enable the
corporate laboratory to refine their models and really maintain a
continuing projection of the course of the business and assist management in making the kind of decisions it must make along the way.

A MANAGEMENT INFORMATION STUDY

One of the most important and far-reaching studies at present is
United Air Line's Management Information Project. In this study we
are not trying just to simplify or improve our present information
systems or to look for computer applications, but more basically, to
try and obtain an understanding of the kinds of decisions that need to
be made within the company and what information systems currently
exist.

Since this project will require a great deal of effort, it may well
be asked: What is the basis for management's approval and what we
expect to get out of it? Here are some of the specific reasons drawn
from our work during the past five years:

- Many of our information systems are based on government, legal,
  and financial requirements. They do not adequately serve planning
  or operating needs at various management levels.

- Time lags within and between information systems cause or contribute to company problems and can be costly.

- Managers are often handicapped rather than helped by existing
  reporting and control systems. The interaction and relationship
  between different decisions is not brought out.

- The company needs a blueprint or plan to guide it in applying to best advantage the benefits of "information technology."

These reasons are hardly peculiar to one company or industry; they exist in all, generally differing only in degree and intensity. It is simply an area that has never been adequately studied and needs research badly, especially since so many of the problems are common to all organizations.

We are mindful of the study's magnitude and aren't banking on spectacular results, but we do hope to gain some understanding of the company's needs, the direction we should take, and where effort is required. The project itself, however, has been set up with some rather specific goals so that no one will lose sight of the ultimate targets. The goals are as follows:

- A firm understanding of the company's internal requirements for management decision and control information.

- A detailed understanding of the present information flow systems and of their interaction.

- Specifications for the development of analytical tools with which to evaluate alternatives, performance, and decisions.

- Detailed recommendations for improved information flow systems.

- A blueprint for integrating the technical advances in data communication and computer techniques into the data gathering, processing, and evaluation systems of the company.

We believe this study is going to give all of us in United Air Lines a better understanding of just how our company operates and how our information and control systems can be improved. We expect that many problem areas common to all companies and industries will be found. These we hope will receive the kind of research and attention they deserve.

SUMMARY

Every management, whether it realizes it or not, is engaged in an economic struggle and is seeking winning combinations. To my way of thinking, there are no easy solutions, but perhaps an answer may be found in trying to better understand and utilize the untapped resources that exist within each human organization. Worthwhile research can be undertaken to study and understand the interaction between key elements in a business organization and the basic information control principles which must be met to bring about the desired interaction and meet the enterprise's objective. This means that managements must somehow balance their expenditures in developing better physical products with research into the processes and systems by which they produce these products and manage and control their enterprise.

DISCUSSION   (Following Mr. Alberts' presentation of his paper)

D. G. MALCOLM: You have brought an entirely new dimension to our discussion. The concept that an organization design itself is a management control dimension that we haven't yet faced up to. The concept of a functionally organized company will have an impact on our present thinking of organization structure. It poses the question as to whether or not it is possible to do laboratory research on organization.

W. E. ALBERTS: I think one of the problems today is that research in the management field is being done apart from where management is managing. I do not think that the kind of management or operations research that needs to be done today can be done from without; it needs to be done from within. This does not mean that valuable insights cannot be obtained by working with basic structures and simulating their behavior. It does mean that the data should be drawn from real life.

N. J. REAM: I was happy to hear the point that computers are not necessarily going to solve the problem. I feel very strongly that the computer is only a tool and must be used properly. If I might draw an analogy it is like an automobile. To someone who knows how to drive, it is a very useful vehicle; but to somebody who doesn't know how to drive, it is probably the most destructive device in human hands. In the same way, I think that too often we try to apply computers, or people like to talk about their application, and really don't know how to apply them.

A. W. RATHE: I would like to say that United Air Lines is one of the three pioneers in this whole field of managerial planning and control, and there isn't anyone who has worked in this area who has not indirectly or directly learned from them. Some of the work done at United has been to deliberately use a different approach than others. But the result, after twenty years, is the same. That is a perfectly delightful thing, because if you are exploring the same territory, using different approaches, and you come up with the same conclusion, I think that bolsters the conclusion.

D. G. MALCOLM: Is it your contention then that you can shorten the route?

A. W. RATHE: Yes, but not necessarily with a computer.

D. G. MALCOLM: Is there anything we can generalize from United Air Lines' experience? Are we agreed now that this is the type of organization that one should move toward?

A. W. RATHE: I don't know that you can draw that conclusion concerning the organization. However, here is the first agreement I have heard as to what management, fundamentally, involves.

W. E. ALBERTS: I don't think there is any one right way, because I feel that the philosophy of organization control, no matter what the best way, is always going to be a reflection of the man in the top job.

R. L. SISSON: Your conclusion that the research on management controls should be done within a company disturbs me a little bit. I would hope that there would be a group doing some theoretical work and that somebody like yourself could do the engineering work. In part, our difficulty in doing it now is the lack of a suitable theory.

W. E. ALBERTS: I said that research should not be apart from an organization. Now this does not mean that a group such as SDC working in science and theory should not work in this area. My suggestion was that if they probe into companies they should chose a channel which knows the inside of a company.

R. L. SISSON: It keeps occurring to me that most of the advances in other sciences are made by people who are quite far removed from the physical experiments.

W. E. ALBERTS: I am not saying that organizational research or systems logic or control philosophy cannot be developed in a closed room which might revolutionize the whole. I am not saying that organizational theories or control philosophies cannot be developed in a closed room. I am saying that when you start translating results for use, they are going to have to be translated into and tested in real-life situations.

A. SCHULTZ: I think that is a very important clarification.

C. K. SIMON: How far can a research group advance before they must go to the one or more—or any number of corporations—to create realistic problem areas, in order to evaluate what they have done? Without practical corporate application won't they lose themselves in a cloud nine operation?

R. L. SISSON: I have a very strong suspicion that you can work for about ten years in that research and come up with many good ideas, and still not be ready to go out and implement them, because as soon as you get one idea, you have five better ones that you want to continue to work on. At the end of seven to ten years you will come up with something that is so revolutionary you will say: "Now I have to go out and test it." I think there hasn't been enough of this kind of research.

M. O. KAPPLER: I believe it is possible to operate in the science link without looking at some specific company problems or at a group of companies. This is undoubtedly a difficult problem to solve.

W. E. ALBERTS: I agree with this conclusion. We can proceed by looking inside our own company, and when we run across what we think has general import and are areas of research which are common to many companies, we can feed this to a more theoretical group. However, I still don't see why you must wait seven years for the one best idea when you have had fifty good ones in between. I think, too, industry has a responsibility to provide more than just a problem dictated in half a day and sent off in a letter. I think we have an obligation, if we are interested professionally in this area, to work and spend one or two man years to come up with something worthwhile. We should go as far as we think we can in identifying the basic problems which we do not have the skills to tackle.

W. R. FAIR: We have twenty-five people here and, I would say, among them ten industrial organizations represented. I am sure there are many other organizations who have people who would be in a position to make an excellent contribution to this area but simply don't know about it. Now, this doesn't mean that the person or company who goes along with the research effort does not get some benefit. They're going to; it is inevitable that they will get some personal and proprietary benefit. But if the stage is set in advance and there is a clear-cut admission that there is going to be some proprietary advantage, it would seem that fairness is insured.

C. K. SIMON: What we are really discussing is a communications problem. If these communications are mostly incoming rather than outgoing it might solve the problem. Suppose that most of the input is not just from United Air Lines but from a cross section of industry and that you control the output of information. Maybe this would solve the problem.

W. E. ALBERTS: I think the biggest step has been taken by SDC in recognizing an important field, and then in gathering together people who have some practical appreciation of what makes business tick, but who also have theoretical skills and abilities. If industry acts as an advisory council, recommending significant problems to work on, you will find there is enough to be shared by all.

Management controls in business

CHAPTER **B** by ALEX W. RATHE

INTRODUCTION

A Brief Glimpse at the Laboratory of History

Control has been the problem of the world since its population grew from one to two. Perhaps the oldest record of managerial activity dealt with what is still a key control problem, the accounting for funds. It was a set of clay tablets, estimated to be now some 4500 years old; it recorded the coins collected by the Egyptian ruler of that day.

Some 1500 years later, a papyrus recounts how the first known strike in history, during the construction of the pyramids, was brought under control. At the same time, the Constitution of Chow, the foundation of the Chinese realm for centuries, was drawn up to include a provision for audits.

The first fundamental contribution which remained basically unchanged in the 2500 years which have since passed was the attempt to control governmental operations in Athens by dividing them into the Ecclesia and Boule—line and staff as we know it today.

Another great addition to the management scene followed a similar trend of organizational control through the establishment of decentralization as the mode of operation in Rome. Started in the Greek city states, this principle was developed in the Republic of Rome to an effectiveness as yet unequalled anywhere. It enabled the Eternal City to control the largest Empire the world has ever seen as it included all of the globe then known.

28

A different attack on the problem of control was made during the Middle Ages by the invention (or resurrection) of the idea of monopoly. The German guilds and indeed many other organizations used this principle to keep themselves in power for a long time; it gave way only when a more fundamental idea proved itself once again. This was one of the supreme laws of nature, namely the recognition that man can not control his fellow men indefinitely against their desires.

Yet like other attempts at control which history has shown time and again to be brittle, monopoly continues as a phenomenon today in many parts of the world where it still operates effectively—to the temporary advantage of at least one group.

Control and Management

Management reflects society, of which it is an integral part. For thousands of years, management has developed in tune with civilization, with which it is creeping along on a cruelly slow trek.

On its way it has been the witness of much misery from war and oppression. From the days of the ancient realms on the banks of the Nile to more recent centuries, anywhere on the five continents, it can relate but a handful of inspiring sights: the birth of religion and the beginnings of democracy.

As any wanderer who lives off the land he traverses, management has absorbed much of what it passed through. Today it reflects the horrors of the years which it saw come and go as well as the benefits which they produced. It is this heritage of ancient and medieval cruelty to individuals which is retarding our advancement in the twentieth century.

It is thus not surprising that today's business operations are not as far removed from the climate of olden years as the time which has elapsed appears to propose. History saw five centuries go by after the Magna Carta was proclaimed before the truth became self-evident that men are endowed with certain inalienable rights. Not quite two hundred years have passed since our forebears pledged to the support of this philosophy their lives, their fortune, and their sacred honor. Yet the ideal of government by the people is but partially achieved in 1959.

Only at the turn of this century did the wave of human evolution begin to lap at that fortress of grim impersonal power: business. This was the time when some of the very characteristics of democratic living which have contributed so much to the development of our national existence were introduced into business.

At first, business, too, defied the human soul to find satisfaction within the range of its chimneys' soot. How could we expect, in such an atmosphere, ready acceptance of the managerial counterparts of our philosophy that governments derive their just powers from the consent of the governed?

Was it not folly to hope for immediate realization of such legacies, which to comprehend takes a longer span than is given each of us in our lifetime? To accomplish this demands the concerted power of all of us. But this runs counter to the image of control which history has handed down.

While these pages deal with business, the observations made here with regard to the control of commercial and industrial activity apply in their fundamentals to other organizations as well. In government and agriculture, in hospitals and schools, in the home and indeed all other human endeavor, precisely parallel roads are being traveled. In the past few years, progressive business has possibly taken the lead, at least by its recognition that the problem of control is not only at the root of success but at the base of many failures as well.

Similarly changes in control—its locus, its scope, even its philosophy—are perhaps more typical traits in the forward march of business in our generation than any other element of management.

Consequently, control is one of the thorniest problems of management today. It is worthy of even more careful examination. To thoughtful study should be submitted not only the full tool kit of control practices but the underlying theory as well.

THE SIGNIFICANCE OF CONTROL

What Is "Control"?

The term "control" appears often in key functions of business. We speak of:

- Production control.

- Quality control.

- Budgetary control.

- Safety control.

- Labor control.

- Inventory control.

Then there are, outside the business world:

- Currency control.

- Traffic control.

- Pest control.

- Arms control.

- Land control.

- Heat control.

- Government control.

- Rent control.

- Birth control.

- And many others.

When a politician controls votes, he exercises influence. When we control our temper, we suppress something. The airport control tower gives the pilot landing instructions. A control valve regulates temperature. A control experiment provides comparison data. A pitcher has control of the ball if he can land it where he and the catcher want it to go.

Norbert Wiener defined control as the "sending of messages which effectively change the behavior of the recipient." Recent hearings concerning the fixing of TV quiz programs provided this novel yet interesting definition: "Control is the conscious matching of contestants who are informed in the same categories of knowledge."

"Control" has just too many and too different meanings. Figure II-B-1 reproduces a random sampling of the connotations attached to the word.

In the majority of these meanings, control has the connotation of domination; it conjures up the picture of penalties. This so thoroughly negative approach is at the bottom of so many failures of control. Why think, as a matter of everyday occurrence, of the need for domineering—for tyranny—for retribution?

Attached to every one of these is the memory of bygone days which we wish we could erase from the pages of history. Tied to every one of them is the record of enslavement and ultimate rebellion. Each sets forth the proposition that only the one who controls is competent and reliable, that all others—the vast majority!—do not qualify for such trust.

People have realized for centuries that slavery is immoral. We are learning just now that it is also uneconomical.

Today's Meaning of "Management Control"

Many leaders in business have given thought to the proper role of control in management. In some of its more extreme uses, "control" has become completely synonymous with "management." In most applications, however, its realm is much more restricted.

---

57 Varieties
in the
Connotations of "Control"

Account	Number
Act	Object
Administer	Observe
Boss	Overpower
Check	Overrule
Command	Persuade
Compare	Prevail
Correct	Prohibit
Curb	Quantify
Direct	Query
Dominate	Question
Drive	Regulate
Enforce	Reprehend
Expose	Reprove
Fit	Restrain
Forestall	Rule
Govern	Shackle
Guide	Supervise
Hinder	Suppress
Influence	Sway
Inhibit	Test
Join	Undertake
Judge	Unite
Know	Uphold
Lead	Verify
Manage	Warn
Manipulate	Watch
Measure	Weigh
Negotiate	

Figure II-B-1.

Representative of this more useful scope of control are the following two explanations:

• In an address before the American Management Association in

1954, Harvey O. Edson, Controller of the Illinois Tool Works, stated when speaking specifically about cost control:

> "Control is established when differences between planned and actual costs are understood and when operating personnel establishes effective measures to avoid excesses in all known areas of importance."

- We are indebted for an even more penetrating discussion to the late John E. Bassill, President of American Enka Corporation. This truly great and successful manager who portrays the best in U. S. management in so many ways, stated before the executive and staff departments of Algemene Kunstyzidje Unie, N.V., at Ainheim, Holland:

> "The control function embraces all those activities by which our company's operations are guided and motivated to the attainment of a desirable end. It is the final step in the performance of a completed job. It involves objectives, planning, and appraisal.
>
> "Very often when the word 'control' is mentioned, some people shy away from it. It's because they think of it as something restrictive, whereas it is really the means by which management can, with confidence and safety, delegate authority and responsibility broadly.
>
> "The process follows a regular cycle:
>
> 1. Control begins with planning—in the determination of objectives through the medium of profit goals, work programs, procedures, quality standards, and the like.
>
> 2. Once decisions have been made and the job is being done, these management tools and objectives permit the individual to better accomplish the task at hand and to gain the inner satisfaction which comes with a performance that meets the objective.
>
> 3. The process of control includes the appraisal of performance by those who have delegated authority and are responsible for seeing that the job is done properly.
>
> 4. On the basis of appraisal, it is possible to ascertain the points at which performance has varied from planned objectives or standards and to determine the reasons for variance. Either performance has been inadequate or our goals were incorrectly set.
>
> 5. The cycle is completed with the planning function again

coming into play to determine how performance can be improved in those cases where it has fallen short of the objective.''

The Management Cycle

One of the hallmarks of progressive management in this stage of our development has thus become the recognition of the need for a "systems" view of management. Managing is a cyclical process. As its most basic essentials, the management cycle (Figure II-B-2) contains the three elements of:

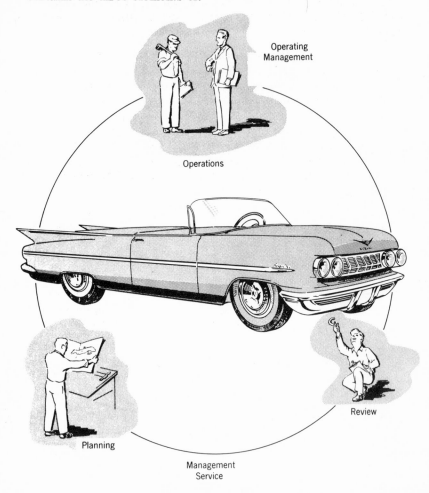

Operating
Management

Operations

Review

Planning

Management
Service

Figure II-B-2. The Management Cycle.

- Planning:

  Goals are established for the organization as a whole as well as
  for every one of its components. Available resources are examined
  to determine whether they permit the realization of these targets.
  This establishes the best way by which the objectives can be
  reached under the prevailing conditions.

- Operations:

  A decision among possible alternative plans is made. Necessary
  instructions are discussed with all concerned. Activities proceed,
  under the direction of management, as closely in harmony with
  the plans as possible.

- Control:

  Actual results are recorded and interpreted so as to distill those
  conclusions out of the effects of operating which are useful for
  future plans.

Because of the uncertainties inherent in the meaning of the term
"control," this third* element of management is referred to, ever
more frequently, as "review." Other terms are also in use, such as
General Electric's "measurement."

In this framework, "review" is more passive. It is perhaps best
characterized by its service trait in that it, as well as planning, exists solely for the purpose of making better operations possible in
the future.

"Control" in the sense of "holding the reins" must, unflinchingly,
remain a prerogative of "operations" because it is there that activities are directed. Of course, this "control" is based on "review"
because we need measurements and interpretations of performance
for the purpose of drawing conclusions; and it depends, equally, upon
"planning" as it is there that these conclusions are utilized in the
form of new blueprints, which now include the lessons from past
operations.

During the early fifties, there was a trend to call the sum total of
planning and review "Management Control." More recent practice
seems to abandon this terminology in favor of designating these two
elements more appropriately as "Management Service."

This strikes me as indicative of a really significant development.
It gives expression to the recognition that we always deal in management not only with economic problems such as money, markets,

---

*The number of elements into which management's most basic tasks may be
divided, varies in the literature from two to forty-seven.

technology, materials, etc.; a co-equal partner at all times are social considerations, i.e., people—be they groups of employees or customers or owners or suppliers, or be they individuals. What a delightful calling card the twentieth century would leave to posterity if we would be able to conclude forty years from now that the change from "control" to "service" was something more than semantics.

The Mission of Review

There is an interesting parallel between the two components of Management Service, planning and review:

- Planning looks ahead, determines what should be done; review looks back, establishing what is actually happening.

- Planning thinks about operations in advance; review thinks out the lessons represented in the realization of these plans.

- Planning might be considered the organization's windshield, review as its rear view mirror

Like planning, review has two distinct though, of course, interwoven parts:

- The first is the measurement of performance.

  This requires the observation of operations wherever they might take place—in a department or group, by an individual or the firm as a whole.

  Results are recorded, preferably in clear-cut facts and figures.

  Data are checked and arranged so that they facilitate the second part of the review.

- The second part of review is the appraisal of the findings.

  This entails the examination of the symptoms just registered so as to be able to state a diagnosis.

  Cause(s) must be detected whose presence is indicated by the measurements just taken.

  Such interpretation supplies meaning to the figures as only the surrounding circumstances give specific significance to any fact.

We said earlier that the concept of review as a service is of a more passive nature. The tasks just outlined show that it is also a most needed, a practical and indeed profitable service. Without review, we do not profit from experience; and those who can not learn from the past are condemned to repeat it.

Characteristics of Effective Review

Review and Planning

From the point of view of usefulness in business practice, perhaps the foremost trait of profitable review is the need to be recognized as an element in its own right but one that engages in liveliest interplay with planning.

As a matter of fact, many instances could be cited where planning and review are mixed up too much. For instance:

- The same functions are referred to by some firms as "production planning" while others label them as "production control."

- Many tasks of quality control are pure planning, such as the design of sampling plans, the setting of tolerances or of control limits, machine-capability studies, etc..

- Standards are frequently mentioned as control devices; yet as they designate planned amounts of quantitites (of cost, of time, etc.), they are really bona fide residents of the planning sector.

- This lack of differentiation prevails in government as well; for example, investigating committees of a legislature are an outright contradiction of the fundamental separation of the three distinct powers (elements) of governing (managing).

This is carrying interplay too far. We need to distinguish between planning and review. Each has its specific niche. Both have to dovetail. But each looks different.

At best, review can point out failures after they have happened; planning can prevent some of them from happening in the first place.

This principle is at the root of a significant trend of current business practice, the shift of emphasis from review to planning. In materialistic terms, we can state unequivocally that a dollar spent on planning is likely to bring higher dividends than a dollar spent on review.

Here is just one out of a multitude of possible examples of this development; more and more firms "control" inventories not by stopping purchases when a specific turnover limit is reached but by planning stock in advance and in harmony with the volume of activities they are to supply.

But planning does not intend to take the place of review. It would make little sense to plan if we did not find out how plans come out (review). From this, we can formulate a second principle which is also gaining wider acceptance in business these days: "Planning is the prerequisite to control."

If our records show, for instance, that this quarter's expenditures have been three times as high as those in the comparable period last year, the meaning of this fact is obscured until we know first what expense level we had planned, secondly what results we expected, and thirdly how both of these two "plans" actually came out in operations.

The interplay between planning and review as well as the two principles just cited can perhaps be summed up by stating that "the better the planning, the easier the control." Put another way, it is clear (although not yet standard practice in business) that we can not control matters sensibly unless we have first planned properly.

Foremost among the needs of review which planning has to answer is a clear and specific statement of:

- The objectives which should be accomplished.

- The results which are anticipated.

- The center and scope of responsibility which have been established.

The close interaction of planning and review is evidenced also by the fact that some planning tools are simultaneously review instruments. The budget is a good example: it first stipulates the amount of (capital and expense) expenditures needed to execute the plans made; it then records actual outgo; the difference between the two, when stacked up against results achieved, permits an evaluation of the original plans and their execution in operations.

Review and Feedback

The second most important characteristic of review is its need for feedback to planning. It is this feature which bestows a systems character upon management although the management cycle is indeed not a "closed loop" in the strict technical sense; it does, unfortunately or happily, not adjust automatically when output differs from expectations.

The link from the review of past operations into planning for the future is quite frequently the weakest part in practice. As feedback depends upon communications (once the necessary information is at hand through appropriate review), this phenomenon appears less phenomenal as communications are among the least explored of all human activities.

This is true of business as well as of the rest of the world. It is particularly the case with written communications; and performance or progress reports, the usual feedback vehicle, are generally in writing.

It is the mission of managerial feedback to make future planning sensitive to the results of previous plans. This keeps the enterprise dynamic and responsive to new conditions and new ideas. As in its counterparts in other areas of the natural and living sciences, its job is "regeneration."

At best, feedback makes available the sum total of every shred of useful information from the company's own past experience. Yet in many cases, we need additional facts and data. This suggests the expansion of the basic management cycle (Figure II-B-2) through the addition of an auxiliary. For want of a better name, I like to call it "Management R & D" (Figure II-B-3) because it does for the function of management precisely what we have come to expect from R & D for any other area to which they are applied. Figure II-B-4 represents the management cycle in another form. Here Management R & D is shown twice; first as it affects the planning problem, and, second, as it affects the review of several problems.

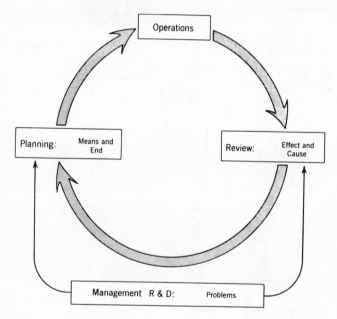

Figure II-B-3. Management R & D and the Management Cycle.

Management R & D

The purpose of this auxiliary is the feed-in of additional intelligence. It has a triple objective; the first two parts cover the "development" and the third represents the real "research" work:

• It procures supplementary information.

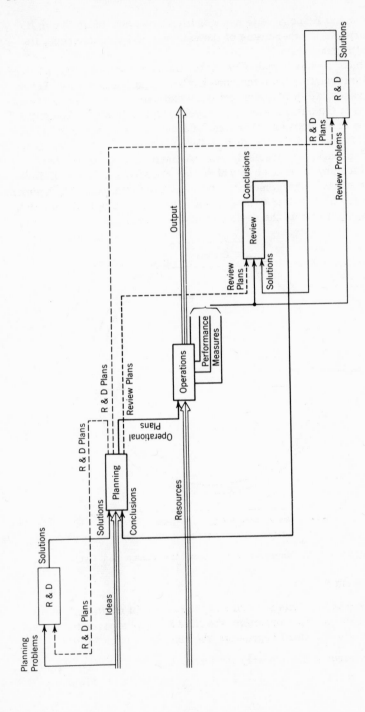

Figure II-B-4. The Management Cycle.

This is generally done through surveys; topics cover anything
that has an influence upon company operations—industrial and
other business activity, population growth, interest rates, legislation, etc..
Many sources qualify, such as trade associations, government
agencies, banks, credit bureaus, societies, the literature, foundations, research corporations, universities, etc.

- It processes existing data by enlisting the magnificient potential
  of statistical, mathematical, and computational techniques.
  It is perhaps surprising to note how recent the adoption of these
  tools into the business realm really is; with the exception of a
  small handful of firms, the first beachhead was established by
  this formidable trio just about twenty years ago.

- Most important and as yet least utilized, however, is the third objective, that of true management research.
  Its purposes are in the area of management exactly the same as
  those entrusted with research elsewhere, i.e., truly scientific
  search for new knowledge which makes it possible to crack old
  problems, to find new alternatives or solutions, and to discover
  the reasons for previous failures.
  Examples of this third category could be market research and
  economic research, as well as what a number of us consider the
  true mission of operations research itself.

Why Review?

In this framework, "control" in the sense of "review" constitutes
an approach which as yet only a minority of American business firms
follow. Yet their number has been increasing with such vigor, their
results have become so outstanding, that this concept deserves to be
presented as destined to be as typical in just a few short years as anything will ever be representative in the face of the U.S. fondness for
variety.

It merits this position because it also facilitates—better than any
other concept or arrangement—the mission which progressive management is setting for itself. To be the innovator of progress—the
most important obligation in the entire executive portfolio of responsibilities.

KEY PROBLEMS OF CONTROL

As this paper discusses control as synonymous with review, the
major problems confronting it are spelled out in its twofold mission:
to measure and to interpret performance.

Measurability

The Four Corner Stones

Managerial performance measures are heirs of generations who did not see management as we do now, namely as an activity by itself. We recognize today that there is quite a difference between doing something ourselves or supervising others who do it. We know that each demands different abilities and knowledge.

But this realization is of recent origin. Our predecessors, in some cases even our present colleagues, in management believed that the cause of any managerial problem was to be found in just the one function which happened to show the effect most prominently.

If a new product line does not sell well, it is still not uncommon for executive attention to focus on the marketing aspects to the exclusion of all others (such as design, manufacture, quality, pricing, etc.), in the expectation that this will assure complete remedy.

The function which was at first singled out persistently for prime attention was finance. Nothing else mattered except as it influenced the financial picture. At that time, review started and ended with the recording of the financial aspects of performance; control concerned funds and money, cash and other assets. It was this period which established the accountant in his unique position within the review or control picture which he still holds in quite a few organizations.

Closer to our lifetime, concern with technical problems, mainly those of manufacture, was added to the attention of financial considerations.

If we take a look at the performance-measuring techniques which predominate even in top-notch firms at this moment, we find "money" and "production" as the key ingredients. To wit:

1. Accounting. Concerned exclusively with financial data, it is the review technique with the longest record of splendid and effective achievements.

   Speaking from the point of view of management, accounting furnishes executives with financial (including cost) data in every detail; its usefulness is enhanced by its ability to summarize hundreds or millions of data in such statements as a balance sheet, an income statement, etc.

   While statistical methodology is bound to invade the area of cost accounting farther, today's business operations use almost exclusively general accounting (not statistical) principles and tools for the specific purpose of keeping track of costs.

   In an attempt to honor the fine service which accounting has rendered management, the executives have actually limited the usefulness of many a "modern" accounting setup. This happened when two conflicting missions were assigned to it, namely:

a. The continuation of its original custodianship, i.e., to give a historically and legally incontestable account of the receipt and use of monies.
This imposes the obligation to keep records comparable over the years; it requires strict observance of many laws (taxes, SEC, etc.); it introduces a definite degree of inflexibility.

b. The extension through the more recent mandate to provide data in operationally meaningful form.
This emphasizes the future instead of the past; it puts stress on reality, not on law books or tax regulations.

One example of this dual recording obligation can be found in entries to depreciation accounts; in most cases, they are as high as Internal Revenue rules permit, say 15 per cent per annum. Yet the equipment involved may have lost much more than that fraction of its value after the first year of use because of technological improvements, obsolescence for other reasons, inadequacy, or whatever the causes may be.
Thus the first and oldest review technique, accounting, is faced with distinct problems in its endeavor to continue serving management as well as it has in the past. The remarks on Controllership (see page 57) will contain a partial answer which the accounting profession has developed so far.

2. Work Measurement is another old-timer. Its domain is the time aspect of output.
Today work measurement is firmly established in most well-run organizations. But even in the best, the likelihood is high that its scope remains the same as when this technique was first introduced into business some seventy-five years ago, namely routine repetitive plant operations.
This limitation of existing recording techniques to their original habitat, the plant, is also typical of:

3. Production Control, which reflects this restriction even through its name. Its realm is quantitative considerations of performance. Representative production-control data might be:

● Production rate.

● Production volume.

● Share of economic lot sizes in total order runs.

- Efficiency of individual operators or groups.

- Inventory turnover.

- Out-of-stock situations.

- Equipment capacity and utilization.

- Types and frequency of emergency repairs.

All have in common the natural characteristic of being concerned with quantities as well as the unnatural confinement to stay within factory walls.

4. Inspection is the fourth member of the quartet of recording techniques. Its mission is to record quality characteristics of output. Data might include:

- Defectives.

- Their division into reworkable or scrap parts.

- Information on the kind of defects encountered.

- Malfunction rates.

- Productivity of inspectors.

Once again, an outstanding feature of this technique is its shyness in venturing into non-manufacturing arenas.

These four techniques constitute the bulk of managerial performance measuring in today's business practice. They have two common denominators in which is wrapped up much of the cause for dissatisfaction with the way "control" has worked in many cases:

1. Each of these tools has acted like the hermit of the Middle Ages who, once settled in his retreat, refused to leave it for better pastures.
Therefore, all give us information on manufacturing with more detail and greater accuracy as well as with higher precision than on any other activity of business.

2. Every one of these four instruments measures only material aspects—finance, time, quantity, and quality.
True, these are four of the most common factors of any performance; there is nothing wrong with attention to each as long as this does not draw a borderline beyond which interest shall not advance.

Is it any wonder that the executive whose view is limited to these four considerations finds himself confined in the splendor of isolation.

Is it surprising that review techniques which were born as slaves to such narrow objectives became specialists which span in ever-narrowing circles.

Is it not just natural that, once aware of their limited scope, they kicked over the traces and transformed themselves at times into control of the rankest ruthlessness—control which restrained and wrecked, which became punitive rather than preventive.

It is control of this caliber which decapitates needed expenditures in the frantic search for more working capital, to the point of rationing paper clips; which makes the president of a plastics firm retain approval of every expense over 100 dollars within an authorized company budget of 8 million dollars and which has the executive vice president of a food concern personally sample every routine test batch, which ties him up some seventy-five times in an average week, or once every thirty minutes during the regular business hours.

If examples of this sort appear out of order in the enlightened atmosphere of today's management, it is necessary only to recall the actions of too many executives in the 1957-1958 recession who resorted to just this way of establishing the fiber of U.S. business confidence and skill in the face of a temporarily adverse, although clearly predictable, situation.

Progressive managers have shown the way out of the jungle of such narrowness. They have added three lanes to the review road:

- They have widened the application of these four recording tools from exclusive use in the plant to establishing all of them in other phases of business activity.

- They are demanding measures of non-material, i.e., the human component of business.

- They require the design of yardsticks and the collection of data on activities and factors of performance which none of the recording instruments discussed so far can provide.

Beyond the Factory

The adaptation of accounting and work measurement, or production control and inspection to non-manufacturing tasks is paying off handsomely. This is why better cost data are now becoming available in, say, research work. This is the cause for seeing ratio delay studies applied to the executive's own tasks.

This is the underlying reason why design and copy writing, for instance, can now be measured with fundamentally the same techniques which were formerly in evidence only on assembly lines. This is the means by which the output of an Accounts Payable Section is inspected in the same way which has so long been common in the Parts Fabricating Shop.

The migration of these techniques is fortunately not limited to industry; many other fields of business are opening their doors to them, at least on a trial basis.

Personnel "Measures"

As to the second point, the measurement of the as yet most unmeasurable of all "things," the human being, the situation is not yet encouraging. The fundamental reason for this is the sad fact that we still know so little about Homo sapiens—what makes him tick?; what does he really want?; why is he doing so well in one situation and so miserably in another?

But we certainly know this: We cannot put people under the same sort of inspection microscope which examines products for "go—no go" or "acceptable—reject."

People are individuals. Each has his own individual and (for him) purposeful goals and actions. Each has a value by himself which can not be totaled arithmetically; it can not be averaged with standard mathematical tools. In many cases, it is the exeptional rather than the average or normal behavior that really matters. And furthermore, what constitutes "normal" in human dealings in general or in a specific company or department?

Tex Antoine, one of the TV weather reporters in New York, makes the wise observation that "normal is just a collection of abnormals." While he made this observation with respect to normal temperature, it is easily extended to statistics.

This is why so many statistics have little meaning in a human situation; for example, it is a "scientifically established fact that the average executive has been married 1.7 times and has 2.3 children." It is hard to find a single colleague who pleads guilty to at least the first portion of this statement of indisputable facts.

But difficulties in measuring an individual are only the beginning. What we need in management is a yardstick that shows what this individual is doing in the group of which he is a member. It is his contribution to his unit that counts on the dial of executive performance. And for this purpose, we know of no single application in business, although results from sociometric research may change this situation before long.

True, any good recording setup of a company includes data on such personnel matters as:

• Accident frequency and severity.

- Training hours.

- Absenteeism.

- Turnover.

- Number of requests for transfer.

- Number of grievances.

- Number of disciplinary suspensions.

- Number of unauthorized work stoppages.

- A skill inventory.

- Measures of depth (of succession) in management ranks.

The scantiness of this list highlights the conclusion that in this key area, non-material aspects of performance, we are faced with the proverbial case of the missing yardsticks.

More Management Review Data

This is the reason why the third trend, the demand for new measures, i.e., for additional management review data, is now so prominent. In this area, management still has a good bit to learn; it can readily do so from the many facets of everyday life. For example, would baseball still be so fascinating if there were no records of the number of runs, hits, and errors in each game; if these scores were withheld from the fans and the players themselves; and if these performance indicators were not made known at once? And the same holds true in golf, football, bridge, and in many other activities. Yet in business, we still ask men and women to work eight hours a day, for forty or fifty years; and millions of them are never given any score on how well they are doing. This failure is much more telling than the principles psychology has given us, since it is the one undisputed maxim that man is a goal oriented animal. He will, invariably, perform better if he knows how he is doing.

When we do provide yardsticks, we have the unhappy faculty of putting matters rather negatively. For instance, the usual occurrence is to measure quality in terms of "reject rates," or "defectives"; in baseball, we take the opposite, i.e., a positive approach: "He bats .295"; one never hears this expressed as "He misses .705."

In progressive companies we find, steadily, new and additional yardsticks of performance which are not the result of the four review techniques listed above. While accounting gives us a measure of total sales volume, more and more firms demand its breakdown, through non-accounting means, into sales by:

- Customer category.

- Geographical territory.

- Product line.

- Profitability.

- Distribution channel.

- Promotion.

- Etc.

Any field of business activity qualifies for treatment that produces numerical values. Decisions on stockholder relations, for instance, are obviously easier in an organization which has at its disposal data on:

- Composition of stockholder ranks.

- Proxie response.

- Number of repeat stock sales (and their value).

- Attendance at stockholder meetings.

- Etc.

Relatively few companies can claim today that they have equally useful data on every phase of their activities. The General Electric Company pioneered in this area when it embarked, several years ago, upon the task of measuring every one of its departments as well as the corporation as a whole in what it calls its seven "key result areas," namely:

- Profitability.

- Market position.

- Productivity.

- Product leadership.

- Personnel development.

- Employee attitudes.

- Public responsibility.

Especially the last category, public responsibility, makes the point that we can measure whatever we wish today provided only that:

- The executives involved are convinced that this is desirable.

- We do not expect scientifically precise yardsticks.

Measuring "Intangibles"

It is the exception rather than the rule that measurements which are in wide use today can stand the test of scientific accuracy. Take the dollar, for instance; its significance as a measure of values is distorted by the functions in its purchasing power. The balance sheet of a firm shows items with quite different unit impact, such as:

- Cash (at its current purchasing power).

- Fixed assets (at their original price, adjusted by depreciation).

- Inventories (at a synthetic—FIFO, LIFO, etc.—valuation).

We blissfully add these items up arithmetically, disregarding the fact that we really total turnips and oranges and artichokes.

At this stage of development, the attempt at obtaining more and better measures hinges upon our being satisfied with approximations in many cases, at least as a first step. Experience has shown time and again that even rough yardsticks can be refined quickly as long as they are used consistently. With this qualification, we can proceed to measure any aspect of performance by designing yardsticks specifically for each situation. The provision of these indicators is an integral part of the planning task. It has just one hurdle: we have to know clearly just what we are after before we can measure it.

It is the lack of this knowlege which has, in my experience, been the cause for at least nine out of every ten failures in any managerial measurement project. Why did Pete Porter fail to work out as a salesman in the Wayne County territory although everyone who interviewed him before hiring considered him such an excellent choice.

The answer is likely to be ignorance on the part of those who selected him as to precisely what personality traits, spheres of interest, motivation stimuli, etc. are needed in this particular job. Of course, the more materialistic matters, such as product knowledge and attractive speech, were known prerequisites; but how about the others? Did we ourselves know just what they should be? Did we check whether they were present before the man was put on the payroll? Or did we notice their absence only after he failed in a mission we had not analyzed fully in advance?

The pioneering case for measuring the "unmeasurable" is the Bell Systems' assortment of Service Indexes. They measure such activities as:

- Information service.

- Installation service

- Manual exchange service.

- Repair service.

- Collection service.

- Directory service.

(As a supplement to the usual financial, time, quantity, and quality yardsticks.)

How do they operate? In each case, the activity involved is carefully examined for the two or three or four key contributors to success. In the case of Information Service, there are speed of answer and accuracy and courtesy in the opinion of the customers. These two are made measurable by:

- Ascertaining how much weight each factor has; telephone users told the company, in a 2:3 ratio, that accuracy was more important to them than speed of response.

- Assigning a corresponding point value to each factor; for a maximum attainable total of 100 points, accuracy then is entitled to 60 and speed of answer to 40 points.

- Attaching to each factor a statement of what constitutes "standard" performance; for instance, speed of answer is set up with a twenty second threshold figure.

- Establishing an allowable tolerance for each component; if more than 6 per cent of all calls, for example, take more than 20 seconds for the operator to come in, performance is below par.

- Devising a scale of demerit points for deviations in performance which are larger than the "standard tolerance."

- Totaling the points which "speed of answer" and "accuracy" earn in each case.

By having Service Observers monitor calls, according to a predetermined sampling plan, each Bell System exchange thus measures its information and any of its other services through clear-cut numerical values.

Since its first publication some five years ago, this approach has been used by a number of firms in numerous ways. As different as these applications are, they have in common the fact that they have made "intangibles" measurable and that they are paying for themselves handsomely in the unanimous opinion of the companies who use them.

Facts versus Opinion

Returning to the first prerequisite for the establishment of yard-

sticks, the willingness of executives to see them established, it is
clear that this is much more easily stipulated than done—even by the
man who really wants to give this idea a whirl.

Once again, tradition and other historic precedents account for a
considerable share of the existence of this situation. In the public's
mind, an executive is not yet a man who studiously analyzes problems, carefully weighs the evidence and then decides. He is rather
the Daddy Warbucks type—with five phone sets on his desk which are
in use constantly because the boss barks orders into one, crushes the
competition through another, buys square miles of waste land in the
Antarctic via the third, dispatches a nuclear-powered air fleet with
construction crews and equipment to that region on a fourth trunk,
etc.—all off the cuff, at the spur of the moment.

The crux of this perhaps slightly exaggerated scene is the in-
stinctive omission of the need for establishing facts; it does not lie
in the error in public conception as such.

Too little has been known about management in the past to permit
facts to play a key role. The record of operating in this straight
jacket produced some of the most successful (and ruthless) Captains
of Industry who built the greatest economic empire the world has
ever seen—with iron fists, with fabulous results, on hunch and guess.
It has also assembled a tome of failures whose consequences are now
at the disposal of possibly less formidable men because facts begin to
emerge.

Because of this drastic change in the situation, disregard of facts
which was once the norm for executive strength has now become a
hallmark of managerial weakness. But such a transition is not easily
accomplished in one lifetime. Many managers still have to learn a
cardinal principle which was formulated by one of management's all-
time Great about fifty years ago: "If we allow ourselves to be governed by opinion where it is possible to obtain facts, we shall lose in
our competition with those who base their actions on fact."[1]

Mr. Gantt went one step further when he added the warning: "We
have no right morally to decide as a matter of opinion that which can
be determined as a matter of fact."[2]

The one thing that is sure to occur when we prefer opinions to
facts, is disagreement; different people are bound to judge things
differently. Perhaps the most glamorous of all witnesses to this fact
is the Miss America Contest; in the many years of its existence,
there has never been a single decision which met with the full agreement of all present although this particular project concerns matters
which are at least in part measurable.

As we need facts in management, measurements must be expressed
in numerical values if they are to be fully useful. This is the reason

why more factual measures are mandatory before managing can
reach the state which it paradoxically attached to its name many
years ago, namely "scientific management."

Interpretation

The second category of key problems of control goes with the
second part of the mission of review, the interpretation of data for
the purpose of extracting from them conclusions which are useful for
the future. Much less progress has been made in this segment.

Techniques

Quite naturally, the caliber of such an appraisal depends upon the
facts at hand and the diagnostic skill of the man who goes to work on
them. Preceding pages addressed themselves to some of the more
basic problems with regard to measuring performance. As far as
the evaluation of such data is concerned, the manager has even fewer
techniques at his command. There are:

1. Financial Audits: a fixture in as yet too few among the smaller
    companies, this activity has nevertheless had wide acceptance;
    accounting operations are "inspected" for the purpose of analyz-
    ing their strong and weaker features so that recommendations
    may be formulated on how to improve things.
    As they are based upon accounting work, the scope of these audits
    is limited to financial considerations.

2. Quality Control: its appearance in addition to Inspection, which was
    discussed earlier, is a significant landmark in the development of
    review; it highlights the shift of emphasis from merely being sat-
    isfied with the recording of results (inspection) to pinpointing
    their causes (quality control).
    This is a trend in all phases of review work although this par-
    ticular technique is operative only with respect to one aspect of
    performance, namely quality.
    It is gratifying that in a small but growing number of firms pro-
    duction control is being broadened similarly so as to include not
    only the measurements but also the interpretation of the quantity
    aspects of output.

3. Personnel Appraisals: few topics are likely to raise the heat of
    a discussion as rapidly as this complex problem of reviewing a
    person's performance in a specific position.
    Attempts at making this tool more useful have been quite numer-
    ous. Results have been disappointing because of the extreme
    difficulty to distinguish a man's performance as such from the

personal characteristics of the individual who produced it. This is
why personnel appraisals have, in so many cases, turned into
one mortal's judgment of another person's personality which took
personal traits into consideration much more than they had influenced results.

The most experienced manager turns rank amateur when he gets
himself trapped into trying to assess—or change—people's personal characteristics to any extent; this is a matter for the psy-
chiatrist. Business is exclusively concerned with work performance; that is a proper matter for management.

Where these pitfalls have been avoided, personnel appraisals
have taken on much more the shape of:

4. Management Audits: they represent the endeavor to forge a man-
   agement-wide audit tool from the lessons of the three techniques
   just discussed.

   As yet they mostly cover just parts of the total management
   picture; purchasing audits or audits of time standards, procedure
   or policy audits are becoming commonplace in many of our leading companies; however, they are conducted more often at haphazard intervals than as a periodic routine.

   Yet a true management audit looks at the full scope and orbit of
   the management of each function in all its responsibilities. It is
   performed regularly, not just once in a while. And it is characterized by the fact that it is probably the least used of all review
   tools although the one that has by far the greatest potential.

   Everyone who have tried his hand earnestly at management auditing, will agree that they are destined to become, very soon, a
   fixture in the habits of progressive managers as planning has
   become a trusted mainstay in the past ten or fifteen years.

   I believe that the rate of development in the use of management
   audits may even surpass the amazing speed with which planning
   made a place for itself at the executive desk after World War II.
   This prediction is based on my conviction that today's executives
   have progressed so well on the road to making our occupation into a true profession that the searching self-criticism which management auditing promotes, is bound to be recognized as one of
   the most potent helpers toward that challenging goal.

The Riddle of Relationships

We have to be aware of all forces which affect a given problem
before we can have a full understanding of the existing situation. Yet
until very recent years, the dynamic nature of management, which is
really one of its key traits, has had but scantiest recognition in prac-

tice. Even today, organization charts are still shown in two-dimensional "models," indicating "lines of command" as the channels of communication. Yet the crux of any organization is not so much the static arrangement of its components which the "normal" organization chart pictures but rather the dynamic relationship between them as the whole system operates, which the chart does not show.

This matter of relationships is as crucial in management as it is in anything that is alive. Wherever a pattern exists, there is usually more significance in the relationship among the parts than in the intrinsic substance of each element.

It is not, for instance, the existence of some so-called line and staff functions per se which causes difficulties but their relationship or lack of proper interaction. To cite another example, it is not the absolute amounts of available capital and the existing market, respectively, which are important but their relationship. Fifty thousand dollars is a nice sum with which to operate a corner grocery store; a population of 100,000 is a delightfully sizable market to court. But put together, these two cannot work as there is relatively much too little working capital for a mass of customers this size.

Any figure, any fact therefore has meaning only as its relationships to other pertinent elements bestow upon it. Thus the interpretation part of review is more important and more difficult than the measurement portion.

Managerial Decisions Are Influenced
by Considerations of:

. Product and market.
. Equipment, facilities, and location.
. Finances and capital structure.
. Ownership.
. Other functions and their utilization.
. Personnel.
. Relations with—Customers and suppliers.
                —Employees and unions.
                —Stockholders.
                — Financial, educational,
                  and other institutions.
                —Community.
. Existing plans.
. Own and related industries.
. Economic, political, and legal situations.

Figure II-B-5.

The multiplicity of relationships makes interpretation of facts difficult. In every business situation there is bound to be quite an assembly of factors which influence even the simplest matter. Figure II-B-5 lists a mere ten which tentative conclusions from research still in progress appear to show as always present in any business decision.

All these forces swirl around a given problem, constantly altering their impact upon one another and the subject matter, which itself is not fixed but rather moves and changes all the time—unless it has been anchored securely to a specific target, i.e., specific plans. We can therefore greatly facilitate the interpretation of an existing set of facts if we accept as the datum line the plans which have been made for this particular situation.

Too often, however, comparisons to other performance values are preferred in business as evidenced by the large number of reports which stack current actuality, for instance against:

• Last month.

• Previous year.

• Cumulative results.

• Percentage of change.

• Past high or low point.

Such evaluation is of course useful as long as it keeps in mind that it is being made exclusively from the point of view of historic developments.

As the past, though prelude to the future, is nevertheless gone forever, business is more concerned with different perspectives. That is why other comparisons have become popular, such as those with other plants of the same corporation, with other firms in the same industry, with different industries, and with the regional or even the national economy as a whole. Once again such appraisals are significant because they reveal our relative position to somebody else.

What counts most, however, is how we manage ourselves in the orbit we have chosen for our activities. This is laid down, unambiguously, in our plans. Thus they, and only they, should be "par" for the course. Setting "par" properly is not easy—either on the golf links or in business; but this is not a problem of control but rather of planning.

Even the most capable and successful manager of 1959 looks for additional help in his interpretation tasks. And help is coming from the experience and research in the systems and in other fields. The results of Warren Alberts' simulation projects on behalf of United Air Lines and Ford Dickie's investigation of common parts inventory patterns at General Electric are examples. Approaches and results of this caliber provide some really bright rays of hope; so does SDC's interest in these matters as evidenced by their research efforts.

For the time being, the vast majority of business executives rely upon their judgment when it comes to cutting through the maze of relationships. The more facts they have at their disposal, the later will judgment have to enter and the lower will be the strain to which even exquisite judgment is exposed. But for now and for a few years to come, it appears certain that judgment will remain the key ingredient to executive success. It has been that in the past and it will continue to be in the future when it will be brought to bear at an even later stage in the decision of a problem.

TWO IMPORTANT DEVELOPMENTS ON THE CONTROL SCENE

Integrated Data Processing

The key characteristic of "integrated data processing" is not a computer, not five-channel tape, and not miles and miles of interconnecting wires between plant or office locations, but the existence of a true network of managerial intelligence.

Data on which management bases its decisions must be the result of a systematically planned system of indicators; they have to stand guard at every sensitive spot within the company and outside. For example, inventory "control" procedures in the stock room and in bookkeeping should be integrated, not merely superimposed. Shipment records in the traffic department, in production control, and in accounting should be matched together—deliberately, not coincidentally.

These observations are a sidelight on a principle stated earlier in somewhat restricted form; it means that all review procedures should be planned out as carefully as the operations on which they are to report. This should involve not only the substance of performance yardsticks needed; it ought to include methods of collection and interpretation, frequency and form of the resulting reports as well as scope and speed of their distribution.

Naturally mechanical and electronic gear can contribute materially to the effectiveness of the collection and interpretation process of data. But it is, in my opinion, a facility which, like all other instruments, must remain subordinate to that of which it is an instrument.

Controllership

Few fields which have the advantage of a long tradition have adjusted themselves so effectively to the changing business scene as this peculiarly American function, the Controller.

In the classic text,[3] which is still the "latest" book in the field, Dean Jackson describes the major functions which are associated with the function of the Controller as:

Usually:

1. Accounting—

- Policies and procedures.
- General accounting books.
- Cost accounting.
- Payroll accounting.
- Tax accounting.
- Property records.

2. Interpretation—

- Financial statistics.
- Financial statements.

3. Internal auditing—

And often in addition:

1. Office management.

2. Insurance.

3. Economic studies.

4. Clerical systems.

With this scope, the Controller is properly designated as the Chief Accounting Officer.

Shortly after this book reported this picture as generally prevailing within U.S. business, the Controller's Institute's Committee on Ethics and Eligibility Standards submitted to the Board of Directors the following concept of Controllership, which was approved in 1949:

"1. To establish, coordinate and maintain, through authorized management, an integrated plan for the control of operations. Such a plan would provide, to the extent required in the business, cost standards, expense budgets,

sales forecasts, profit planning, and programs for capital investment and financing, together with the necessary
procedures to effectuate the plan.

2. To measure performance against approved operating
plans and standards, and to report and interpret the results of operations to all levels of management. This includes the design, installation and maintenance of accounting and cost systems and records, the determination
of accounting policy and the compilation of statistical
records as required.

3. To measure and report on the validity of the objectives
of the business and on the effectiveness of its policies,
organization structure and procedures in attaining those
objectives. This includes consulting with all segments
of management responsible for policy or action concerning any phase of the operation of the business as it relates to the performance of this function.

4. To report to government agencies, as required, and to
supervise all matters relating to taxes.

5. To interpret and report on the effect of external influences on the attainment of the objectives of the business.
This includes the continuous appraisal of economic and
social forces and of governmental influences as they
affect the operation of the function.

6. To provide protection for the assets of the business.
This includes establishing and maintaining adequate
internal control and auditing, and assuring proper insurance coverage."

The following conclusions are suggested:

1. The concept of the management cycle and the view on controllership just cited, are fully compatible.

2. The question of whether such controllership represents still primarily an accounting job is wide open; some firms answer it em-
phatically in the affirmative; others take the opposite view.

3. Even after ten years since the introduction of this far-reaching
view on controllership, which differs fundamentally from the
"classic" picture, relatively few companies have adopted it.
Those who have, are enjoying its benefits in many ways, including
sizably improved means of profit management and spectacular

rise in the contributions which controllership makes for every sector of the business and the organization as a whole.

4. The crystallization of the concepts of the management cycle and of this new controllership has placed the matter of whether (planning and) control tasks should be centralized or decentralized into proper perspective: The decision on this is a part of the broader problem of whether all management activities should be centralized or decentralized.

I happen to be one of those who are firmly convinced that decentralization is not just a fad or a fleeting fashion. I believe it represents a more refined form of managing because it brings into play the decision-making power of the many.

As such it is, in my opinion, one of the voices who testify to the deliberate and effective introduction of more democratic ways of doing business. The decision on centralization-or-decentralization thus has strong philosophical overtones in addition to many other considerations. Of course quite a few situations make decentalization possible only after developments take place which are sometimes beyond the immediate influence of the organization itself.

The original pioneer installations of the concept of management control or management service do not supply conclusive evidence. Two companies took the centralized road (United Air Lines as well as General Somervell at the U.S. Army during World War II and later on at Koppers Company); the other (Hudson American Corporation) chose the decentralized approach. Since then, the Defense Department changed the operation of its wartime Control Section fundamentally in the legislation which aimed at the unification of the Armed Forces. Koppers and UAL have decentralized their respective setup, but Hudson American has merged into a firm which so far shows no inclination for decentralization.

These as well as later applications in other firms bear out, as a minimum, the proposition that organization of controllership must go hand in hand with the arrangement governing other phases of management.

CONCLUSION: RULER OR ROGUE?

Is "control" a means or an end? Is it the prerogative of one man or of just a few selected individuals? Is it the obligation of every individual so to self-discipline his actions that they contribute the optimum share to the common objective? Is "control" power?; force?; ability?

At first sight, these questions may appear to belong in a discourse on philosophy. They certainly do, but they have also been quite frequently posed in deliberations of practicing managers which it has been my privilege to attend over the years.

One of the true management clasics, Mary Parker Follett, explains that "power might be defined as the ability to make things happen . . . and control as power exercised as means toward a specific end."[4] This establishes "authority as vested control"[5] and adds another powerful voice to the thought advanced earlier that contemporary changes in the exercise of control are a most encouraging indication of the use of democratic experience in business.

Management is unquestionably a leadership function. In a free society, we remain leaders only as long as we have followers. When we have followers, there is evidence of control as long as we admit that the authority which brought about our following is balanced by sensitivity to the reaction of those we direct.

In such a climate, control is a prerogative which is not available to lightweights but only to men of courage who know that they have to stand for something lest they fall for anything.

Thus we have just one choice: to produce economically lucrative and socially acceptable results or to abdicate. The control concept outlined, much too briefly, in these pages, has proved itself as one practical approach toward that aim. As a by-product, it assures for us escape from the most deplorable of all fates: to be born, to subsist for many years, and then to die—without every having lived.

REFERENCES

1. Henry L. Gantt, Industrial Leadership, Yale University Press, New Haven, Conn., 1916, p. 89.
2. Ibid., p. 88.
3. Hugh J. Jackson, The Comptroller: His Functions and Organization, Harvard University Press, Cambridge, Mass., 1948.
4. "Dynamic Administration," The Collected Papers of Mary Parker Follett, edited by Henry C. Metcalf and L. Urwick, Harper and Brothers, New York, 1942, p. 99.
5. Ibid.

DISCUSSION   (Following Mr. Rathe's presentation of his paper)

A. J. ROWE: Although the planning function requires human judgment, farsightedness, and the willingness to take risks, it may be possible to automate control.

A. W. RATHE: You may well be right; it is difficult to find the demarcation between analyzing what happened last year, reaching conclusions which affect plans for the future, and the actual planning for next year. Depending upon where this line lies, creative thinking would reside either in the control or the planning function.

W. E. ALBERTS: I think one of the most significant things you have said is that the control function isn't only in the area of controls. It is also in operations, planning, and in research. It probably could be likened to self-control in a human being, which I am sure we learn to exercise for good reasons. In the same way, to do an effective job a company must exercise a certain amount of self-control in all phases of its operation.

A. W. RATHE: A cardinal point in management controls is the distinction between totalitarian and democratic management. Although this is an oversimplification, I think one prerequisite for making democracy work is self-control or self-discipline. We have often decentralized—one example of democratic management—and have run into trouble where there was no self-discipline or self-control.

H. O. DAVIDSON: To me "democracy" has to do with the process by which authority is vested in the chief executive, and not with the extent to which he delegates it. Totalitarianism, on the other hand, does not preclude the decentralization of control.
I don't believe we are primarily concerned with the way in which management authority is created or with the way in which this authority is limited by constitution, by statute, or indeed by physical law. I think we should recognize that, within some limits, management is fundamentally totalitarian. This may be a bad word, but I say it is true. If it is not true, I am unable to define management control. If the limits become so narrow as to dictate the decision, or if the executive is required to consider his staff and subordinate executives as an electorate whose majority wish prescribes the decision, we should then no longer have a management control process in the sense I conceive it.
My point is that the choice of terms tends to mask the generality of your argument. I believe you have made an excellent exposition on the delegation and control problem which is generally applicable, irrespective of whether the executive authority is created by democratic or by totalitarian political processes.

A. W. RATHE: I agree with the need for a more precise definition of the term "democratic" in our discussion here. What I meant to indicate by it was not merely the delegation of decision making to lower levels but, very much also the existence of an effective two-way flow of information and sensitivity to the reaction to the exercise of authority.

A. SCHULTZ: It is obvious that each of us has in his mind an entirely different conception of what a control system is. One of the first steps is what we might term the design of the system or the structure. Another step is planning; and perhaps control follows in some cases. I think it is important for us to recognize these different steps.

W. E. ALBERTS: Recognition of the need to design a system or even of the need to do research in management systems is a demonstration of control.

J. F. LUBIN: Very often, in meetings of this kind, the participants discuss those cases in their experience in which managers had the insight not to use the control system available. Perhaps the systems designers believe that these illustrations are reflections on their competency; much time is spent rationalizing and justifying these "exceptions." I suggest that such "exceptions" are worth study and that less time be spent on justification. We all know of the ability of a modern system designer to develop control systems analytically and logically. But, often there is a small unspoken reservation: "It is unfortunate that many intuitive managers do seem to make good decisions and run enterprises successfully. These are so difficult to explain, and they do mess up our analyses badly." Worse, sometimes reservation is swept away: "Let us ignore these cases and go our way into the future, a way made beautiful by logic and consistency. Have no doubts; intuition is chaos; rationality is all."

Management control
in the military departments

CHAPTER **C** by GORDON O. PEHRSON

This report is but a small drop in the cascading flood of attention
to the subject of "Defense Program Management." The findings and
recommendations of special commissions established to study the Defense Department crowd the files of government offices. The linear
measurement of new text dealing with large and small segments of
the subject grows in exponential pattern. Large "in-house management staffs" exist at all levels in the defense organization to improve
management of the largest single department in our government. Management consultant firms move in and out of problem areas on study
contracts. Management training courses are established, grow,
merge, subdivide and form new groupings to raise the level of individual competence for dealing with all parts of the defense management problem. A full range of professional associations, covering
selected subject fields of management interest exist, and vie for
membership from all parts of the defense establishment. In short,
the organized, documented, and continuing attention to defense management problems finds its definition and measurement in the same
superlative terms of size and variety that apply to any description of
the defense program itself.

There would be no purpose served here by drafting a detailed blueprint of the scope and content of the defense program. Some familiarity with these matters must be assumed if the subject title of this paper is to contain any interest. Let a few numbers suffice to place this
subject in useful focus.

The Defense departments own, and are responsible for managing, about 150 billion dollars worth of property. About 30 billion dollars of this is real property. The balance of 120 billion dollars consists of military and production equipment and supplies of all conceivable kinds.

The military departments have proposed operations for one year (fiscal year 1960) that will require the appropriation of about 41 billion dollars. The use of these funds, in broad classifications, are divided into five parts:

- Major procurement of equipment   13.3 billion dollars
- Military personnel   11.6   "   "
- Operation and maintenance   10.5   "   "
- Research, development test and evaluation 3.8 "   "
- Military construction   1.6   "   "

There are almost 1.1 million civil service employees in the military departments. The total number of military personnel is somewhat in excess of 2.5 million.

These kinds of data can be, and usually are, furiously heckled with qualifying footnotes. These distractions can be ignored. The purpose of this stark recitation is simply to establish the fact that the scope of the "things to be managed" in the defense program is large beyond any useful terms of personal reference with which the average reader may be familiar.

The volume and variety of activity for which the Defense Departments are responsible is greater than the activity represented by the gross national product of all but a few of the largest countries in the world.

SCOPE OF MANAGEMENT CONTROLS IN THE MILITARY

The title of this chapter—Management Control in the Military Departments—contains no qualification as to its scope of coverage. It should; and, I wish first to identify those matters which are set aside from this discussion.

First there is the wide range of intelligence activities and military operations. The subject of command operations will be noted only in the essential coupling of "consumer and producer" logistics planning as this relation bears on management control.

The management of military personnel is also essentially set aside, even though military persons represent over 70 per cent of the total

"controlled labor force" of the military departments. In defense
planning, military force levels are considered to be highly interchangeable military assets. The various controls that apply to their
use involve special considerations that justify their exclusion from
this paper, other than to note the existence of a special group of military persons (principally officers) in the management picture at all
levels of responsibility. There is no counterpart of this arrangement
in private industry. The pros and cons of this military-civilian "mix"
have been examined repeatedly and exhaustively, but always incon-
clusively. As a personal summary assessment, I believe that the
programs for military officer selection, career assignment, and
training make available a higher level of executive talent for defense
program management than would be possible by any other known
means.

As a final broad exclusion, I do not propose to discuss the controls
designed to keep people honest. Here the Uniform Code of Military
Justice, and the body of laws, regulations, and codes that control government civilian conduct have resulted in outstanding records of hon-
esty in the defense departments. Controls have been important to this
result, but I believe there is another point of important and special
influence. The atmosphere of self-censorship, and the holding to high
standards of personal integrity do have somewhat unique derivation
from the disciplines of military training. This is a point, not to be-
labor, but at least to recognize for its implications on management
control systems and principles.

Setting these three areas of consideration aside, there remains
the problem of defining the defense management problem in a manner
that will permit an understanding of controls in terms broad enough
to ignore Service Department differences, yet meaningful enough to
provide useful points for discussion.

I believe this can be done within a framework that separates the
defense management problem into three parts.

1. The Management of Materiel.

2. The Management of Field Agency Operations.

3. The Management of Programs.

This classification is but one of many ways in which this total subject can be divided for discussion. I believe it to be a useful way in
which to identify control principles and procedures; to point up the
complex interplay and contradictions of some of these control mechanisms; and to highlight the need for new concepts of management that
will better resolve problems existing in and between each of these
different, broadly defined areas of management responsibility. The

opportunities for applying operational research approaches and electronic computer techniques to these problems can also be identified.

SUPPLY MANAGEMENT

Consider first supply management broadly defined. The military departments have responsibilities for managing an inventory of equipment and supplies valued at 120 billion dollars.

The problems associated with managing intentories of these dimensions are, of course, staggering. They are common to all Services. The commodity groupings into which supply management operations are classified differ between the Services; and these groupings keep changing with new patterns of need. But in all cases the functions of supply break down into the simply stated problems of determining what is needed, getting it, storing it, maintaining it, distributing it to points of use, and finally disposing of the unneeded items through sale, salvage, or destruction.

In the handling of these problems of massive supply support to the military demands of a dynamic defense program, the departments have quite naturally turned to electronic data processing systems (EDPS) for solutions.

Under Defense policy directives the Service departments have developed long-range projections for the use of automatic data processing systems covering their "business type" operations. Over 175 major computer installations were approved by the end of the fiscal year 1959. This number is projected to increase two and a half times during the next two years. The application of computers to logistic and supply functions has been given priority in these plans.

It is in supply management that the most clearly demonstrated benefits can be established for obtaining project approval under criteria that list in order (1) to reduce current direct costs; (2) to prevent major cost increases; and, (3) to solve system deficiencies.

It is from projects in the third of these categories that the most important improvement of supply management will come, with return benefits of the kind listed in the first two categories.

Application of EDPS to Supply Management Control

Developments in the field of EDPS provide new and exciting terms of reference in which logistic operations of the past can be re-examined, and military concepts of future operations can be confidently planned.

There are few technical advances in the non-weapon fields which

have so directly challenged the limitations on which so many past decisions have, of necessity, been based. EDP systems give to the defense departments what is truly the most limited resource with which
to plan and program logistic effort. It gives time, the most perishable
of all resources. Time is the one asset that cannot be accumulated in
reserves, but can be saved only in operations. The full potential of
EDPS has required that the departments think in the new compressed
measurements of time that represent the core of the EDPS advantage.
The range of things that can be done "in time" through EDPS applications will direct inquiry into every corner of the total military
logistic responsibility.

The Services have only begun to inventory the possibilities. These
possibilities are not merely related to improvement in procedural
details, nor to improvement in the administration of management
control systems now operative. The basic concepts on which these
systems rest; the organizational, command, and staff relationships
which these systems support, are being re-examined. It is being found
that many of these concepts are based on two limitations which can
now be challenged by EDPS.

The Limitation of Time

A few examples are illustrative. The lack of time to process supply and demand knowledge at central supply and stock control points
has dictated in large part the physical and functional characteristics
of the defense supply distribution system. More rapid and accurate
knowledge of where "things" are, where they are needed and being
used, and where they can best be shipped from, has already permitted
reductions in military inventories totaling hundreds of millions of
dollars. This is the classic application, where better use of better
information directly substitutes for expensive ownership and wide-
spread physical distribution of material. The opportunities for further
exploiting these profitable substitutions are just beginning to emerge.

There is another, more subtle but more difficult, problem that
derives from the limitations of time. The lack of time in which to
classify supply data for the many different points of executive and
staff interest has dictated the establishment of awkward, compromised information control apparatus throughout the Departments of
Defense. Budget and program analysts, and the other functional staff
and supervisory groups, dissatisfied with information that reaches
them through these compromised systems, seek to use data organized
to meet the different needs of operators and commanders. The frequent misuse of these data through misunderstanding has created
great barriers of distrust and dissension between powerful staff

authorities and gravely responsible command or line elements. Again, the opportunities for synthesizing data into arrangements of new perception, and in time to serve the pressured purposes of central staff, can be found through intelligent application of EDPS.

The Fallibility of Man in Information Processing

The second great limitation on which so much in control system and organizational structure has been built might be called, for want of better words, the assumed or real fallibility and errors of men. This limitation has been particularly severe in the supply management field where elaborate and expensive doctrine, supervisory, and resource control apparatus has been established. EDPS has permitted review of many decisions based on this limitation. In a very fundamental assessment we can note that progress has always been represented by an extension of the number of important operations which can be performed without thinking about them. We now know that many of the supply data-processing functions can be performed easily and naturally by EDPS. We know that, when firm judgment factors can be expressed numerically in advance, the machines can make discriminations which have the nature of what we now call decisions.

On this fact, fully recognized, the existing structure of echeloning supply supervision can be revised. Large segments of the present problem of tracing, identifying and measuring the impact of program changes through the thousandfold parts of supply supporting systems can be solved—accurately and quickly.

The Economic System Analogy in Supply Management

But until the military departments develop better ''demand-sensitive'' supply management reputations, the principal controls in this area of responsibility will continue to be through fund controlling procedures established under the Defense ''Financial Management Program.''

In supply management the fund controlling procedures operate at two levels. First, there is control of the funds made available to military ''customers.'' The need to use material or supplies for various purposes must be justified in detail through the budgetary process. If this need is approved, then funds are made available to the ''customer.'' He then ''spends'' these funds in ''buying'' material from the military supply system. These monies move from military ''buyers' '' pockets into military ''sellers' '' pockets, called Stock Funds. The receipts from these ''sales'' accumulate in the various Stock Funds where they are supposed to be available to supply managers for use in maintaining proper supply system inventories. At this point, however, the funding authorities again move into the picture and impound these "sales receipts" until the seller can justify really spending them to buy material for the supply system from commercial and industrial sources.

In conceptual terms this arrangement means that the military departments are trying to operate internally through an "economic system" with buyer and seller relations established by procedures based on fund transactions.

The economic system analogy is complete even to the inclusion of periods of acute economic depression. The services, from time to time, find they have warehouses full of material which they want to use but cannot get out of the warehouses because the material is "owned" by the supply managers and there is inadequate "purchasing power" in the pockets of the military command customers. Actual bartering and script arrangements are sometimes resorted to as a form of "relief"; but in some cases desirable programs starve in the midst of plenty.

A recent example of this sort of thing was reported to the Congress during the present legislative session. The Army had a surplus of 67 million dollars worth of canvas. The National Guard had thousands of tanks and other vehicles in open storage rusting because of the lack of canvas. But the supply could not be applied to the demand because "funds were not available with which to buy this material from the Army stock fund."

This is not an isolated case. It is the kind of a problem that was predicted would result from trying to install concepts of a "free economy" into large internal supply operations without providing adequate counterparts for the well-developed banking and credit systems and the "turnover" of money that keeps free economic systems operating with disciplined viability.

Assuming the conceptual soundness of "dollar transactions" between the elements of the defense department as a spur to efficiency and economy in supply management, then in this "control area" there are indeed great opportunities for more imaginative design of financial systems than have been installed to date.

It is not visionary to assume that the military departments could establish the most efficient supply supporting system that has ever been conceived in or out of government. The factors required for such a demonstration are controlled in a way that will never exist in the market play of a free economy. The problem basically rests on the sheer difficulty of processing relevant information to points of logical decision. It is possible to develop adequate capabilities for rapid processing of supply data. It is possible to tie this capability to communication media that will permit continuing or statistically validated "market analysis" of usage. It is possible to identify and assess the effects of program changes on future supply demand. And it is possible to tie supply operations together with fiscal systems designed to permit control of funds and to replace the present funding systems which are designed to control supply operations.

In this scale of possibilities the essential role of automatic data processing systems is quite obvious.

MANAGEMENT OF FIELD AGENCIES

Moving next to the problems in Management of Field Agencies, we again find that the scope of activity is measured and defined in the maximal terms suggested by the ownership of over 30 billion dollars worth of real property. The elements of the total defense field establishment range from small posts, camps, and stations to huge industrial, depot, research, and test complexes supporting the manifold operations of the defense program.

In this area of defense department responsibility we find many direct counterparts with the management control problems of business. The functions performed at the government plant or laboratory level are virtually identical with those carried on in similar installations operating in our private business structure.

At this level of operations the management control systems, locally operative, have familiar patterns. The control system effort includes, for example, establishing sound operating budgets supported by useful modern cost accounting systems. Operational performance data is systematically organized and reported based on engineered standards. Modern production control methods, and the complete array of modern management techniques have been introduced with varying degrees of effectiveness.

What has been done on balance at these local installation levels compares quite favorably with what would be found in a comparable cross section of American industry at plant levels of operation. The profit and loss statements prepared under government plant industrial funding procedures permit "profits" to conceal inefficiency about as effectively as they do in private industry of equal size. And "losses" are about as responsive to factors other than operational efficiency to about the same counterpart degree.

The point is simply that unusual management problems related to field agency control do not originate at the local levels. The nature and size of problems which are somewhat unique to the defense department in this area of responsibility derive from three principal "external" causes. These causes are: (1) the bigness of the organ-

izations of which these agencies are individual parts; (2) the complex
interrelations between the many parts and layers of authority in these
big organizations; and, (3) the changing nature of the total defense
programs to which these field elements must make supporting ad-
justments.

Figure II-C-1 is a rather strange looking attempt to represent in

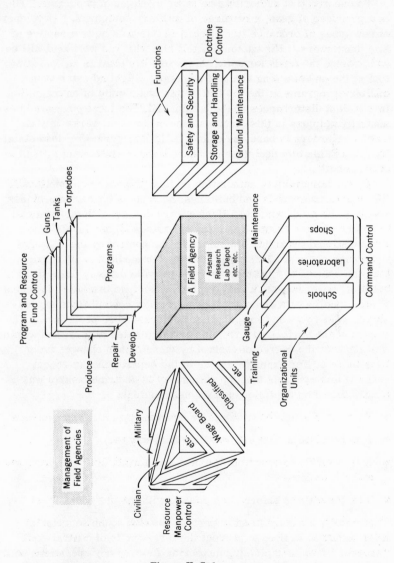

Figure II-C-1.

a single figure, the main elements of the field agency management problem. All field agencies are captives of "higher authorities," and the station commander or plant manager is required to turn many different faces to these different authorities. To each of them, therefore, he has a different appearance. In the chart, for example, four of his "faces" are depicted.

To one group of authorities he is a "manager of programs." (He is a producer of guns, a repairer of military equipment, a developer of new types of ordnance items, etc.) In this role he is a captive of his "customers." His customers tell him what his workload will be and provide the funds for doing this work. His plant is an operating tool at the end of a long chain of command. Slight adjustment in military programs at the top end of this chain quite often magnifies into violent disturbances at the bottom end. The local manager is essentially helpless in this circumstance because he works only on customer orders in hand. He cannot build long-term workload stability through his own decisions or through the operations of a "sales department".

To another group of authorities he is a "manager of functions". (He maintains grounds and buildings, he handles boxes, he provides security, he kills rats, etc.) Here we are dealing with the powerful influence of staff groups operating at various higher levels in the organizational pyramids of authority. The control by these groups is through doctrine. This control is less immediate in its impact than the control by "customers" who provide the only funds he has, but it is, nevertheless, a very real influence. He is audited in terms of his compliance with doctrine. This type of control finds expression in vast volumes of regulations and prescribed procedures. The record of the various departments on this matter differs; and within departments the degree of control by these means changes from time to time. For example, in one of the departments in recent years it was apparent that the philosophy of doctrine control was firmly based on the following four assumptions:

- There is a single best way to do everything in all field agencies.

- It is possible to find out what this best way is.

- It is possible to describe this best way for all field agencies, and make it understood.

- It is possible to enforce compliance with the use of this best way.

Fortunately, a change in an important position at the secretarial level occurred in time to prevent the large staffs of central staff "experts" from completely smothering field agency operations under a heavy blanket of regulations.

Large industrial concerns go through these same cycles and face continually the problem of maintaining balance between prescribed doctrine and useful procedural guidance from central staff sources. In the defense departments the existence of military command relations and the patterns of military regulations makes it more difficult to maintain this proper balance in establishing management relations between echelons of authority.

To a third group of authorities, the installation manager is a "landlord" for various organizational units put together into a multipurpose agency. Strong command lines of authority exist between elements of his agency and counterpart groups at higher levels. These groups control through their authority over organization, facilities, personnel selection and assignment, and management audits.

And, finally, to still another group the plant manager is a "manager of people." From this source of authority he receives allocation of manpower ceilings and prescribed staffing patterns. This is a very complete control of an essential resource. The chart suggests a few of the many classifications of personnel under which this control is applied.

This total picture is somewhat overdrawn, and a great deal is being done to strengthen the position of field agency managers in their relations to the higher command and staff elements. The largest problem, however, remains and is not easily solved. This is the problem of a constantly changing defense program; and planning and controlling the use of the defense field agencies in a way that will permit their most effective use in supporting these changes.

THE MANAGEMENT OF PROGRAMS

Actually the operation of government facilities under the new realities of defense planning represents only a small part of a much larger problem, for which the solution is only beginning to appear in dim outline. This larger problem involves new concepts of organization for tying the resources of our entire country to the new demands of present military programs. In the past it has been possible to support a large part of the military's requirement either from standard peacetime goods or by "beating plowshares into swords" at times of national emergency. Today, the dynamics of modern technology and the awesome military products of modern science have created a need for new terms in which industrial response can be effectively coupled to military purpose.

The production miracle of World War II is becoming as irrelevant as the "power horn and musket" response of 1776 would be to the realities of present defense problems.

This matter is most clearly noted in the field of guided and ballistic missiles with all of their associated supporting subsystems. These complex weapon systems have no counterparts in the civilian economy. They have no counterparts in prior military planning on a number of vital points of difference. First, they need be few in number to serve their intended purpose. A few of these weapons carry the destructive power of hundreds of thousands of prior weapons. This means there is no need for mass production of these weapons. But there must be "enough" and they must be ready. Being ready in mobilization production plans will serve little purpose.

Secondly, these new weapon systems are continually being made obsolete by rapid changes in technology. This fact coupled with the fact that the weapons are fantastically expensive further supports a case for not building large weapon inventories based on frozen designs.

These points alone have been enough to dictate a new look at all prior concepts of production planning within government facilities and with private industry. It has become increasingly apparent that the defense program is "calling out" a specialized industry in which the elements will be unlike any before established in this country. It will be an industry in which combinations of government and contractor operated public facilities will be tied to private industry through many different and new patterns of prime, associate, and subcontracting relationship.

In these emerging complexes of research, development, engineering, test and production facilities, and organizational resources, the defense departments must squarely face up to the role of their own field agency assets. The tremendous values represented by these investments in facilities and experience must be sensibly merged with the new kind of weapon industry that is now needed.

A more difficult appraisal in clearly objective terms is hard to imagine. The subject is badly clouded with interservice proprietary feelings toward their own agencies. Vaguely disturbing half convictions about the benefits of "free enterprise" are forcing a halting "desocialization" of much activity previously carried on in the defense field establishment. There is haphazard "picking at the spots" of newsworthy difficulty by congressional committees. Contractors, and the communities supported by weapon industry payrolls, maneuver crudely for advantage and then cringe from the label of "munitions lobby."

These influences and others equally extraneous will always be present in a free and democratic society. But they need not be the dominant, dictating influences that now prevent the military departments from putting together a sound military-industrial, public-private combination of resources that will serve as the new kind of technologically dynamic base needed to support the new kind of military problems we face.

Only a small fraction of the effort expended in the design and production of specific weapon systems is being applied to this problem of organizing the new weapons industry. Yet the value of this supporting base is vastly more enduring than the performance of any single new weapon system now under development.

Again we turn in our need to operational research and information processing techniques for better means by which to make the complex assessments, and best combinations of resources required.

Finally as the third major part of this approach to the defense management problem, there is that area of responsibility which is called management of programs. In outlining briefly the supply management problem and the problems of field agency management, I have returned to a single principal difficulty, the difficulty of adjusting supply decisions and field operations to the changing nature of defense programs. If a single source of control had to be identified as the principal discipline in defense management, in most cases the answer would be "It is program control."

Control Programs

Each of the services have "Program Systems" which are designed to provide for development of balanced programs in terms of forces, facilities and material which will be in accord with war plans, existing resources and anticipated fund availabilities for varying periods of future time. In the Army for example, there are five "Control Programs" established as the framework within which all planned effort of the Army is to be defined. These programs are "Troops, Installations, Materiel, Reserve Components, and Research and Development." Responsibilities for the preparation, revision, performance review of and reporting on these Control Programs is assigned to various high levels of authority in the Army General Staff.

Within the framwork of these Control Programs all of the planned effort of each command or agency in the department must be defined, scheduled, and priced out in terms that will permit determination of consistency with all other effort that is required to achieve common "program objectives".

The other military departments have similar Control Program approaches with variations in their classification, and differences in the organizations and procedures through which total planning is carried out under this control concept. Figure II-C-2 illustrates this concept of "program planning" by identifying and showing the complete interdependence of major factors in one part of a total depart-

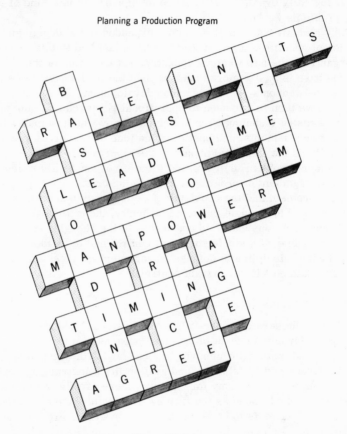

Figure II-C-2.

mental program. (The example might represent a proposal to produce a quantity of rockets.)

Complete staff work in the preparation of such a part of a total plan would require that consideration be given to each of the listed elements. These considerations must respond to policy guidance and the controlling "program objectives" in each area where they apply.

In more specific terms, this means in our example:

● The "Item," number of "Units," and "Timing" would involve review and approval from various operational staff groups who approve the "requirement" for the proposed procurement with consideration of "Troop" and "Material" Program Objectives.

- The "Item" itself may involve research and engineering staff review and approval as to its readiness for procurement. This would involve referral to the staff responsible for "R & D" Control Programs.

- The production capacity "Base," the proposed "Rate" of production, and "Stowage" facilities involve considerations of peacetime and mobilization readiness planning. The changing policies and Control Program Objectives related to these matters are applied through "Material" and "Installation" program authorities.

- "Leadtime" factors involve both production facts and funding policy. These matters receive the attention of procurement and fiscal authorities.

- "Manpower" as it involves government employees (military and civilian) is a controlled resource. To the extent that a production plan involves the use of government employees the requirements of separate manpower authorities must be met, as they too are included in the review and approval chain.

- "Loading" is listed as an element to indicate the involvement of still other authorities when part of the plan requires work in a government field agency such as an ammunition depot. Here the total station workload (of which a specific production proposal may be a part) receives the attention of "banker type" authorities in the Defense Department and the Bureau of the Budget. Most of the industrial-type operations of the Defense Department are funded through "operating capital allocations," which are maintained by "receipts" from "sales" to "customers." The "bankers" can influence the level of a station operation by their action on the "line of credit" they extend as operating capital.

- Finally, there is the element of "Price," which is the key that unlocks the entire plan to the attention of Comptroller staffs. These groups use this "authority over money" as the basis for examining and auditing all elements listed.

This is a very brief sketch of the difficulty of responding to program guidence even for simple proposals and even when guidance is made available through well-documented and formalized Control Program systems.

The Need for Better Information Processing

In this example, the elements of the plan are interlocked and interdependent. Remove one element and the pattern comes apart. Yet it is not possible to even present such a total plan to a single authority who can agree to it. The elements of the plan are, as noted, presented to different "program review" staff groups who have authority to act only on "their parts" of the plan. Unfavorable action by any one of these groups can negate the favorable action of all of the others.

Multiply this simple, single example by the multi-thousand parts of the effort involved in the totality of a 41 billion dollar defense program. The enormity of the job of effecting program control as a basic discipline over all defense agency activity quite clearly points to the need for electronic computer assistance. Man simply cannot identify, sort out, arrange, cross reference, and assess the importance of the many actions which bear on program decisions to be made, and translate the effect of these decisions into known and meaningful responses. With long-range stability in these decisions this problem might be solved through massive staff effort. Under pressures of change and time, the defense departments will have to turn increasingly to the new "information technologies" for help.

The seriousness of this program is clearly unfolding in Washington today in shaping up the defense program for the next fiscal year. The Defense Appropriation Committee of the House in its report stated:

"The President, the Secretary of Defense, the Congress and the American people have a right to expect a better job from the (Joint Chiefs of Staff) . . . in the way of military guidance. ance. . . . There is something wrong in our present military planning."

The House of Representatives then proceeded to make major revisions in the President's Defense Program through action on the FY 1960 budget. The Senate in turn has differed with both the House and the President's plans for defense, and has set forth its own version of what this defense program should include. With this kind of confusion at the highest levels in our government there is small wonder that management through "program control" has been very difficult to establish. Yet, it is the only sound approach that can be responsibly advanced.

The established military authorities must be permitted to recast their decisions into the terms they are supposed to be most qualified to use. It has been suggested that these terms are "strategic retalia-

tion, continental air defense, limited war and antisubmarine" functional forces, rather than the present Army, Navy, and Air Force
designations. If these are the terms in which a modern military pos-
ture has meaning, then they are the terms into which all programmed activity should be fitted.

From decisions in these terms, the entire management of total
approved programs can unfold. Given total cohesive "program
packages" to administer, there is abundant talent to provide effective and efficient management of all of the activity involved in their
accomplishment.

Description of Program Management

As a final summary presentation chart, I believe the case for program management can be presented in the form of a management
matrix. (See Figure II-C-3.)

Note that the "things to be managed" represent the total true
content of a military program. The decision to create a kind of a
military capability includes, as it must, material, men, and the operational and logistic supporting projects that are required to bring men
and material together to points of military application. Given a job to
do in these total most meaningful terms, then the "means of management," which are quite familiar, can be applied with properly balanced emphasis and reflection of sound management principles. In
the use of these means, as a point of personal appraisal, I would
judge the greatest current need is for strengthening the programming
function. Computers are needed for this job. The mass of interacting
forces cannot be handled adequately by other means.

In this matrix there is an overlay of familiar-type controls. In
the defense department today the strongest control apparatus exists
for the control of resources—money and manpower. Doctrine and
supervisory controls tighten and are relaxed with changing patterns
of central staff influence. But what should be the most effective and
meaningful control—that of information—has been the least effective
of all. There is need for better ways to separate relevant data from
the irrelevant; better, more accurate means for sorting out the in-
consequential variants from those matters which require the exercise of human judgment and knowledge; better and faster ways to
measure the impact of failure or success in accomplishing a planned
event on the probability of meeting other future planned and scheduled objectives.

These needs always bring attention back to new information processing techniques and proven statistical methodology. In these
fields of new knowledge there is encouraging progress. The decision-

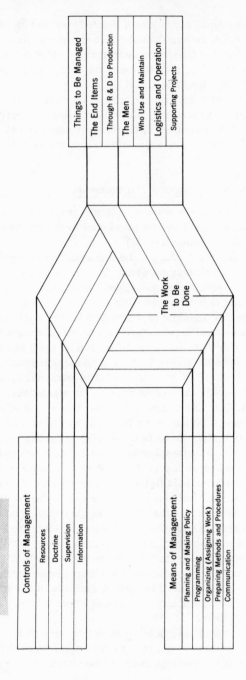

Management Matrix
A Weapon System Program

Controls of Management

Resources

Doctrine

Supervision

Information

Means of Management

Planning and Making Policy

Programming

Organizing (Assigning Work)

Preparing Methods and Procedures

Communication

The Work to Be Done

Things to Be Managed

The End Items

Through R & D to Production

The Men

Who Use and Maintain

Logistics and Operation

Supporting Projects

Figure II-C-3.

making and management control problems for defense operations, even those of the present scale and complexity, can be reduced to manageable proportions.

DISCUSSION   (Following Mr. Pehrson's presentation of his paper)

A. J. ROWE: Would you call "in-time" control equivalent to what Mr. Kappler has reffered to as "on-time" control?

G. O. PEHRSON: Yes. If you are talking about a problem which is unique in the military operation—that is, keeping track of things while they are happening.

A. O. MANN: Were you differentiating between peacetime and wartime operations?

G. O. PEHRSON: The primary difference is that in war there is more frantic behavior, and the same attention is not paid to the results of the control.

A. O. MANN: But doesn't the command structure change?

G. O. PEHRSON: Since it does not always change on paper this is one of the real problems. In peacetime people are given responsibilities, and yet their behavior is prescribed in a manner that makes them comply with what other people have told them to do. And yet in a case of emergency these same people are expected to remove the peace time reins of control and become very resourceful administrators. There has been no serious fundamental thinking about peacetime controls and their effect on wartime operations. It is, of course, clear that in a wartime situation (such as World War II) the accommodation of control procedures to a free economy would no longer be necessary. The country would be operating under a controlled economy responsive to military needs.

W. E. ALBERTS: Doesn't the personality of a military organization change when, at some very high levels, you have an influx of reserve officers who have different attitudes toward control systems?

G. O. PEHRSON: They have different attitudes and talents. In a war there is a tendency to throw the book away and get man back into the picture. In this regard, General Somerville's operations in the Army during World War II were very interesting. He accumulated some very fine people around his Army Supply operation. As soon as the war was over, the Army changed his whole supply command structure. Yet, when the Korean War came along much of his operation was changed back to what it had been during World War II.

The need for compact management intelligence

CHAPTER **D** by NORMAN J. REAM

Today, there is a growing complexity both of the business enterprise and its internal management environment, and of the economic, governmental, and social climate in which it exists. There is also the growing specialization of management which creates an ever-expanding requirement for planned objectives, basic understanding, and intelligible common management language. Without this common language, top management decisions, however right, will never become fully realized.

Management continues to seek means to cope with the myriad of problems resulting from the increasing size and complexity of their corporate structure. They are continuing their quest of means to develop an organizational structure that will provide a proper delegation of responsibilities and authorities, and relationships within the organization that will allow an individual to function effectively, and which will achieve a higher level of profitability through individual, group, and corporate effectiveness.

In the past few years members of management have heard, read about, discussed, devised, and experimented with innumerable management techniques. In view of the large number of management problems, this profusion was inevitable. But this fact in turn has found management with an extremely confusing problem—the problem of choosing the right techniques. Today, there is sufficient evidence that the choosing has been haphazard, biased, and ill-formed. The

prime problem facing management today is not "What is the technique?" but "What is the problem?"

The problem is to find the means for the development of an integrated management structure.

Twenty years ago it was possible to envision the management of
most business enterprises mechanically as an assemblage of functions,
but today we know that when we talk of management, separate functions do not in reality exist. We speak of business profit, risk, product, investment, customer relationships, etc. The normal functions
are irrelevant to any of them, yet we do recognize that work has to be
done by people who specialize because no one person thoroughly understands the entirety of a given function, let alone all the functions
of a business. A basic problem then is how do we translate functional
knowledge and functional contribution into general direction and profitable general results?

If the basic problem facing management is the development of an
integrated management structure, it would appear axiomatic that
functional knowledge and functional contributions of the various levels
of management must be integrated. These functions would be focused
in accordance with their individual responsibility requirements by
means of a compact set of management intelligence as the output of
an integrated management information system. This can only be developed by a dynamic analysis of decision criteria, which, when followed, tend to lead to decisions in all parts of the management structure which are most profitable or desirable for the organization as a
whole.

MECHANIZATION VERSUS MANAGEMENT INFORMATION SYSTEMS DEVELOPMENT

Little progress has been made to date in the development of a compact set of management intelligence. Almost without exception, corporations are focusing their attention solely on cost reduction in a
frantic effort to compensate for their having failed in the past to provide proper and balanced functional management guidance to their
efforts.

Efforts to date have generally been devoted to the use of electronic
data processing systems, or other hardware, as a substitution for
clerical paperwork efforts. Little effort has been devoted to a dynamic
analysis of the entire management effort to determine the interaction
of its components and their informational requirements.

As a result, the typical situation that currently exists within a corporation is that the plan for information flow to the various echelons

of management is not in accord with that which should be available to properly carry out their assigned management responsibilities. Available information normally consists of a conglomerate of usable and unusable information that complicates rather than simplifies their decision-making role. The tendency has been and continues to be that of increasing the flow of information rather than to refine the flow through the establishment of required decision criteria. This practice inhibits the development of an integrated management information system by promoting a continued functionalization approach to the problem.

M. E. Salveson in his treatise "Dynamic Organization Planning"[1] states "that the many and expensive control systems used in business, such as cost control, production control, quality control, etc., often compete or conflict with each other in managerial decision-making. The competition is due to inadequate articulation and communication of decision critera from top management. Thus, the decisions are often less profitable or effective than they might be. The same potential competition and conflict exists in any organization in which the decision criteria have not been determined through a dynamic analysis."

The challenge is not just to mechanize. The real opportunities are in our ability to develop a compact set of management intelligence that will permit us to take advantage of the required functionalization of management and at the same time allow for full-planned coordination of a corporation. This was recently emphasized by Peter F. Drucker in his article "Long-Range Planning—Challenge to Management Science"[2] in which he stated:

> "We need to know how to 'translate' from business needs, business results and business decisions into functional capacity and specialized effort. There is, after all, no functional decision, there is not even functional data, just as there is no functional profit, no functional loss, no functional investment, no functional risk, no functional customer, no functional product and no functional image of a company. There is only a unified company product, risk, investment, and so on, hence only company performance and company results. Yet at the same time the work obviously has to be done by people each of whom has to be specialized. Hence for a decision to be possible, we must be able to integrate divergent individual knowledges and capacities into one organization potential; and for a decision to be effective, we must be able to translate it into a diversity of individual and expert, yet focused efforts."

RESPONSIBILITIES OF MANAGEMENT

Let us turn for a moment to a discussion of the basic responsibilities of management. Certainly the planning of management's information systems in a company must be addressed to the responsibilities of that management.

We can in a broad sense, define the responsibilities of management as the guidance, leadership, and control of a group of individuals toward a common objective. This broad definition indicates a purpose, but fails to give us insight as to how results are obtained. Therefore, it is necessary to define the responsibilities of management by defining their five basic processes:

- Planning—that is, determining what shall be done. As used here, planning covers a wide range of decisions, including the clarification of objectives, establishment of policies, establishment of programs, and determining specific methods and procedures.

- Organizing—that is, grouping the activities necessary to carry out the plans into management units, and defining the relationships among the executives and workers in such units.

- Assembling resources—that is, obtaining for the use of the business the personnel, capital, facilities, and other things needed to carry out the established plans.

- Directing—that is, issuing management directives. This includes the vital matter of indicating plans to those who are responsible for carrying them out.

- Controlling—that is, seeing that operating results conform as nearly as possible to the established plans. This involves the establishment of performance standards, motivation of people to achieve these standards, comparison of actual results against the predetermined standard, and initiating necessary corrective action when performance deviates from the plan.

All management engages in the processes I have enumerated and it is clear that the individuals who comprise the various levels of management spend varying amounts of time at each.

The various members of management are divided in their functional specialities in the areas of sales, research and development, engineering, manufacturing, finance, industrial relations, etc. Each of these functional areas may in turn be divided into the five basic processes of management that I have previously enumerated. (See Figure II-D-1.)

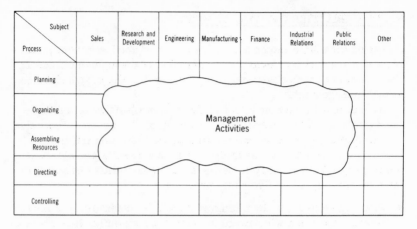

Process \ Subject	Sales	Research and Development	Engineering	Manufacturing	Finance	Industrial Relations	Public Relations	Other
Planning								
Organizing								
Assembling Resources								
Directing								
Controlling								

Figure II-D-1.

THE MANAGEMENT PYRAMID

The various levels of management may be regarded as the management pyramid. (See Figures II-D-2 and II-D-3.) The base of the pyramid is first line supervision—for example, the foreman. The procession up the pyramid of management levels proceeds through the general foreman, superintendents, branch managers, division managers, middle-management group executives, and finally top management (including the Board of Directors). The bulk of the operating decisions are made in the lower regions of the management pyramid. As we proceed up the pyramid, the role of the decisions change from operational to those more directly concerned with the planning and control phases. Accordingly, each successively higher level of management requires less detail concerning the individual functions; the requirement as we progress upward is for consolidation of information and reports pointing out deviations from pre-established standards, together with analyses of the causes of the deviation. This principle is axiomatic in the development of a proper management information system in order to furnish management with a compact set of management intelligence.

Traditionally, we like to envision top management as exercising full planning and operating control over the business enterprise. However, in actuality members of top management have found that it is necessary that they devote their major efforts to the planning and control phases and that they delegate the operational control to lower echelons of management. This represents a delegation of authority

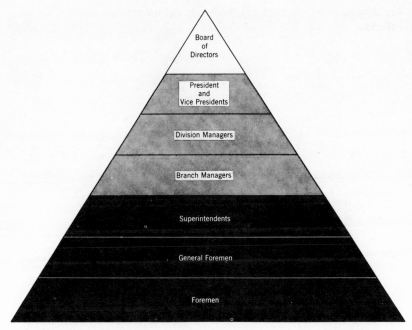

The Management Pyramid

Figure II-D-2.

but not a shift in basic responsibility and is characteristic of decentralized management.

The result of this shift in top management efforts has led to a
requirement for the development of performance measurement techniques which are much more precise than has heretofore been required. The absence of such performance criteria inhibits effective
decentralization and delegation of authority, and precludes the use of
management by exception reporting principles.

The establishment of performance measurements in a corporation
determines action—both on the part of the person measuring and the
one being measured—and as a consequence directs, limits, and causes
the behavior and performance of the corporation.

The types of performance measurement devised and their ultimate
use determines what information will be considered relevant in the
operation of a business. The results desired must be built into the
management processes in such a manner that one can determine
whether or not expectations have actually been fulfilled—including
a knowledge of the deviations. Otherwise, management cannot plan,

for they have no information feedback and no precise control of their efforts.

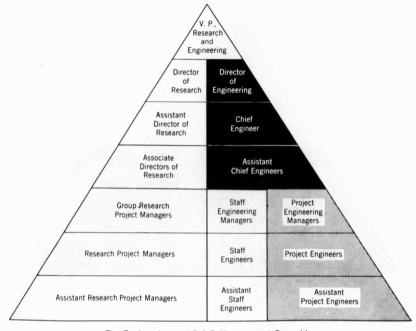

The Engineering and R & D Management Pyramid

Figure II-D-3.

To emphasize the critical requirement for the development of a fully integrated management information system with its inherent development of a compact management report structure, one only has to review the dominating growth factors that are characteristic of those successful companies that are a major part of our industrial economy. The dominating growth factors according to the Company Planning Research Section of Stanford Research Institute[3] are:

"Long-range planning; product research and development; marketing research; and acquisition and expansion into new high growth fields."

Long-range planning has been defined by Drucker[2] as "the contin-uous process of making present entrepreneurial (risk taking) deci-sions systematically and with the best possible knowledge of their futurity, organizing systematically the efforts needed to carry out these decisions, and measuring the results of these decisions against the expectations through <u>organized, systematic feedback</u>."

The stress that is placed on "organized, systematic feedback" is a direct demand for the development of a dynamic management information system and the accompanying compact reporting structure.

STRUCTURE OF REPORTS

The output of the management information system is determined by the nature of the responsibilities assigned to each level of the organizational structure. A basic problem encountered, however, is the determination of what point in the organizational hierarchy we find the transition made from operating reports to management planning and control reports.

In developing an integrated management information system, it is necessary to stratify the levels of reporting in the enterprise and to clearly understand the basic characteristics of each of these levels. Essentially, these levels are concerned with:

- Management Planning.

- Management Control (performance measurement).

- Operational Control.

- Legal and Governmental.

It is important to note that each of these report levels is dynamic in nature, and that each must necessarily change in response to changes in the socio-economic and political environment. Legal and governmental reporting requirements, for example, while varying from industry to industry, have become an important part of the report structure of every company. Various industrial-governmental associations and committees have been created to facilitate the exchange of information between governmental agencies and industry.

The essential differences between management planning, management control, and operational control reports may be enumerated as follows:

Planning Reports

The basic objective in the planning report structure is to evaluate the company position in the industry with other comparable entities. Also included are the alternate courses of action available to management under a series of predetermined premises.

Control Reports

The basic objective of the control reports structure is to inform top management of functional operating performance as compared to predetermined performance standards. These reports activate changes in planned performance as such action is required.

Operating Reports

The basic objective of the operating report structure is to inform functional management of the current performance of operations within a given function. Normally, this report structure includes a comparative analysis of current operations and operations for a previous period, as well as current performance compared to predetermined detailed performance standards for immediate action.

If we refer to the "management pyramid" (Figures II-D-2 and II-D-3), we find that the responsibility for management planning and management control increases as we approach the top echelons of management, and that operational control receives its greatest emphasis at the base, or lowest management, level. It is recognized, of course, that planning and control responsibilities are inherent in every level of management. The basic distinction lies in the emphasis on the nature and degree of the planning and operational control responsibilities found at each distinct level of management.

THE MANAGEMENT INFORMATION SYSTEMS CONCEPT

It is well recognized that a corporation can no longer continue to operate as a series of uncorrelated functional organizations. Therefore, the one paramount problem facing management today is the development of an integrated management effort. Admittedly, the development of a completely integrated organizational effort on the part of the management is something that will not be attained in the immediate future and will require the continued use of functional organization structure, management committee actions, etc. The ultimate solution of this vital problem, however, rests with the development of an optimal integrated management information system, the output of which can and will contribute heavily to the eventual development of integrated management operations.

Further, the development of an optimal management information system requires recognition on the part of all management that data requirements do not recognize existing functional organization lines and must flow freely between them in an impersonal manner where-ever required. The second requirement is a recognition that such an optimal system requires the maximum utilization of all known data-processing techniques, including clerical and machine systems, electronic data-processing equipment, electronic source data automation and communication equipments. Information processing is not confined to the use of electronic data-processing equipment alone.

Indeed, fundamental to the development of an integrated management information system is the need to clearly identify and to understand those pertinent factors that affect the conduct of an enterprise, and the basic information required by management to properly plan, control, and operate the business.

The development of such a system requires a recognition of three basic phases in its evolution:

- A clear definition of the problem.

- A definitive outline of the logic of the system to be employed.

- A detailed definition of the techniques to be employed to implement the system.

The final step, a detailed definition of the techniques to be employed to implement the system, is clearly the responsibility of the systems planner, and involves the use of data-processing hardware and techniques. The first two steps, however, require that a close working relationship be established between those in the planning effort and all levels of management, and that management actively participate in the development of the integrated management information system.

The achievement of the basic goal, however, will be possible only after extensive research is conducted in the areas of identifying and understanding all factors which affect the operation of a business. Merely applying data-processing equipments to the refinement of existing information systems may speed up the production of existing reports, but it does little to further progress in the development of an integrated information system. Unfortunately, much effort has been expended in systems projects in many companies which follows this "computer application" approach. This approach has been followed in the main because many managements feel that the basic information problem they have faced is concerned with the organization of existing data on a faster, more timely basis. The management information systems concept, however, is more basic and profound in that it requires dynamic analysis of the entire management problem (as shown in Figure II-D-4), with emphasis on the development of an integrated management intelligence system, not merely the refinement of single existing functional reports.

Development of Management Information

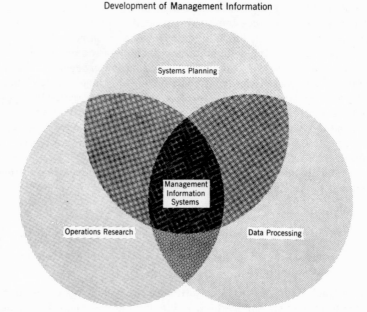

Figure II-D-4.

The criteria of a planned management information system that will provide the required intelligence are (see Figure II-D-5):

● It facilitates planning and control, and provides top management with a comprehensive understanding of those factors, both external and internal, which influence the conduct of the business.

● It provides for performance measurement of functional responsibilities, and at the same time, presents top management with the means for over-all review of company-wide operational results of a consolidated nature.

● It provides all information requirements for dynamic operational control in all areas of the management structure that are profitable or desirable for the organization as a whole.

● It provides for the development of those informational requirements that are essential to the continued development and application of advanced scientific management techniques.

● It is dynamic in nature, capable of change to conform with shifts in the socio-economic and political environment in which the business must survive.

REFERENCES

1. Melvin E. Salveson, "Dynamic Organization Planning," Center for Advanced Management, New Canaan, Connecticut, 1959.
2. Peter F. Drucker, "Long-Range Planning-Challenge to Management Science," Management Science, Vol. 5, No. 3 (April, 1959), pp. 238-249.
3. "Companies Must Grow—or Die," News Front, Vol. 3, No. 5 (July, 1959), pp. 13-15.

THE IMPACT OF COMPUTERS ON THE DESIGN OF MANAGEMENT CONTROLS

SECTION **III**

An appraisal of current computer applications

CHAPTER **A** by ROGER L. SISSON

This chapter consists of two major parts and an appendix; the first part deals with the computational requirements of the management control process (as herein defined); the second part describes and evaluates the use of computers to perform these functions. It is shown that, all things—especially profitability—considered, computers are being used for the functions for which they are most suitable; but it is certainly true that they are not being used for all appropriate functions in all companies.

COMPUTATIONAL REQUIREMENTS IN MANAGEMENT CONTROL

Definition of Management Control

Consider a production manager. He is a decision maker. His job is to determine the present status of the manufacturing operation, measure this against the desired position according to company policy

---

*Ideas in this paper came from many sources. In particular, I am in debt to Joel Kibbee of System Development Corporation for pointing out the analogy between the multi-dimensional view of business status and the "phase space" used in physics, and also for editorial suggestions; to Dr. Ernest Krause of Aeronutronic, A Division of Ford Motor Company, for ideas on the need to consider the flow from marketing to machine tool control as an entity; and to Burt Grad of General Electric, and Richard G. Canning for many fruitful conversations on management control.

97

and specific production requirements and issue orders so that the
desired results are most nearly obtained. The orders which the production manager issues are general in nature, such as "produce at
the rate of six hundred units per day." These orders have to be translated into exact directives to the manufacturing and warehousing activities. An <u>order translation</u>, therefore, takes place. Upon issuing
the orders, the <u>activity</u> takes some action, generally in a direction
to fulfill the directives. It is not enough to stop here, however. Some
method must be established by which the manager can determine the
new current status to see whether further orders must be issued and
further action taken to correct the situation. In order to accomplish
this measurement of status, data is recorded about activity in the
manufacturing area. These progress reports, in the form of time
cards, job cards, stock room receipts, and so on, are fed to some
sort of a data processing facility, which may consist of a few clerks
or a complex electronic computer installation. The purpose of the
data-processing facility is to record the activity in such a way that
reports can be prepared which are meaningful to the decision maker—
the production manager. We will call these <u>functions file</u> processing
and <u>status analysis</u>. We will examine below to a greater extent this
kind of data processing.

Figure III-A-1 illustrates a method of summarizing this typical
management control loop. When I use the term "management control"

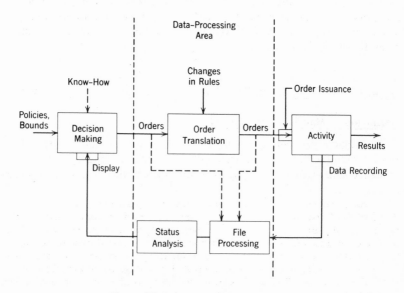

Figure III-A-1. Management Control.

in this chapter, I am referring to the entire series of processes which compose a typical management loop as just discussed. This is a "model." It is a highly abstracted picture of the basic management control system and is based on an analogy between management control and servo control systems. This analogy is not entirely valid, but is extremely useful in organizing our discussion of the computational aspects of management control.

Figure III-A-1 represents the basic steps involved, in some form or other, in the functioning of every level of management; from the machine tool operator to the chairman of board.[1],[6] Recognize that a complete business enterprise consists of an entangled network of such management loops. There is "cross talk" between decision-making units and between various activities. Many facilities are shared by the various activities. We will largely ignore these latter complications in the interests of emphasizing the basic computational problems in management control. One comment, however, might be directed to the problem of isolating one of these management loops. The key seems to be to <u>isolate the decision maker</u> who has the effective authority for guiding an activity. Once the decision maker is isolated, the various parts of the loop can be distinguished. Let us investigate these parts in further detail, following Figure III-A-1.

Decision Making

The "policies" and "bounds" guiding the decision maker are, in effect, the orders from the next higher management loop. (There is probably a psychological significance in the fact that one issues "orders" to a lower level but prefers to think of oneself as acting under "policies." Certainly, they are the same type of directive.) The possible examples of decision-making units are endless: a machine tool operator is a decision maker in the sense that he observes the status of the machine, compares this with the order in the form of written documents and blueprints and directs the machine controls to insure that the result meets the orders. A materials manager observing inventory levels and issuing necessary shop and purchase orders is a decision-making process. Going on to a high-level executive such as general manager, the situation is diffuse, but of the same type. The general manager operates ideally under rather clear-cut policies from the board of directors, as well as bounds placed on him by financial and legal rules. He observes the status of the company by studying a wide variety of management and trade reports as well as by direct conversation with other executives. His orders are often in the form of general policies to the upper management.

The importance of "know-how" brought to a job by a human decision maker must not be underestimated. It is in mechanizing this know-how that many OR studies run aground. Such know-how includes the personal experience of the decision maker and his current knowledge of the status of the trade, of general economic conditions, and of activities of the competitors.

If one must be quantitative, it is probably correct to say that about 20 to 30 per cent of business decisions by type are computational in nature. (We will use "computational" and "mechanized" to mean a procedure which can be precisely defined, and therefore, possible of execution on a machine; computable in the Turing sense.) The remaining decisions generally involve human factors such as the choice of an executive, and are, to date, beyond expression as computational procedures. If, however, one looks at the number of decisions made in a given enterprise, for a year, the percentage which are computable is probably in the 80 to 90 per cent range. Computable decisions are exemplified by all sorts of materials ordering decisions, be they for stationery, purchased parts, manufactured parts, subcontracting work, new facilities, etc. Almost any allocation of materials or facility capacity among a variety of possible activities is a computable decision. This includes the allocation of capital as well as the allocation of inventory, machine tool capacity, and so on. Many routine engineering decisions required to make product modifications to meet customer specifications fall into the class of computable decisions.

It is clear then, that in the decision-making area, a great quantity of decision making can probably be mechanized and that these decisions are those being made by the lowest levels of supervision and in part, by the class of management generally called "middle Management." It is the key product and personnel decisions of the higher levels of management that at the moment appear beyond mechanized processing. It should be emphasized that when I say "A decision is computational in nature," I mean that:

- The factors involved can be isolated and quantified, and

- Relations can be expressed which relate the decision outputs to these factors in such a way that

- The computations lead to effective (purposely avoiding the word "optimum") decisions.

This does not necessarily lead to simple computational procedures; it means the result is a concept that could be reduced to such formal procedures.

Order Translation

The principle outputs of the decision maker are orders or directions to a controller set of activities. The orders, as we have noted, from a decision process often need further translation before the "doers" can interpret them. Let us continue the example mentioned above: a marketing manager may decide that a product should be produced at the rate of three hundred per month for the next six months. This requirement must then be translated into requirements for individual parts, purchased and manufactured, required to build these products. Estimates must be made of manpower required, the machine, or more generally, facility loads required, and so on. One order causes much "confusion." An order on the part of an insurance executive that, henceforth, the company should provide an insurance coverage for personal liability damage, of certain forms, would also cause much activity on the part of actuaries and legal groups to prepare the exact documents which are, in effect, the product.

One can think of these order translation processes as analogous, if not in fact equivalent to, a language translation. The rules for making the translation can be grammatical rules (expressed as logical or analytic relationships) or by a dictionary process (a file look-up procedure). In the marketing example above, much of the data is obtained by a "dictionary" supplied by engineering and/or production planning. The dictionary is formed by the bill of materials, planning cards, and so on. With the present level of dynamicism in business, these dictionaries change extremely rapidly; such changes being in the form of engineering changes, production methods changes, the reflection of facility availability changes, and so on. In the insurance example above, the premium and dividend rates are computed from statistical data by analytic and statistical relationships; that is, rules are used, in part, rather than a dictionary.

It is interesting to note that the outputs of an engineering activity (with its own management control loop) are changes to the order translation process of another loop, e.g., manufacturing.

Where the order translation process is analytic or logical, a large part of the proceedings are computational in nature. In some cases, e.g., where involved legal judgment is required, the possibility of reducing such translation to computational procedures is small.

In the area of manufacturing it has been recently shown that a great variety of translations between customer orders and manufacturing activity can be related by relatively simple logical and analytic relationships, rather than by time-consuming dictionary look-ups. But by either method, in the manufacturing fields, probably 95 per cent of the translation is computational. Where the relationships

between the detailed orders to the activity and the general orders
from the decision maker are empirical, a dictionary must be used.
Where a dictionary is used procedures are certainly subject to routine data processing manipulation. The usual process of looking up
bills-of-materials to determine what parts to order in the manufacture of a given item is certainly a data-processing procedure of the
most routine nature.

We might emphasize again, something just touched on; that in many
cases where dictionaries are used because the relationship appears
empirical, further study will indicate that there are indeed basic
logical relationships and that the processes of obtaining the output
orders can be related to the input orders by simple relationships. It
is always worth investigating for such relationships since regardless
of the type of data processor, logical manipulations are usually easier
to perform than file maintenance. All in all, nearly 90 per cent of the
order translation processing is computational in nature, and simple
computations at that.

Activity

The detailed orders created in order translation are then sent to
the activity. We will not dwell upon the procedures within the activity.
Where the activity is another lower-order management control loop,
the present discussion will apply. Where the activity is a physical or
financial process leading to an end result, the problems are not properly a part of "management control." We are not discussing manufacturing engineering, salesmanship, stock keeping, or the like.

Note, however, the two little boxes which couple in and out of the
activity in Figure III-A-1. We may call these order issuance and data
recording. The problem here in most non-automated industries, is
essentially one of man-machine instrumentation. We must couple the
orders issued to the human who executes the activity. We must then
measure this activity performed by a human and the tools he controls
and translated back into an information signal. This coupling from the
information system to the man-machine activity has been given attention only in isolated ways. The design of forms to make them more
readable would be a simple study in this area. Attempts to feed signals directly to machine tools indicates progress in automating this
coupling.

Likewise in the area of data recording, some activity is noticeable.
Efforts are progressing to create the so called "shop recorder,"
which permits the operators of manufacturing facilities to record
their activities simply and accurately. Results of the work on character sensing and recognition will assist data recording. Here the job

is to read data from the results of activity, for instance, bank checks. directly into the data processing system. Since, in most cases a human is involved in these couplings, the problem is difficult. I feel however, that little attention has been given to over-all problems and approaches to the information system-man-machine coupling problem indicated here. Work going on in the instrumentation field may provide analogies which will give clues to good solutions to these problems.

File Processing

Historically speaking there is really only one reason why the functions in the feedback path entitled, status analysis and file processing exist. In the small business, where the decision maker may directly observe and comprehend the entire activity under his control, very little "paper work" is required. The situation is directly observable and the general trend of the situation may be computed in the man's head. Key factors and policies are memorized and do not need compicated written procedures. It is obvious that this situation no longer exists, even in small companies. The diversity of product lines, the complexity of the products, the rapidity of engineering changes and changes made at customer request precludes any one person or group of persons comprehending the entire situation. Some way is needed to take the data recorded about the activities and maintain it up-to-date, so that various management reports can be quickly obtained. In effect, this data-processing activity becomes the eyes and ears and in fact, the preliminary interpretive processing for the manager. The insertion of data processing between the activity and the manager has the disadvantage of removing the manager one step from the actual activity, but appears to be the only feasible way to permit him to obtain an over-all, reasonably accurate view of the situation.

It is useful to think of files being processed as an "analog" of the actual business activity. The data about the business: the capital used, the decisions made, the activity that actually occurs (both services and material processing), and the financial results of the activity are all recorded in files. Thus, at any moment the files reflect the actual status of the business. With this analog it is then possible to manipulate data and extract it so that management can get a picture of the status of the business which in ancient times a business manager obtained by "walking through the shop." Examples of files are numerous. Any updated list, card file, tabulating card deck, or computer master tape is a file, and specific examples will come to mind easily.[7]

As will be discussed below, nearly all file processing can be stated as a formalized process capable of mechanization.

Status Analysis

The step of status analysis is often not explicitly recognized as a control function which is being performed outside of the decision maker's area. For this reason its importance is often underestimated. By "status analysis" we mean the process of deriving data from the file system and manipulating it in such a way as to produce abstract quantities which are meaningful to the manager. For example, a list of all of the jobs in a manufacturing shop showing their location at various stations and the quantities being processed is not particularly meaningful. A summary of these, which compares the present location with the orginally planned location, becomes more meaningful. In other words the procedure given the name of "management-by-exception" is a simple form of status analysis. The status is portrayed by isolating exceptions or deviations from a planned program.

Take the case of a marketing manager who obtains a figure of dollar sale by salesman for various territories in the country. The concept of dollar sales per salesman is an abstraction, which is derived from the individual activities of a large number of salesmen and customers. This summary figure, however, can be correlated by the decision maker with certain goals he has established and, therefore, is a more useful control tool than any direct observation of the salesman's activities or even a direct item by item report of the sales made. In fact, the process of obtaining any of the classical control factors would be included in our definition of status analysis; such factors as: current ratio, percentage of profit on sales, sales trends, quality control charts, etc.

In the Appendix to this chapter, an attempt is made to present a more formal approach to organizing the status analysis activity to insure that management gets an over-all, accurate picture of the company's status at a given time. We might note here that "status" includes not only the present situation, but measures of various trends to aid in predicting future situations.

File processing and status analysis are almost, by definition, completely data-processing or computational procedures. The maintenance of a filing system should conceptually be merely a process of recording information in the correct form; certainly a pure data-processing problem. Status analysis, as we have indicated, is a procedure in which the decision maker delegates to the data-processing system the problem of preliminary interpretation and summarization of detailed data about current activities. One delegates that type of status analysis which can be computed and processed in the most routine way, since we wish to leave all judgment decisions, including the judgment involved in interpreting data, within the decision maker's area. Thus, status analysis also should be purely a computational function.

Display

The final step of the management control loop is to display various measures of status to the decision maker. The present method of "display" is almost exclusively to present tabulated reports and sometimes simple graphs to the manager. This is again another "instrumentation" problem in which we must couple the information system to, in general, a human decision maker. Considerable work is going on in military management control systems for the visual presentation of data to the manager.[4] Figure III-A-2 illustrates several

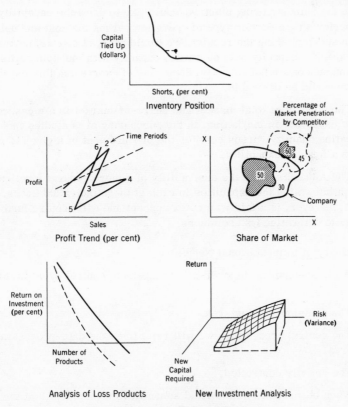

Figure III-A-2. Possible Displays.

possible displays which might be more useful to the manager than the charts and reports he often gets.[2] These concepts are discussed in a little more detail in the Appendix to this chapter and we will not go into the problem of display here. This is an important coupling, however, and at the present time, unfortunately, a manager's over-all ability is sometimes determined to a large extent by how patient he is in examining detailed management reports in search of exceptions and general trends which should have been computed for him and displayed in a more graphical manner.

We might note that the displays in Figure III-A-2 permit the visualization of capability as well as present status. It is important for a decision maker to know what he <u>can</u> do as well as where he <u>is</u>. The computation of capability is undertaken only in very limited areas in present management control procedures and might well be given further attention in the future.

Here are some examples:

In the manufacturing plant we would like to know the capability for performing a certain type of operation versus the cost and delay in accomplishing the results. We would have, of course, normal capacity, capacity with overtime, capacity with multiple shifts, and subcontracted capacity. Some way of expressing this capability would be desirable.

The concept of total market and share-of-market is a measure of capability in marketing. In the purchasing area studies indicating quantity versus cost for the procurement of a given item is a form of capability.

The Appendix notes the desirability of a more general function which integrates the capacities in each of these individual areas. This, however, is a fairly complex concept and will require further study to determine its usefulness.

Summary of Computational Needs

We may consider the over-all management control cycle in three parts:

- The decision-making area.
- The central area, which we will refer to as the data-processing area.
- The activity controlled.

When observed in a historical sense, it is no accident that the data processing area in Figure III-A-1, which includes order translation, file maintenance, and status analysis, is subject to almost complete mechanization. At one time, the manager could observe the entire activity and do all of his data processing in his head. As the organization has grown, the manager has delegated more and more of the routine parts of his decision-making procedures and management control procedures to separate data manipulating agencies. Naturally, the decision maker has (or should have) delegated those parts of his procedures which can be stated as a formal mechanized routine, retaining for himself those which require judgment.

Of course, a manager does not do this perfectly, so that some of the decision-making procedures performed by managers can actually be mechanized, and some of the processing delegated to the central part of the management control cycle may require judgment decisions. This is especially true in the early states of order translation, and in status analysis. Sometimes the orders given by managers are sufficiently vague or the rules or dictionaries sufficiently incomplete so that judgment is required to develop specific orders for the activity. Also in some cases, the interpretation of the data gathered and maintained in files into terms meaningful for decision making requires judgment decisions.

It should be the aim of the system designer to create a system in which the judgment decisions are indeed either properly mechanized or retained by the manager.

THE USE OF ELECTRONIC COMPUTERS TO PERFORM MANAGEMENT CONTROL COMPUTATIONS

Figure III-A-3 summarizes in a rough way the extent to which computers are used in various parts of management control, and also

Function	Percentage of Activity Computational in Nature	Percentage Economically Feasible on Computer	Percentage Actually on Computers
Decision Making	80*	30	5
Order Translation	90	45	10
File Processing	100	50	20
Status Analysis	90	50	10

*By number of decisions made, probably representing only 30 per cent of the types of decisions made.

Figure III-A-3.

gives this author's estimate of the extent to which they <u>could be</u> used. It is interesting to note that there are still many areas where computers are not suitable at the present time, largely because of economic rather than technical reasons.

Computers in Decision Making

We have noted above that the decision-making area includes specifically those items which are given time, require judgment decisions. Therefore, the use of computers in this area is, almost by definition, difficult. The use of computers for decision making depends almost entirely on developing techniques for formalizing the decision-making procedure. We might digress here to make the distinction between a <u>formal</u> procedure which <u>mechanizes the judgment decisions</u> made by a manager and an <u>optimum</u> procedure which <u>goes beyond</u> the decisions made at the present time and (supposedly) develops a technique which makes more profitable decisions. Computers can be used to execute procedures developed from either process. The only requirement is that the procedure be capable of definite statement.

One of the most interesting problems in relation to decision making is that the tool—the computer—appears to be providing a method for developing techniques for improving decision making. The work of Dr. Simon,[5] Dr. Forrester,[3] and others in developing "learning" simulations of business processes on a computer may lead to computational procedures which tend to make better decisions than could a human. It is this area that computers offer real hope in assisting decision making. Otherwise, computers are used only to carry out mechanized procedures which are well known and which could be carried out by clerks except for the time factor. A couple of examples may make this clear. The process of reordering in a lower level materials situation by using procedures such as the famous EOQ formula are often considered decision making. By the definition given above, it might be better to classffy such procedures as order translation, since they are completely formalized, if not optimized, and can be mechanized by routine procedures; computers or clerks. The process of linear programming is more complex. Here is a process which could, in theory, be mechanized by clerks, but the time factor would be so great that we are almost forced to say that the advent of the computer has actually made a decision procedure possible. This is further emphasized by the fact that the extent to which a linear programming procedure can effectively be applied often depends on how clever the technician is in developing short-cut techniques for solving the problem on present speed computers. Thus, in one sense, the advent of linear programming mechanizes a decision-making problem and permits it to be delegated to the data processing area. But, this in turn, has been possible only due to the advent of a special data-processing tool, the computer. <u>I would expect this trend of the transfer of judgment decisions to data-processing procedures to continue at a rapid pace depending principally, as we have noted, on the development of powerful computers</u>.

We might emphasize the fact that computers have also provided a tool for research in decision-making procedures principally through the technique of simulation. This is a case in which a device is both a research and an operational tool.

Finally, in regard to decision making, I would like to note another way in which the data processing, in particular the file maintenance, and decision making interact. During the process of making decisions, it is important to be able to get as much information as possible. To do this, <u>inquiries</u> are made by the decision maker (human or mechanized) into the data files. In rapidly moving businesses the need for inquiries is especially acute, and it is this that has led to the accent on good displays and "random access" files; a data-processing tool which provides the inquiry facility.

In conclusion then, we might say that computers are a tool for mechanizing decision making and transferring these procedures from the manager's area to the data-processing area (a process that can have a large payoff in profits). Computers are also a very powerful tool for research in decision-making techniques. Ultimately, computers may become decision makers in the sense that they can learn. It is evident that in this case the manager becomes involved more and more with the extremely long-range decisions, interrelating global considerations.

Let us now go on to look at the parts of the management control system which, as we have already noted, should be almost completely subject to mechanization. Of course, the fact that they <u>can</u> be mechanized does not mean that they <u>should</u> be from an economic point of view. In many applications, clerks are still less expensive than computers.

Order Translation

In general, computers have been used extensively for order translation where this is a routine procedure. Examples include issuing paychecks, utility bills, or the like. In these cases the final order results from the initial input by simple (although often extensive) rules.

It is well known that computers are more adaptable to executing analytic or logical rules than to dictionary look-ups. It is not sur-

prising, therefore, that computers have been found less adaptable
to the issuance of orders in manufacturing application where reference must be made to lengthy complicated bills of materials. Considerable work has been done, in particular by General Electric, in
expressing the shop orders as a function of customer or productions
orders by means of rules rather than by dictionary look-ups. Such
procedures reduce the total computing load and make the use of
computers more economical. Such procedures might also, of course,
make clerical procedures more economic.

The other factor which makes the use of any inflexible tool difficult in manufacturing order issuance is the extremely high rate of
changes, principally engineering changes. Systems, whether using a
computer or not, must be designed to handle such changes expedi-
tiously. System designers have had difficulty, first, in recognizing
this, and second, in designing adequate systems. We are now on the
verge of being able to develop systems which will be flexible in the
face of extreme engineering changes, and therefore, will be adaptable to computers. This is done to a large extent by going away
from dictionaries wherein every change means changes in some
lengthy file, and going towards rules for the order translation
process. Better equipment techniques with more rapid random access memories and more powerful logical abilities assist, of course.
Computers, at the present, are used in a few per cent of cases for
order translation and could probably be used economically in a few
more. It will be several years before computational equipment becomes cheap enough for a wide use in this area, even though technically it is subject to almost complete mechanization.

Coupling to the Activity

A few words about the coupling of the data system to the activity
are in order. Three techniques might be mentioned which are in the
process of development which will mechanize this coupling and hopefully perform it more economically and more accurately. These are
the following:

- The development of numerically controlled machine tools which
  permits the data system to direct machine tool equipment and indeed a wide variety of other automatic equipment directly.

- The development of character recognition which permits a data
  system to read printed material and hopefully—in the more distant future—handwritten material. Such techniques would permit
  the data system to accept directly documents from outside the
  company which affect the activity and also permit the data system
  to perform its data recording functions, the process of measuring

present status, by reading documents prepared by the activity for other purposes, such as invoices to a customer.

• The development of semi-automatic mechanisms called "shop recorders" or "point-of-sale recorders," which force the human operator in the activity to record data at the same time he performs his normal operation, such as making change (in retail functions), obtaining the instructions for performing a new job, and the like.

Considerable effort is being expended in improving these coupling processes. At the present time only an extremely small percentage is mechanized. In the future possibly as much as 50 per cent may be mechanized. The procedure will never be completely automatic because there are many activities, such as personal selling, which will require some transcription of data before an automatic input to the data system can be obtained.

File Processing

As we have stated, essentially all file processing can be mechanized. At the present time, probably only some 50 per cent can be economically mechanized. The reason for this is that the basic components out of which computers are made—transistors, tubes, magnetic cores, and so on—are just not cheap enough. In my opinion, however, within ten years, computer components will be developed such that computational costs will be extremely low—much lower than any clerical processing can be—and therefore, probably as much as 95 per cent of file processing will be mechanized. One of the most interesting computerized file maintenance systems in the West, at least, is carried on at Pacific Mutual Life Insurance Company. Here, the complete records of hundreds of thousands of policy holders are processed every day. All changes to policy status, all premiums, dividends, and so on are adjusted in the files, so that at the end of each day, the files represent the true situation as nearly as possible. It is interesting to note that the principle benefit from this mechanization is not the elimination of clerks. Two principle benefits are:

• The ability to handle a growing business without an unreasonable growth in clerical help.

• Certain benefits deriving from faster processing time.

One of the latter is the fact that the company can compute its income requirements more rapidly and as a result of this, had 750,000 dollars less tied up in deferred premiums.

Status Analysis

Status Analysis is a gray area. In theory this should be a mechanized procedure which extracts data from the files and manipulates it so as to compute the magnitude of various abstract factors which are meaningful to the decision maker. Unfortunately, decision makers have not been able to state clearly all of the factors they need. Therefore, status analysis is either very simple, such as computing simple numeric summaries like the current ratio. Or, in other cases, more complex factors are computed, but often they have no relation to the decision-making procedure. In yet other cases, the judgment of financial personnel enters into the "computation" of these factors and, therefore, the manager has unwittingly delegated some of his decision procedures. Examples of this are particularly evident in cost accounting systems in which the methods of allocating costs to various direct and overhead accounts are left to the discretion of, for instance, the controller; whereas in fact such allocations vitally effect the magnitude of these numbers and, therefore, the decision-making material used by the manager. It is my opinion that status analysis is an area for much further research. It is difficult because it depends directly upon being able to state the factors which should be measured about the business, and this in turn depends upon a full understanding of the decision process, which we almost never have. Nevertheless, an integrated study of decision making and the factors required will lead to more exact status analysis which may be mechanized and, therefore, delegated to the data-processing system.

As noted, at the present time, the nature of status analysis is somewhat confused and, therefore, it is hard to tell what percentage might be mechanized. Probably, when properly defined, nearly all of it will be a formalized procedure and, therefore, suitable for computation by electronic devices. Again, it appears that, it is economic to mechanize only a small part of this process.

Displays

The possibilities of mechanizing the output of status analysis to form display is shown in Figure III-A-2. The military has financed a great deal of work in automatic display systems, such as can be seen in the SAGE installation. Relatively inexpensive displays can be developed which will permit management to see the factors which are meaningful to them plotted rapidly and in an up-to-date fashion in such a way as to encourage better decision making. Again, it may not be economical to mechanize the display coupling in a great variety of cases at the present time. Within the next few years, however, with the advent of better computer components and better display techniques, such displays will be not only economical but vital to companies who wish to really understand business they are controlling.

CONCLUSION

In conclusion then, computers have two vital functions in management control:

- They can completely mechanize the functions of the management control cycle which we have included in the data-processing area. At the present time, it is not economical to mechanize all of these, since clerical help and semi-automatic devices are still cheaper than electronic computers. Computers are useful where highly repetitive, high volume applications, or extremely complex applications exist. Within ten years, however, computer technology will bring devices cheap enough to permit mechanization of almost all computational procedures in this area; even perhaps our own personal budgets.

- Computers provide the only tool we have for investigating decision-making processes. This is done by programming the computer to simulate the complex decision situation and its environment. The fruits of this research should lead to significant changes in business management and organization procedures.

APPENDIX

Note on Status Analysis

As a result of some current work I am performing in the design of management systems for a field army, I have found that the information displayed to a manager may be divided into two parts:

- The display of the current status, including the facilities available and the activities in process.

- The capabilities possible, the directions in which the business may move with some estimate of the cost of going in these various directions.

The purpose of this note is to propose that it is useful to think of the condition of a business enterprise at any given time as a point in "phase space." This phase space is equivalent to the phase space concept used in physics. It is an n-dimensional space (for a business probably thousands of dimensions), and a single point in the space

represents the status of the business. The variables which comprise
this space are all of the factors which are necessary to make intelligent decisions (at any level of management) in order to direct the
business. Such variables as: quantities of stock in inventory, number
of customers, dollar sales during the last period, location of branch
offices, and so on would be typical variables. In fact, one might say
that any of the "fields" on a form (where the word "fields" is used
in the data processing sense) is a variable. Some variables measure
quantities, some designate one of a number of possible units such as
operation numbers or employee number, some give geographical location.

At any given time each of these variables has a definite value and
a definite rate of change (where the concept of rate change is applicable). Thus, at any time a single point in the phase space is defined.
The progress of the business may be observed conceptually by noting
the path of this point in time.

The total derivative of this path might be called the total trend and
would give an indication of the direction in which the business is
moving.

We may think of plotting a path in phase space which would represent the "budget" or the desired path. The vector between the present position and budgeted present position we might define as the
exception vector. If one could observe this exception vector, one
would then have true management by exception. Finally, we might define the volume surrounding the point which represents present status
as the capability volume. Within this volume the business may move.
Beyond it, it does not have the capability of moving. The capability
volume must be expressed as a function of time, and probably as a
function of profit; since a business can proceed to do almost anything
if it disregards cost. It is also true that almost all of the variables
involved are statistical in nature and it is probably more proper to
talk of distributions rather than specific points and paths.

It is vital to recognize that for a business phase space, all functions on it are highly discontinuous. Indeed, many of the variables
are discontinuous. If one examines something as simple as the rules
for reordering materials which go into the manufacture of parts, one
can see the discontinuity of the function. Figure III-A-4 summarizes
a typical definition of a reorder rule. Note that the rule to be used
depends upon the status of several variables and depends upon these
in a discontinuous way. This discontinuity causes most business problems to be extremely complex and not capable of analytic solutions.
It is for this reason that we must resort to simulation in order to understand the nature of the business and thus, the need for the electronic computer in business research. We may think of the phase

VARIABLES:

Quantity on Hand	$= Q_H$
Quantity on Order (Excluding Special Orders)	$= Q_R$
Quantity of New Requirement	$= Q_0$
Reorder Level	$= Q_L$
Standard Reorder Quantity	$= Q_S$
Quantity to Order	$= R$

CONDITIONS (Location in Phase Space)	TYPICAL ACTION (Function)
$Q_0 < Q_H$	$R = 0$
$Q_H < Q_0 \leq Q_H + Q_R$	$R = 0$
$Q_H + Q_R < Q_0$	$R = Q_0 - (Q_H + Q_R)$
$Q_H \leq Q_L$	$R = Q_S$

Figure III-A-4. Discontinuities in Functions of Phase Space.
(Simplified to ignore lead-time problems, etc.)

space as being a model of the data represented by the totality of files
in the system, if they are properly kept up to date. Status analysis is
the process of observing the path of the point in space. Three areas
of study suggest themselves:

- How can we get better understanding of procedures for partitioning
  this multi-dimensional space into two- and three-dimensional problems which can be comprehended by humans?

- How can we use computers or other clerical processes to assist
  humans in deriving and displaying the exception vector, the total
  trend, the capability volume, and so on?

- Can we develop logical procedures which permit the deductive solution of problems involving functions which are discontinuous on
  such a multi-dimensional space?

REFERENCES

1. R. G. Canning, Electronic Data Processing for Business and Industry, John
   Wiley and Sons, New York, 1956.
2. George J. Feeney, "A Basis for Strategic Decisions on Inventory Control
   Operations," Management Science, Vol. 2, No. 1 (October, 1955), pp. 69-82.

3. J. Forrester, "Industrial Dynamics: A Major Breakthrough for Decision-Makers," <u>Harvard Business Review</u>, July-August, 1958, pp. 37-66.
4. D. G. Malcolm et al., "Application of a Technique for Research and Development Evaluation," <u>Operations Research</u>, Vol. 7 (September-October, 1959), pp. 646-669.
5. H. Simon and G. Newall, "Heuristic Problem Solving; the Next Advance in Operations Research," <u>Operations Research</u>, January-February, 1958, pp. 1-10.
6. R. L. Sisson, "Business Systems Can Be Engineered," <u>Automation</u>, December, 1955, pp. 2-9.
7. R L. Sisson, "Files in a Production Control System," <u>Journal of Industrial Engineering,</u> Vol. 9, No. 6 (November-December, 1958), pp. 491-497.

<u>DISCUSSION</u>   (Following Mr. Sisson's presentation of his paper)

A. J. ROWE: If management control is to be based on the use of computers, the real problem is in developing the necessary approaches, rules, principles, and methods. It seems reasonable that a computer will be needed to process huge amounts of data to aid decision makers. However, this does not necessairly imply that management control will require computers.

M. O. KAPPLER: I think of the loop of information which Roger described as one of the facets of a pyramid that I described last night. Not only are there flows of information around the pyramid, but perhaps also there are loops which don't always lie on the facets; there are probably also horizontal loops.

R. L. SISSON: A clear example of this interaction loop is where the output of an engineering group is the input to the order translation part of a manufacturing activity. The engineering group creates the dictionary for the language translation.

C. K. SIMON: Are the automation figures shown on your chart limited more by computing capacity or by memory capacity of computers?

R. L. SISSON: They are limited almost entirely by the fact that a clerk can simply do some jobs cheaper than a computer. This is especially true where there are a fair number of exceptions.

C. K. SIMON: Does your percentage change at all when you start considering the use of a large computer with extensive random access memory, rather than memory in the form of a tape?

R. L. SISSON: It is true that large computers are more efficient than small ones; and you are more likely to find an economic justification for the large job (whether it is one big process or many little ones) than for the little job.

I am also wholly in agreement with the idea of looking at the whole system first before making changes in parts of it. But I think that this idea is unrelated to the use of large computers.

C. K. SIMON: Instead of a large computer with a small capacity memory core, such as the 704, what about computers with a 20 million digital storage? Would this change your thinking?

R. L. SISSON: No. You can't answer that detailed a question in the abstract. You have to relate it to how much it would cost you for storage.

A. J. ROWE: Aside from mechanization of clerical functions there are many decisions which may be uneconomical to formalize.

R. L. SISSON: That is right. The human brain is still pretty cheap.

A. J. ROWE: When you say that judgment enters a problem, what you are saying is that it costs less to use judgment than try to formalize all the possible alternatives that might arise and which would have to be put in the computer.

R. L. SISSON: That is probably right; however, you are bringing the level of discussion up to another level of abstraction.

M. O. KAPPLER: One thing we may be overlooking here is the possibility that you may not want to formulate a problem completely and explicitly, because it may prove uneconomical; but at least you could formulate something which presents the decision maker with alternatives. He could at least apply a measure of judgment in selecting the one that appears to deal adequately with the center of the distribution of responses which are expected of him.

A. J. ROWE: But then the computer isn't making the decision; it is presenting information to the decision maker. The question is, can we mechanize the whole process and do without the person?

M. O. KAPPLER: I am inclined to resist that. I lean toward using the computer as an aid when it is most economical to do so.

A. W. RATHE: I think there is one rather serious danger, and that is to make things too easy for the executive. There have been instances where companies have improved their planning so magnificently that some executives have become lulled into a false sense of security; then an unexpected emergency arose and the people who had been excellent before in ad-libbing had lost their skill to do so. I think a little bit of that same problem can exist at the other end of the scale. Too much mechanization, even if it were economically feasible, could, in the long run, stifle the innovation and the creativity of the human being.

A. J. ROWE: Of course, the other side of that argument is that if we could eliminate all the routine concerns of top management they would have more time to innovate.

A. W. RATHE: There is nothing wrong with getting rid of the routine, but this will often mean getting rid of some people in top management.

J. F. LUBIN: There has been the implication in some remarks made here that the weakest element in the operation of a system is the manager of that system; further, the ideal system seems to be one which requires no management as such. Once again, we find the concept of the omniscient system designer and the deficient system operator. In contrast to this concept, I believe that the manager-decision maker is the essential element that must be studied in this research.

R. L. SISSON: If you're talking about systems research, you have to try to be abstract. When you design a computer, you make an idealistic picture of the situation. For example, in the design of a 10-megacycle computer you can get into trouble if you forget the time it takes for electrons to travel along a wire. You start by making an idealistic design. Either through tests or final analyses you gradually make it more realistic. Finally, you build the computer, and then you get the rest of the bugs out of it, and eventually it works. At our present stage in management control systems we can be pretty remote from reality and still find a lot to think about. After we understand these abstract problems better, then we may find that the manager can't always depend on the status analysis, but may have to have access directly to the data. He may even have to go and walk in the shop. Thus, in practice, I agree wholeheartedly with Mr. Lubin's comment.

J. F. LUBIN: Is it not the function of managers to manage, to create and operate the system which they supposedly head? Is this not why they are well paid, often better than system designers?

M. G. HOLMEN: When you have a product to turn out for an important client, you don't get this done by having a production manager take a tool from a lathe operator. I object to the manager's going down and getting involved in these functions because it keeps him from doing the things he is supposed to do.
To use the analogy of a football game, the coach should never try to play the quarterback's role during the game. He should retain his role as coach at all times, and not decide to kick or to pass on a particular play.

J. F. LUBIN: A coach of a football team often should (and does) send plays in to the quarterback. A good coach knows when to do this and when not to do so. In my opinion, it is usually incorrect to attempt to design a system which prevents these actions.

R. H. GREGORY: What are the demerits of having the coach go into the game and make a play once in awhile?

R. L. SISSON: You have to distinguish between interfering in data processing and interfering in activities. I think the manager has to be able to change an activity, but not necessarily actually do it. Also, the manager must be able to get at data, but not necessarily be the data processor.

N. J. REAM: I think the manager states that as being his responsibility, but he doesn't participate because it is not his full responsibility; it is only a side responsibility as far as the system designer is concerned.

C. K. SIMON: Isn't it possible, as management controls are put on computers, that the quarterback of the management control team may become a coach; and then shouldn't go into the game?

W. E. ALBERTS: I would like to state the reverse situation. Most of the barging in is done the other way. Very seldom do managers at different levels go down and grab raw data, but staff and line people frequently feed management with irrelevant data which cannot be interpreted, placing them in a very poor position to make decisions.

M. G. HOLMEN: In our System Training Program, one of the ways we deal with this is to have the battle staff positions filled temporarily by people from the subordinate jobs. After dealing with a mass of unrelated paper they go back to their jobs and send up organized data instead of bits and pieces; and the numbers of pieces of papers and bits of information that come up are much fewer. They realize the need for correct kind of staff work, after having tried to operate at that level during some exercises.

M. O. KAPPLER: Don't we have to distinguish between levels of management? I seriously doubt whether we have done so at any time today in talking about management controls. Perhaps the difficulty is in interpretation. I think we carefully have to distinguish policy management and policy decision making from the routine kind of decision making that can be put into model form. What has gone before has not been management controls but the elimination of management through controls. If indeed you can call the supervisory management level management. I am personally interested in the kind of control that can be developed for higher-level management, policy management, in making the critical decisions; and none of this has evolved today.

Organization of the data-processing function

CHAPTER **B** by JAMES D. GALLAGHER

Much has been written of the contributions that data processing can make toward the establishment of effective management planning and control techniques in American business. Unfortunately, the analytical techniques used in the development of management information systems have not always been applied to the development and management of the data-processing function itself, with the result that data processing has been hindered in its advance and acceptance, and has not always met the goals set for it by management.

Because of the multi-project nature of an integrated data-processing program, it is of great importance that continual management control and review procedures be established and followed in order to maintain proper control over each project, and to effectively direct and orient the entire program.

The necessary prerequisite to control is planning, and it is here that the majority of data-processing programs are most deficient.

There must be a substantial improvement in the organization and management of the data-processing function for most businesses if any degree of the full potential of data processing is to be achieved, and this improvement can only be carried out by all levels of management who must exercise a continual and active role in the planning, control, and review of the over-all program.

DEVELOPING THE ORGANIZATION AND MANAGEMENT OF THE DATA-PROCESSING FUNCTION

The development of any management information system is always conditioned and influenced by the dynamic nature of the business. The systems planner must never consider that he is working in a static management environment in which he can develop a management information system as if it were a pure laboratory project. Changing economic conditions, technological advances, the aggressiveness of competitors, company programs of expansion and diversifications, etc. are but a few of the factors that the systems planner must take into consideration in formulating an approach to the solution of major systems problems within a company, and in the organization of a management plan designed specifically to develop the full potential of the data-processing program.

A basic problem that has hindered the advance of data processing from its inception has centered around the difficulty of establishing proper lines of communications between the data-processing organization and operations personnel, and between the various departmental groups within the data-processing organization itself.

If a data-processing operation is to achieve any measure of success, it must integrate its activities with the operational activities of the company. It cannot consider itself as a separate and distinct entity, apart from the company, functioning as a pure service agency or as a captive consulting facility.

This integration cannot be achieved, however, unless the data-processing departmental groups have established a clear understanding of their own individual responsibilities and the nature of their departmental job relationships. Further, the management of a company should not establish a data-processing function unless it first tailors the organization of the data-processing group to meet the information requirements of the company in such a way that the organizational structure of the company is not adversely affected.

In addition to the requirement for a comprehensive organizational-management information flow analysis and a clear definition of data-processing departmental responsibilities, it is also necessary that management develop a program which describes the intelligent use to which computers and associated equipment will be put.

This latter requirement of defining in advance, and in substantial detail, the objectives of the data-processing program and the applications to be placed on the equipment has been surprisingly lacking.

All too often, we find that data-processing equipments are ordered with vaguely stated objectives that are not supported by a systematic

orderly study of the total information requirements of the business.
As stated by Richard F. Neuschel of McKinsey and Company:

> "There is no question but that electronic equipment (and in-
> deed, punched card equipment) can produce more informa-
> tion faster than can be generated by any other means. But,
> because this is true, one wonders if our ability to generate
> information has not far outstripped our ability to assimilate
> it and use it intelligently in the running of the business. In
> any event, all levels of management face the persistent dan-
> ger of becoming so fascinated by the lure of office automa-
> tion that they lose sight of a far greater need to sharpen
> their skills in determining what information is of real
> worth.... The real need in applying high speed computers to
> the management of large scale enterprises is not so much
> that of using such machines to manipulate existing knowledge
> as it is one of identifying much more clearly what are the
> factors that affect business health and in what specific ways
> or to what degrees each of these factors exerts its influence
> in any given situation."[1]

BASIC RESPONSIBILITIES OF MANAGEMENT

The basic responsibilities of management in the determination of how a data-processing program can be best organized
and used to maintain or improve the company's profit position
are:

- To determine where the data-processing activity will fit into the
  over-all organizational structure of the company. This can be done
  only after a comprehensive information flow analysis is performed,
  along with a study of the organization of the company to determine
  what impact the establishment of a data-processing program may
  have on the organizational structure of the company itself.

- To clearly determine the responsibilities and authority assigned to
  the data-processing function. Make certain that each departmental
  group in the data-processing activity understands its own individual
  responsibility and how it will work with other groups in problem
  solving and the redesign of business systems.

- To establish basic objectives of the program. Provide for means
  of translating these objectives into systems projects designed to
  gain solutions to major systems problems of the business, i.e., the
  reduction of rapidly increasing indirect expense, the production of

management intelligence required to meet competition, the solution of marketing and distribution problems, etc.

These are the fundamental responsibilities which management must assume prior to the formal establishment of a data-processing function. These responsibilities, along with an interest and participation in the program, cannot end with the decision to establish the activity. Rather, interest and participation in every phase of the data-processing program must be active and continual on the part of all levels of management. Without such support, the program cannot be expected to achieve any degree of success and can never reach its potential.

ORGANIZATION—INFORMATION FLOW ANALYSIS

In the past, the responsibility for data processing quite often has been assigned to the function or department which first uses the equipments involved, or which uses data-processing services the most. Experience indicates, however, that a data-processing activity generally becomes involved in many phases of the business, cutting across the various functional responsibilities and becoming vitally concerned with the integration of these functions in attempting to establish a management information system.

Traditionally, the responsibility for data processing has been assigned to financial departments. The reasons stated for this are that financial departments have generally been held responsible for the development of business systems and reports, and the control of costs associated with this important area. In addition, financial departments are charged with the basic responsibility for the maintenance and protection of company assets, the establishment of inventory policies, and other general responsibilities which affect all phases of the business. Most companies, from a corporate viewpoint, have found that the potential of the data-processing program can be best exploited where the financial department is held responsible for the development of an integrated systems program because of the over-all interests of the financial department in all phases of the business.

The important consideration is that the placement of the data-processing function should be made in the organization where it can best serve all functions of the business so that its potential may not be strictly limited to one area.

In order to relate the organizational structure of the company to the stated objectives of the data-processing program, it is necessary to gain a comprehensive understanding of the information flow patterns that presently exist within the company. This is directly influ-

enced by organizational policies pursued by the company; i.e., whether
it is centralized, decentralized, to what extent vertical integration has
been followed, etc. The important consideration at this stage is that
a purely quantitative analysis, such as document counting, monthly,
weekly, and daily peak work loads, and similar studies, is not in itself sufficient. This limited type of analysis, for the most part, has
been the base or foundation for the majority of "computer feasibility"
studies conducted in the past. What is required is a qualitative analysis, designed to point up the flow of information between all levels
of management, and between all of the operating departments or divisions of the company.

CENTRALIZATION VERSUS DECENTRALIZATION OF DATA PROCESSING

The continual trend toward the decentralization of operations in
industry has materially changed the reports structure and information requirements for all levels of management in every company
which has completed this transition, or which is in the process of
moving from centralization to decentralization.

As noted by Mr. Richard Neuschel, "...if decentralization is to
mean delegation rather than abdication, then the executive who used
to 'run the whole show' himself must learn instead how to evaluate the
way someone else is running it."[2]

This requirement for current evaluation has created a communications problem which greatly complicates the establishment of a
meaningful management information system. This communication
problem becomes even more complex in a decentralized company
which pursues a policy of vertical integration. Here information flow
is not only between operating divisions and the corporate office, but
also between the various operating divisions and their reporting plant
locations.

In designing a management information system for a decentralized
operation of this nature, the systems planner must consider several
factors in determining the relative merits of establishing a centralized data-processing facility, or in establishing a data center at each
operating division or subsidiary:

- The physical size of the corporation and the relative size of each
  of the divisions.

- The degree of uniformity presently achieved in accounting practices and in reports issuance throughout the company.

- The nature of information flow that exists between the reporting divisions, based on product-organizational relationships. The proposed system must not inhibit the free exchange of operations data between various departments and/or divisions.

- The investment required to establish a communications system which can serve the combined administrative-data-processing communications requirements of the company if a data processing center is contemplated. If data centers are to be established on a decentralized basis, the fundamental question to be raised should center around the consolidation of the computational results of each center for use by the corporate offices. Admittedly, this poses less of a communications problem, but in the case of a vertically integrated company, it can create a computer-communications problem of some magnitude.

- The ability of the proposed facility to meet the schedule demands made of it by operating management. This will be related to the stated objectives established for the function, and is the factor which will most influence company long-range planning for the data-processing activity and how it will be organized.

These are only a few of the many factors which must be weighed and evaluated in determining whether centralized or decentralized data processing can best serve the management information requirements of a company.

One other development that has contributed to the complexity of this problem is the question of combining business and scientific data processing. From a data-processing operations viewpoint, the division between these two areas has become less definite as new and more powerful solid state computers, which can handle both areas, have become commercially available.

The basic problem is not one of equipment capability, however, as much as it is with the scheduling of the equipment and the administration and direction of the systems and programming efforts.

There are no precise set of standards or set of hard and fast rules which will serve as positive single guides for management in making the final decision whether to centralize or decentralize data processing. The factors noted previously are a few among several which must be studied and which will influence this decision. It is important, however, that this decision to centralize or decentralize not be made in advance of evaluating these factors, and that a data-processing function not be "forced" into the organizational structure of the company.

EXPANSION—EFFECTS ON PLANNING

The effect that an expansion program will have on long-range systems planning have been measured for the most part in quantitative terms. Projected growth of the company is always an initial consideration in the installation of a system. Through simple extrapolation, or perhaps more sophisticated mathematical techniques, it is not too difficult to anticipate future requirements from a quantitative viewpoint which will influence the nature of the equipment involved and the design of the hardware to be installed.

A program of expansion will have its most serious effects on systems planning in a situation where the capabilities of a single piece of data-processing equipment will be insufficient to handle the schedule demands made of it by operating management. In this case the most obvious solution to the problem is the installation of similar additional pieces of equipment, or a data-processing system in a much larger class. This "obvious" solution, however, can create further serious communication problems, and it is extremely important that the systems planner not be preoccupied with only the ability of source data equipment or the data-processing system to process larger volumes of information.

Increasing trends toward the establishment of data-processing centers and the design and development of improved data-processing techniques and equipments have outstripped advances made in the development of communications equipments and systems. Therefore, while it is entirely feasible to install very-large-scale data-processing systems at central locations to handle increased work loads, the basic problem becomes essentially one of moving large masses of data from many reporting locations to the data processing center, not just the use of more powerful computers. In a rapidly expanding company, the systems planner must always consider that a data-processing plan which resolves the information-processing requirements of a company at the present time may be quite inadequate where the information processing requirements of the business reach certain critical volumes. Singular devotion to a principle in data processing, such as the data-processing center concept, can ultimately lead to disaster if the systems planner is not flexible enough to recognize situations which require a basic shift in long range policies which determine the direction and nature of the company-wide data-processing program.

A few factors that must be considered by the systems planner in measuring the potential effects of expansion on the development of an integrated management information system are:

- The capability of the communications system to handle increased data traffic loads without causing periodic breakdowns of the transfer of information, or requiring a disproportionate investment in the communications network.

- The ability of the over-all data-processing system to adjust to sudden increased schedule demands made on it by operating management.

- The effects of expansion on the present distribution system, and the impact on the data-processing system if substantial changes are made to the distribution system because of expansion policies.

- The effects of expansion on the organizational structure of the company, i.e., smaller divisions or subsidiaries becoming an increasingly important factor in the conduct of the business, with information handling problems that may require processing on a decentralized basis.

- The fact that expansion policies may substantially change the original charter under which the company data-processing program was initiated, and completely re-orient the company data-processing program. An example of this could be a data-processing program which may be initiated as an accounting-financial consolidation program, but of necessity changes to a customer service-sales support program because of considerable emphasis being placed on marketing and distribution services as a part of deliberate product expansion policies.

DIVERSIFICATION—EFFECTS ON PLANNING

The effects of a diversification program on the development of a management information system are more far reaching and complex than the effects of an expansion program. When a company diversifies, invariably we find that the organizational structure of the company changes and reporting relationships that have determined the design and development of the existing data-processing system change to the point where they have little relationship to the requirements of the new system.

This is particularly true in a case where diversification policies result in a vertically integrated organization, where information flow is entirely conditioned by product-organizational relationships. Here the flow of information is not only between operating divisions and corporate management, but also between the various operating divisions and their respective reporting locations. The management information system must be so engineered that it does not inhibit the transfer of information between these locations, and facilitates the development of a reports structure which permits the current evaluation of divisional performance by top management.

In a company undergoing a diversification program, there is considerable temptation to attempt to force the existing information handling system on the organization. Unless the new information requirements of the company condition the planning for the data processing activity, however, the potential of the data-processing program can never be reached and the organizational structure of the company may be adversely affected.

In a diversification program where a new product will be developed and marketed by the parent company, the systems planner is given considerable lead time in determining how this new endeavor will affect the existing management information system. He is able to plan for the integration of the new division into the operational activities of the company and can relate the information requirements of this new business to the capabilities of the existing data-processing system. Where acquisition and merger is followed as a part of the diversification program, however, the systems planner does not have this great advantage of time in order to properly plan for changes in the reports structure of the company. Not only is the transition sudden, but the newly acquired business may have already developed an information handling system which must be substantially modified in order to become an integral part of the management information system presently in force for the parent company.

The emphasis should be on integration of the reports system, not insistence on standardization of equipments. All too often, attempts to achieve compatibility in reporting systems has as its start the basic requirement that the integration program be founded on the standardization of hardware for all divisions of an enterprise. This attitude generally fosters resistance, and, needless to say, this integration can only be achieved with the cooperation of the newly acquired organization who must be sold on the advantages of such a move.

Many companies in the past have felt that this integration was completed with the adoption of uniform accounting procedures and the consolidation of financial statements for the two merging organizations. This consolidation is a very necessary and required step. It by no means represents the solution to the management information systems problem and is only the first step toward the ultimate solution of the problem.

A diversification program, therefore, requires a qualitative analysis of information flow rather than a quantitative expression of fu-

future work load volumes, and will require a comprehensive study of the impact that such a program will have on the organizational structure of the company and its attendant information handling system.

Among the important factors to be weighed and evaluated in a diversification program from a systems planning viewpoint are:

- The characteristics of the existing management information system, and the present extent of mechanization in the system.

- The organizational position of the existing systems staff, and the proposed nature of the organizational relationships between the parent company systems staff and the management of the newly acquired company.

- The effects that the acquisition or merger will have on the existing organizational structure of the company, and how changes in this structure will affect information flow patterns.

- The degree of uniformity between the two companies' reports structure, and the compatibility of the accounting systems.

- The degree to which the new organization will be integrated into the operational activities of the company; i.e., whether the newly acquired organization will be a separate company or subsidiary, subject only to financial review, or whether it will be an operating division of the corporation, with firmly established product-organizational relationships which may require extensive modification of the existing reports structure to expedite consolidation.

ORGANIZATION—DATA-PROCESSING FUNCTIONS

In view of the fact that one of the most important objectives of a data-processing program is the improvement of communications between the various functions of a business, it is ironic that one of the most difficult problems faced in data processing is the development of an organization in which each of the various departmental groups clearly understands the nature and extent of its individual responsibilities and how each should communicate with other groups in the solution of systems problems.

Data-processing organizations, for the most part, have been established on an empirical basis, without first properly defining the scope of responsibilities of the data-processing function and the departmental responsibilities within the function.

The most expeditious way of establishing these departmental responsibilities, and how each group will contribute to the solution of complex systems problems is to first gain an understanding of how each group becomes involved in every step of solving a particular systems problem. This can only be done after an analysis of information flow for a particular project is made covering source data creation until final use by management.

The most common organizational problem discussed in data-processing circles centers around where systems and procedures responsibilities end and where programming starts. We have heard much of the "gray area" that supposedly exists between systems work and programming, and the difficulty of coordinating the activities of each group in working on a project.

The simple truth of the matter is that systems and programming, in almost every instance, must work as a team in conjunction with functional operating departments in problem definition and how the system will be finally engineered. The emphasis should definitely be placed on project teamwork. Programmers are not like actors, anxiously waiting in the wings, to come on stage on cue. They, like systems personnel, must be involved in the solution of a particular problem from its very inception.

Care must be exercised, however, in not providing for the elimination of the complete identity of these two departments. There will always be areas in purely systems and procedures work which will require systems specialists, and which will necessitate the separate maintenance of a systems and procedures department and a programming group.

The key to developing effective project teamwork and coordination is the selection of the Systems Planning Manager who is given the over-all responsibility for the development of the management information system. He must be a good administrator who thoroughly understands each technical area, and who can properly communicate with all levels of management in gaining company support for the data-processing program.

MANAGEMENT CONTROL AND REVIEW

Because of the multi-project nature of an integrated data-processing program, it is of great importance that good project progress reporting techniques be established and carefully monitored in order to maintain proper control over each project. Reporting systems that have been established for the control and review of data-processing programs quite often are extremely cumbersome, complex and difficult to comprehend by non-technical personnel. No data-processing program can possibly succeed unless it first has the active and continual support of operating management. In order to gain this support, operating management should be given a clear, concise picture of how each project is progressing and to what degree established objectives and goals are being attained and modified.

It is also important that realistic estimates for job completion dates be established. A common complaint on the part of the managements of many companies who have initiated data-processing programs is that invariably the data-processing or systems-planning staff has materially underestimated the amount of time required to transfer applications to equipments and also to re-engineer existing systems. This has contributed to a lack of control over individual projects and is quite often detrimental to the entire program since projects that appear to be seriously lagging are completed on a crash basis. Experience indicates that wherever this is done investment required to finish the job is quite high and the program requires considerable follow-up and possibly complete redesign at some future date because of the hasty manner in which the final installation was made.

In the final analysis there can be no substitute for good sound basic planning in the development of a management information system. As noted by Mr. Neuschel earlier, it is important that management in business not be totally preoccupied with the installation of data-processing hardware and its early maximum utilization. The emphasis instead should be on the determination of what information is required to efficiently run the business, not on the efficient utilization of data-processing equipment which is busily engaged in turning out large volumes of information that has been used under previous and existing reporting systems.

Finally, the analytical techniques used in the development of an over-all company-wide management information study should be applied to the data-processing program, so that the control and review procedures suggested for the balance of the company also be applied to the management of the data-processing function itself. When this is done, when the objectives of the program are reasonably clearly understood by operating management, and the organizational position of the activity is clearly defined, we should anticipate a substantial improvement in the performance of the data-processing systems planning function.

REFERENCES

1. Richard F. Neuschel. By permission from Management by System, copyright, 1960, by McGraw-Hill Book Company, Inc., New York.
2. Ibid.

DISCUSSION (Following Mr. Gallagher's presentation of his paper)

D. G. MALCOLM: We have talked about management recentralization
as one possible outcome of utilizing computers. We might find, however, that computers cause a movement toward decentralization rather than recentralization.
Another thought is that by the use of computerized systems we may
actually turn business back toward a competitive enterprise and
away from the price administered enterprise as it now appears to be.

J. D. GALLAGHER: We discovered some interesting results in re-
organizing the straightforward and simple function of accounts receivable. We found it possible to develop reports of an interpretive
nature that replaced some fairly highly skilled people.
In the sales aspect of the problem, we ignored the confines of the existing system and developed a theoretically perfect system based on
a compromise between the operating people and the people on the corporate staff.

D. G. MALCOLM: To me there is a basic question concerning managerial decentralization versus centralization: Which is most desirable?

W. E. ALBERTS: A very significant point is that central information
processing doesn't mean central control or central decision making.
Information fed in from all over the country can be fed back to the
salesman at Podunk, who can be a more effective salesman and operate freely on his own because he is better informed.
I think that, if anything, there is going to be a trend towards greater
decentralization of certain functions by giving people down the line
better information and freedom to work with it, plus better measures
of their effectiveness. That is the only way that all of us, whether we
be workers or managers, can realize our full capabilities.

W. R. FAIR: I strongly agree that we should strive to dignify human
work. A political scientist, however, might comment that when people
are given the opportunity to hold power, they hold it closely.

A. SCHULTZ: Some applications of communication systems have the
immediate effects of cutting down time lags. In other types of organizations—those with different processing functions—there might arise
the necessity for a recentralization of plants that were decentralized
prior to the time that a communication system was instituted.

J. D. GALLAGHER: By centralizing data processing in a company it
is possible to create conditions favorable to decentralization of data
processing.
Although this sounds paradoxical, it is not. Because, having a central-

ized communications system, the divisions of a company press very hard to have their own data-processing equipments for applications over which they feel they want direct control.

A. SCHULTZ: The truth of the matter is we don't know enough about the problem because we haven't studied it. However, now that this problem has been raised, it presents entirely new dimensions and possibilities of automation. It also raises the question of the value of the time factor.

I. KESSLER: There appears to be a conflict in the concepts concerning automation of the various functions of a business.
It seems to me that the line of policy management will stay the same, and what we are actually talking about is extending tools to operating management which will enable them to be more effective in their own operations. But this is not to be confused with the assumption of policy responsibilities,which I suspect will stay just where they are, and which I believe should stay where they are.

D. G. MALCOLM: The consensus concerning the question of managerial recentralization seems to be that computerized control systems will tend to aid decentralization.

A. J. ROWE: I think that one thing we have not been concerned about is the systems aspect of the problem. In particular, it is possible for one person to do a terrific job at the expense of the whole organization. We know that this is suboptimization. Computers provide an obvious way to enhance the operating performance of an individual, but on the other hand, there are certain decisions for which the operating person shouldn't be responsible. Lower levels of management are not in a position to see how their actions affect the performance of the system as a whole.

M. O. KAPPLER: This reminds me of some of the things we at SDC learned about suboptimization from our experience with the System Training Program. The way to fight it is to be sure that the team result is visible to the one who is suboptimizing. He must see how his actions affect the total system. If he can't he will fall short of performing a good air defense job.

A. W. RATHE: Kap's point is one of the most significant things I have heard in this whole symposium: to make the team needs visible to every member. That is the cardinal obligation of top management, wherever that top management is. "Top management" is a relative term; its crux is perhaps not so much the setting of policy, as it is coordination or integration, inspiring or encouraging.
Concerning decentralization, again we have a semantic problem—what

is decentralization? Boeing is in Seattle and Wichita, and this is considered by some people to be decentralization because these locations are 2500 miles apart. A more widely adopted interpretation of decentralization is one which implies a wider distribution of decision-making authority. This definition considers the company and all its components as a system, an "integrated whole."

For instance, I don't know of any organization which is more sincerely dedicated to decentralization than is General Electric. Yet with 125 or 150 departments, each making decisions within its scope, there is still a G.E. You have stock in G.E., not in their Fractional Horse Power Department. So, there are corporate reserve responsibilities which cover the company as a whole. Some may view this as centralization. It isn't; it is the over-all, may I say, systems view.

Now, in the rush toward distribution of decision-making authority, some of the corporate reserve authorities are slighted. One division of a company, in its zeal to make a good showing, may on its own make a decision that should have taken some other divisions into consideration.

D. G. MALCOLM: This discussion has pointed up the idea that, in designing a communication-information system, more inclusive values than the dollar efficiency of the system itself must be included. What is an efficient design from a electronic point of view isn't the whole design.

EXAMPLES OF AUTOMATED MANAGEMENT CONTROLS

SECTION **IV**

Integrated systems planning at G. E.*

CHAPTER **A** by H. FORD DICKIE

General Electric has been a proponent of progress through competition for many years. We believe that it is the competitive situation that makes "Progress Our Most Important Product." General Electric's President, Mr. Robert Paxton, speaking on this subject, stated:

"While business competition is an old story to your Company, we are now challenged by a new surge of competition that is even stronger than what we have faced in the past.

[Possibly most important to the country's economy,] "dramatic and challenging competition is coming from foreign manufacturers. The electrical industry in particular has felt the impact of competition from these sources. From giant steam turbines to tiny Christmas lamps, we find that we are sometimes undersold in our own front yard." [One important foreign advantage is often that of] "shockingly low pay scales in terms of the level of living provided working people and their families.

"American industry is going to have to find an answer to the challenge of new competition from abroad—an answer that does not destroy the living standards that we have worked so hard to achieve."

---

*Prepared with the assistance of Mr. B. Grad, Production Control Service, General Electric Company, New York, New York.

Yet, how can we compete? Does the answer have to lie in high tariff walls or sharp import quotas? During the past four years we have been working intensively on three positive ways of establishing industrial leadership.

First, innovation—we have to provide the amount of research required to develop new products and then to introduce these new products rapidly and efficiently so as to maintain a competitive position.

We must give prompt and reliable delivery of a high quality product, offering customer oriented features, backed up by dependable, economic field service.

But most important, we must re-establish cost leadership. The only logical way to do this is through increased productivity, which means fewer direct and indirect labor hours per unit of product. This increased productivity comes not from sweat shop techniques but from designing a product for producibility, from best shop layouts, from best methods, from using the most modern factory and office equipment and, particularly, from planned, integrated, automated systems.

Recent figures on industrial productivity show how slowly we have improved since World War II. The average increase in productivity per year since 1950 has been approximately 2 per cent. In contrast, Germany has increased its productivity by more than 5 per cent a year in the same period. 1958 was the first good omen, when U.S. productivity increased by over 6 per cent, this in spite of a significant reduction in industrial output. It was analysis of this data that caused General Electric's Services' organizations to attempt the design of an advanced automatic system—one that would be able to respond efficiently and more economically to incoming customer orders.

CONSIDERATIONS IN THE DESIGN OF ADVANCED AUTOMATED SYSTEMS

Certain general objectives were established in order to accomplish this task:

- The new system should be economically practical and technically feasible; it should be broadly applicable to many departments of the Company.

- The system should be multi-functionally integrated and provide a close linkage between the office and the factory.

- It should be designed with bold innovation in order to break the historically accepted business systems patterns.

- We hoped through research to develop new concepts and tools for use in designing such new systems.

- We hoped to develop new criteria for technically and economically sound approaches to automation that would help us determine which particular new techniques should be used in specific businesses.

- We wanted to provide a foundation for future General Electric progress through research and development.

To pick an initial area for this exploration, we analyzed some of the current weaknesses of industrial systems.

- Typically, delivery cycles are quite long when compared to the product's cost. This is particularly true of manufacturing cycles in relation to the actual processing time. Work-in-process inventories are correspondingly excessive.

- Indirect labor costs are increasing steadily. Many factories even joke about the fact that they can't make a shipment until the paper weighs as much as the product.

- A third area is the high redundancy of information used in our factory paper work. For example, on a line of shafts used by a successful motor manufacturer, it was found that some three hundred different drawings had been prepared over the course of two years to take care of minor variations, and that on each of these drawings there was some sixty to seventy fields of information. Of these fields, more than 80 per cent were completely fixed. For every shaft only 20 per cent were truly variable.

With these and other significant problems in mind, we sought the areas of an industrial business system that would have the greatest impact on the above weaknesses. We call these areas, which are at the heart of the business process, the Main Line System.

Possibly a review of the steps included in this Main Line System will give a clearer understanding of the particular scope of this project.

THE MAIN LINE SYSTEM IN A BUSINESS

The present Main Line System starts with a customer's order. This specifies what the customer wants in functional terms, such as size, color, rating, and other product requirements. A typical order then goes through certain conventional steps. (See Figure IV-A-1.)

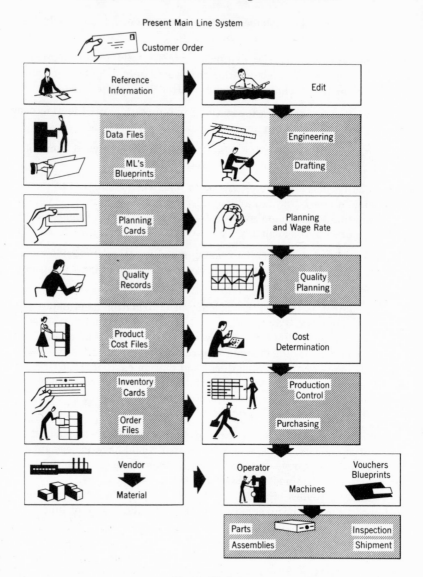

Figure IV-A-1.

1. It is edited to eliminate ambiguities and to put the order into the proper, most usable, internal form.

2. Then this order is engineered, and drafting prepares documents needed, namely blueprints, bills of material, etc.

3. Based upon this design information, the manufacturing engineers then perform the operational planning on how to make the product and what the time allowances should be for the various labor and machine operations.

4. In a similar manner, the quality control procedures are determined, establishing standards, methods, and frequency of quality analysis.

5. And then, using the existing records and files, cost information is accumulated, compiled, and analyzed.

6. Manufacturing control then takes over to determine when the parts are needed as well as how many are to be purchased and made. Typically, this includes the functions of customer promising, scheduling, and inventory control.

7. Finally, instructions in the form of vouchers, purchase requests, etc. along with blueprints and other necessary papers are transmitted to the factory to direct the manufacture of internally made components or to purchasing for outside material procurement.

In each of these steps, information is taken from the previous function, typically in the form of written documents, and used to produce the next document or output with the aid of information reference files: material lists, blueprints, planning cards, cost cards, etc. In short, the Main Line System converts the customer's order into a finished product. Present systems are typically based on human-to-human communication with extensive file reference. The use of mechanical aids is generally still limited. The shop area is often characterized by the job shop type of facilities, high buffer stocks between operations, and long manufacturing cycle times.

Substantial amounts of money are involved in the Main Line System. Normally, 100 per cent of the direct labor and 100 per cent of the direct material is tied up in the Main Line System. At least 40 per cent of our indirect labor and indirect expenses are also in this area. All of our productive raw and in-process inventories are in this category as well as approximately 80 per cent of our plant and equipment investment. In total, this area probably accounts for 75 to 80 per cent of our product costs and a similar percentage of our investment.

THE RESEARCH APPROACH

To perform a research and development job on these multi-functional problems, it was necessary to organize a multi-functional team representing the various business functions: Engineering and Accounting as well as Manufacturing. In this particular study, Marketing and Employee Relations were not included simply because the particular system defined did not require their extensive contribution.

In a decentralized company like General Electric, planning such a program is quite complicated. There are two types of problems that arise:

1. The integration of staff planning people into a closely knit team is complicated by the fact that there is no component in the organization responsible for multi-functional systems work. Therefore, effective work requires mutual participation of the functional services that have no common manager short of the Chairman of the Board, who is the Chief Executive Officer. Basic problems like leadership, budgets, relative functional roles, decision making, reporting, etc. could well have become major obstacles. Fortunately, the merit of the project and the integrating force of belonging to one company was sufficiently strong to overcome these natural organizational barriers.

2. A second problem in a large decentralized company is developing concepts in a framework that will be both understandable and meaningful to the many operating components.

It was our belief that an "ivory tower" approach would not provide an effective atmosphere for integrating systems design work nor would it particularly aid in selling any new concepts which were developed. What was needed was a real live business—a "living laboratory." The selected operation had to be representative of the breadth of businesses in which General Electric engages. These businesses vary from lamp bulbs to large steam turbines, from silicones to guided missiles, from fractional horsepower motors to complex steel mill controls. Also in picking a business, we wished to select one where the existing information was in sufficiently clear form to be readily usable. We looked for a business with a good clear documentation and clean records. Since "you can't automate a mess," we sought a well-run business where we could concentrate on advanced development rather than having to devote time to cleaning up existing problems.

We also felt that by carrying on our research in a particular business, the systems team would have its attention focused on specific, clearly defined problems rather than the more vague, imaginary difficulties. In this way, the creative contributions were concentrated on the areas most needing improvement.

STEPS IN CARRYING OUT THE PROGRAM

After the multi-functional organization was established, a clear and specific work plan was followed. The first phase was that of data gathering. This involved getting all the facts concerning present inputs and outputs, volume of devices, design variations, manufacturing facilities, historical performance, etc. This phase took approximately six months and led directly into the second phase: problem analysis. During problem analysis, all the information gathered during the first phase was digested and reviewed, and an effort made to determine clear cause and effect relationship between changing external conditions and changing internal performance.

The third phase of the program was that of preliminary systems design. This achieved a first verification of what may truly be called the basic system. This lasted approximately one month and brought into play the design efforts of not just the general systems designers but all the specialists in the various areas.

The fourth phase was that of detailed systems design. This refined the specifications in great detail. It clearly indicated those areas which needed to have their technological feasibility proven and those whose feasibility had already been clearly demonstrated in previous work.

The fifth was that of construction of a prototype to demonstrate application of the new ideas. It was, in the vernacular, a bread board model, and not yet an actual operating model.

The last and final phase of any program is that of testing, training, and evaluating. We have been able to test this "bread board" model against a variety of circumstances and have found it to be very satisfactory. We have been carrying out our training objective during the past twelve-month period along with initial evaluations of potential savings.

While these are quite conventional steps, the important new concept that we felt we brought to business systems problems was the use of the scientific or engineering systems approach; the kind of technique RAND and other similar organizations have devoted to military systems problems.

With this systems approach, we treated the entire Main Line System as though it were a big black box with only one transaction input to this black box, the customer's order, and there was only a single basic output, the finished product. All that went on in between was subject to analysis and redesign. The systems approach was intended to design a new Main Line System and provided us an opportunity to ignore present techniques and ignore all of the conventional organizational or functional divisions of work and to really concentrate, without inhibitions, on reconceiving the solution.

We felt that a business system, like military systems, would have five elements:

1. It has information resources including the various decision criteria which are currently in the form of reference files.

2. It must have decision makers capable of taking the transaction inputs and matching them with the information resources to determine a course of action.

3. It must have communications channels enabling it to transmit its decisions and in turn to receive feedback information concerning operating performance.

4. It must have a physical processor which actually transforms material through the use of men, machines, and energy in accordance with the instructions given it.

5. The physical processor must have access to the physical resources of men, machines, materials, and energy.

DEVELOPING AN INTEGRATED SYSTEM

The fundamental concept in carrying out this project was the idea of vertical integration. Integration is currently a by-word, but most new work has been concerned with automating common activities like payroll, inventory control, or processing requisitions across many product lines or the whole business. This might be called horizontal integration. However, we felt that true integration should follow lines of information flow; it should cut vertically through all functions in a product line. With this vertical integration, far broader opportunities for profit will be available. Why? By having all the information processes linked together inside the computer, it is unnecessary for each function to duplicate the others' files. For example, cost will no longer have to maintain independent files of material lists, blueprints, and planning records for every part and assembly. This elimination of file redundancy will be felt in many indirect labor activities.

Further, vertical integration of effort also has a major effect on reducing the information and phsycial processing time cycle. Since all of the decision-making logic needed to completely process an order is in the computer, it is reasonable to expect overnight data processing, and, by having dynamic control of the whole physical process from purchasing through parts making and assembly, it is possible to reduce significantly the actual "make" cycle. This type of control should result in lower inventories, higher promises kept, and better indirect labor efficiency.

An analogy to vertical integrated planning might be drawn from the design of a number of railroads in different states or countries which interconnect at various terminal points. The engineers from the individual companies building the roads and the countries planning to use the roads had better decide in advance certain basic criteria like gauge of track, weight limits for bridges, clearances, motive power, signaling techniques, etc. If this type of integrated planning is not done, the result can be virtual chaos. Vertical integrated planning provides the single gauge approach to business systems design.

A second principle is the need for discovering a logical pattern which formally displays and relates the various decisions such as those in product design, facilities operation, and factory scheduling. In manufacturing planning, for example, by focusing attention on each variation in method or elemental time standard, you can spotlight cause and effect relations and thereby make improvements. Organizing the multitude of detail into a clear, easy to understand framework shows what design characteristics control the various manufacturing process elements, making clear the simplification and standardization opportunities. The use of logical decision patterns in a business should reduce direct labor and direct material through the powerful analytical insights they make possible.

Another new concept was to use computers in the way that they are best qualified to work. It is certainly not true that computers should be programmed to do work the way humans have in the past. We needed to create bold, advanced, computer oriented techniques. We must have the system designed with the computer in mind. Although computers and humans perform many of the same tasks, their relative efficiencies and economic advantages are quite different. To arbitrarily make the computer follow the same routines, the same steps, the same processes as humans is illogical. Rather, the basic system should be reconceived and redirected to obtain maximum performance from the electronic computing equipment.

It was also quite an insight to think about the system as being directed solely toward the ultimate user, ignoring all the intermediate functional outputs that have so commonly become identified with our data-processing systems. The only purpose of having any operating outputs from a system is to cause someone to take action, to cause a buyer to purchase materials, an operator to make parts, etc. The intermediate transformations and hence the intermediate outputs are not essential systems elements but are only a reflection of the particular data-processing techniques currently in use.

The results of this type of work have been quite exciting. We can now automatically convert a customer's order into parts of a specially designed product, performing all of the Main Line System's steps inside the computer. This automatically provides all the factory's action documents: purchase orders, operator instructions, quality instructions, punched paper tapes to run numerically controlled machines, customer promises, bills of material, stock order recommendations, withdrawal notices, shipping papers, etc.

RESULTS OBTAINED FROM THE PROJECT

Many new techniques were developed for use by various General Electric departments to design integrated, automatic systems. For example, new techniques have been developed for decision analysis. New techniques have been conceived for part and product representation and identification. New ideas have been formulated for computer programming. All of these concepts taken together have changed our viewpoint entirely as to the economic feasibility of installing integrated, automated business systems.

We feel that there are many benefits from these concepts. In order to clarify them for you, I should like to describe the nature of each function in the computer and some of the resultant benefits.

The determination of "What to Build" is the key role of engineering, and we believe that the requisition engineering activities can now be computerized. The computer can translate a customer's wants into the specific details of the materials, parts, and assemblies needed to satisfy those wants. In addition, this computerized process can avoid the necessity of having to create many of the documents and records with which we have become too familiar. Outstanding savings can be realized in the preparation of model lists, bills of material, blueprints, etc.

Included in the benefits from this engineering advance should be substantially reduced engineering time and cost through the elimination of many of the routine steps which humans now take. There should be lower drafting expense through elimination of many of the tasks which drafting has historically performed. A clear, logical statement of the engineering scope of a product line should make it easier to obtain an optimal level of standardization. A properly designed computerized engineering system should be easier to change and be more flexible.

With knowledge of the product design details, manufacturing

engineering is then in a position to determine the best routing, work methods, and time standards. We have found that much of this work on "How to Build" the product can also be completely taken over by the computer. The possibility of automatically preparing accurate operational descriptions coupled with correct time standards for every job certainly has considerable appeal.

Another intriguing area is the communication of the computer with numerically controlled machine tools. Three new features should have wide application.

- A single program tape controls an automatic machine for the entire day.
- Machined parts are automatically identified as an integral part of the program.
- Computers are used to automatically generate machine tool programs.

"Tape-for-a-Day" Machine Tool Control

Typically, users of numerically programmed machines have achieved repetitiveness in operations by cycling a loop of punched paper tape. Thus, if ten pieces are required, the operator glues the back-end of the tape to the front and allows the looped tape to run around ten times. In this system, the same objective is accomplished by providing ten machine tool control programs in a single length of tape. Further, the same length of tape also includes a program for all other pieces to be manufactured by the machine that day. Thus, one length of paper tape provides an integrated, sequenced control program for a numerically controlled machine tool for the entire day.

Machined Parts Automatically Identified

Parts processed on numerically controlled equipment are sometimes identified in a secondary manual operation. This can be avoided by introducing an identification step in the machine tool program. For example, parts can be identified with shop identification numbers by spotting a shallow blind hole in a code matrix prestamped on the part itself:

	1A	2	6	51	62	64	75
Identification Hole ○							

A more suitable, generalized version of this code matrix idea would
be:

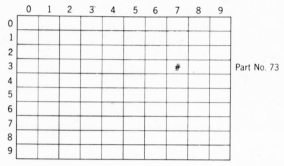

Part No. 73

Computer Generated Machine Tool Programs

The generation of numerical machine tool programs was done on
an electronic computer. This, of course, facilitates developing the
"tape-for-a-day." While electronic computers are not essential,
mechanizing the production of punched paper tapes (or cards) to run
automatic machines improves accuracy and reduces cost.

Among the other benefits is shorter planning time, since the computer takes over a former manual job. There would also be reduced
planning costs, since computers can do this job for less money than
humans. And probably most important, more accurate planning and
time standards should result because of the computer's ability to
follow the exact instructions you've given it.

Quality control can follow a very similar pattern; the key questions here are: at what point to inspect or test, the quality evaluation
method, appropriate time standards, frequency of evaluation, and
criteria for acceptance or rejection. Here again we have found that
a computer program can be prepared which will perform all of these
tasks automatically. This would, in effect, determine how to evaluate
the product and its components. Included in the benefits are fewer
quality corrections through having the proper balance between quality failure and quality appraisal costs. There should be fewer com-
plaints through a careful analysis of customers' needs and product
characteristics. There should also be lower quality costs through
the integrated planning of quality control along with engineering design and manufacturing operation planning.

Cost accounting offers another opportunity. The objective was to
determine appropriate product costs for quotation work or for cost
standards to be used for comparison with actual costs. We find again
that cost standards can be automatically developed and that a computer properly programmed can also be used for establishing work-

in-process inventory value. Through this cost work, we should be able to obtain better cost analyses by having all the facts at our finger tips when they are needed. It should be far easier to maintain up-to-date costs because of the potential simplicity in storing the cost information. There should be reduced expense of cost determination through the use of a computer to replace human effort.

The next area of production control is particularly intriguing to us. Each of the previous steps in the computer portion of the integrated Main Line System have all dealt with tangible product characteristics: what to build from engineering, how to build from operation planning, etc. In contrast, production control, the final element of the computer portion of the Main Line System, develops a fourth dimension by determining the time and sequence in which main line activities take place.

APPLICATION OF RESULTS TO PRODUCTION CONTROL

Production control is interested in when things happen. It has the responsibility of actually carrying out at the right time the data-processing and decision-making calculations necessary to support each function. Production control is concerned with the time inter-relationships of all customer orders. It is responsible for economically satisfying these customers' requirements considering the actual status of the shop.

Production control provides the scheduled release of the factory's action documents:

- Purchase requests.

- Punched tape for automatic machine programs.

- Operator instruction to make and assemble products.

- Quality instructions for inspecting and testing.

- Shipping papers to deliver the customer's product.

In this integrated system the computer should daily schedule shop operations, specify operation release dates and due dates, specify order quantities, review inventory stock levels, and issue customer promises. These orders should not be released prematurely. One key element in computerized manufacturing control is frequent feedback coupled with frequent scheduling for close shop control, using today's performance to guide tomorrow's shop decisions. In the past, a major obstacle to such tight shop control has been the mass of detailed data which had to be gathered and interpreted before any meaningful results could be obtained. Manual and even punched card techniques often sagged under this burden; but electronic computers offer the high speed, low cost calculating ability necessary to cope with this problem.

The Integrated Main Line System has daily feedback of completions from each of the various areas of the shop. This information will be digested by the computer each night and recognized in the releases to be prepared for the following day. The parts to be started the next day will depend upon the exact status of each of the areas of the shop—whether they be behind schedule or ahead of schedule, what their status is on rush jobs, and related information.

The result is a flexible system prepared to respond quickly and accurately to changes. Time displays in handling information are avoided and corrective actions can be initiated immediately throughout the Integrated Main Line System.

Developing manufacturing control rules presents some special difficulties. For example, product performance can be proven in the laboratory, operation time standards can be checked by a stop watch, but how can you pretest a rule for customer promising? General Electric has been instrumental in applying simulation techniques to similar business problems involving many interdependent activities that change with time. The heart of shop simulation is a computer model which realistically duplicates the behavior of the shop as it processes customer orders, making allowances for set-up and processing times, absenteeism, machine breakdowns, and the like. The specific computer model developed for the Integrated Systems Project compressed four months of shop experience into a fifteen-minute computer run. As a result, it was possible to test how well various proposed sets of production control rules would meet due dates and planned cycle times without actually trying them in the shop. In addition, inventory levels, employment stability, and man-machine utilization could also be evaluated and compared. A series of such tests provided the basis for estimating and selecting the Integrated Production Control Rules.

Integrated production control offers several benefits. For example, it now seems quite practical to obtain a shorter main line information cycle—actually less than one day. Similarly, electronic computers can be expected to lower paper work costs. Shorter cycles in the office and factory, as well as improved scheduling techniques, will permit substantially lower inventories. These improvements should lead to shorter customer promises, improved service, and potentially higher sales. Somewhat unexpectedly, indications are that these gains can be achieved while improving employment stability—and without a sacrifice in keeping delivery promises and equipment utilization.

Of course, the only reason for all of this information is to procure the parts that are needed, on schedule, at optimum cost; and to direct the machines and operators in the factory to make the right parts at the right time.

FLEXIBLE FACTORY AUTOMATION

Rather than visualizing automation as a long line of highly special-ized machines and transfer devices, we believe, for our General Elec-tric type of businesses, that the important aspect of automation will be the ability of machines to switch from one task to another at little or no extra cost. The inherent flexibility of the individual machine or group of machines will be a determining factor in the effectiveness and usefulness of these automatic systems concepts. With numerically controlled machines, such as are now available, the set-up cost is re-duced to practically zero; and as those who have worked on inventory control problems will recognize, this implies that the economic lot size can be reduced to one. Hence, flexible factory automation per-mits us to respond to the external customer oriented requirements and not give such heavy consideration to the internal shop.

Through this flexible factory automation we believe that we will be able to lower direct labor costs per unit through replacing hu-man activities, where desirable, by machine operations. Machine accuracy and set-up flexibility will reduce both scrap and rework. Integrated planning and control with the right tempo will result in shorter manufacturing cycles.

PROBLEMS STILL TO BE RESOLVED

The future of integrated systems planning is an exciting one, but some of the problems which we face are certainly significant. A list of some of these problems and opportunities will provide a feeling for the scope of future work.

Decentralization has many advantages, but one problem is the lack of suitable computer equipment for performing such massive data-processing tasks. We find in General Electric individual locations which cannot by themselves justify either medium- or large-scale data-processing equipment. What should be done in these areas? Is there a possibility of combining the needs of a num-ber of these locations to support a computer? We've discussed hav-ing a major business locate its plant on the periphery of a wheel whose hub was the plant headquarters. We have wondered about con-necting these plants through wire transmissions or microwave so that the information for decision making could be fed to the hub location for processing and the answers radiated back out to the individual plants.

In new plant location studies, we have always made a careful analysis of the size of the plant and the amount of labor available in the community, the water and power supply, etc. However, now that indirect labor exceeds direct labor in many cases, now that the major improvement opportunities are available in data processing, why should not the economic availability of electronic data processing be an essential consideration in plant site selection?

Also, we have become aware that while we have concentrated on reducing our data-processing operating costs, we have given inadequate attention to the start-up and maintenance costs of our computer installations. Intensive research is now required on ways to accelerate the installation of a new system and ways of reducing the cost of maintaining and modifying its programs. This compression of the innovation cycle can be a major factor in our ability to compete effectively in the future.

An interesting economics problem is posed by the impact of these automatic systems on our fixed and variable costs. With the higher investment both in factory and office equipment and the simultaneous reduction in the variable cost per unit, we have business systems and factory systems dedicated to growth, since with growth the full profit-making potential will be fully realized. What will this kind of business system mean in terms of inventory accumulation and in terms of product pricing?

It has been our experience that as the breadth of an application increases, the complexity of conceiving and installing a system grows with something like the square of the number of functions involved. We must establish tools and techniques for coping with this increasing systems complexity to allow our systems designers to get their mental arms around the problems.

As with any new development, there is, at least temporarily, an acute shortage of competent, trained systems designers. These men will have to be developed by the colleges and through on-the-job courses and training. This implies the development of a body of knowledge to draw on so that systems design principles and tools may be properly taught. These systems designers must learn to extrapolate wisely from basic fundamental ideas to develop the best system that should be installed in a given plant.

Returning to the problem mentioned earlier, we have to face up to organizing such broad systems studies. Who in the business organization should be made responsible for determining the need for such work and for actually carrying it out? Because of the multi-functional nature of these problems, how can effective cooperation be insured, who should take the initiative? In General Electric there has been developed, over the past ten years, a clear concept of the work of a manager and the work of an individual contributor. We have carefully defined the responsibilities of each individual function of the business. In this same way, we must now analyze in detail the mortar that holds these bricks together. We must describe the kinds of people and the kinds of responsibilities that are required to constitute the most effective kind of mortar. It is even conceivable in some daily operating areas that the mortar will take over the whole operating responsibility, sort of like going from a brick building with mortar in the interstices to a concrete building, which eliminates the individual bricks entirely.

Our evaluation of new systems is generally quite inadequate. We must devote substantial research effort to deriving and determining better measurements of business performance. We have got to stop palming off the decision-making problem on intuition. We have to quit blaming the lack of progress on the intangible nature of the savings from new equipment and new concepts. As a starter, we suggest that at least three factors need to be considered: Time, Cost, and Accuracy. Time includes not just elapsed time between two events such as between the receipt of an order and its delivery, but also response time—how quickly can a business change direction when external conditions require it, how quickly can it innovate? In considering Cost, we have to think not only about actual operating costs but also investment cost and modification cost. We have to stop applying broad overhead factors because the base of our overhead—direct labor—is fast disappearing.

The Accuracy factor is quite complex. It includes not only the quality of the product but our ability to meet promises, degree of employment stability, utilization of equipment, reliability of forecast, etc.

CONCLUSION

To close, I believe that there has been one idea which alone has been more important than any of the individual techniques developed by our integrated systems planning work. It seems to be the fundamental principle underlying the success of our multi-functional team studies and clearly pointing the way to future progress. This is SYNERGISM, the sort of a situation where 1 + 1 = 3. Where two things taken together have a greater total effect than the sum of the individual items taken alone. To us "synergism" is the key that will open the door to future industrial progress. We have seen creative men of widely varying functional backgrounds agree on a common goal, forget their functional bias, forget today's conventional business system, and achieve results that are inspiring, results that are most rewarding.

DISCUSSION   (Following Mr. Dickie's presentation of his paper)

J. F. LUBIN: In my opinion, the Integrated Systems Project (ISP) at General Electric is the most exciting and revolutionary work that has been done in business control systems. However, how are we to insure that information about discoveries and knowledge such as ISP will be disseminated? This problem is substantial. Projects such as ISP show us the great potential of imaginative system planning. Recalling the horseless carriage analogy, we are at last designing "automobiles" and not gasoline powered buggies with false heads mounted on front. It is becoming clearer that we should not do patchwork improvements on existing structures. Indeed, we are perhaps now in need of a general theory of system development and should think less about work on specific operational problems. This might well be the most valuable area for research in management control systems.

R. L. SISSON: I think you are asking for something that is one step beyond what we are ready for. Einstein could reach many of his conclusions because tensor analysis was available and he was able to represent his ideas in extremely concise symbols. The first problem in the data-processing area is to create a language of symbols. Then if I write a few symbols you will immediately know what I mean. There is considerable information in a compact symbol such as an integral sign with a few associated symbols. You know exactly what is meant. We should work on the language problem, if not before, at least simultaneously with, trying to get this flash of insight that will tie this all together.

J. F. LUBIN: Good work has already begun on the common language concept. For example, the efforts of IBM at their Yorktown installation indicate what can be done. But this and all the other work that is in progress is just a beginning, a genesis. We find it difficult to discuss this field intelligently because these developments are so recent and so different in concept from business system analysis up to this time.

C. K. SIMON: I was recently asked by IBM to explain the PERT system. After doing it, they said, "We are talking about the same thing, but have each used a different language." This illustrates a need for a new and common language.

W. R. FAIR: The things that have come out of your model seem to imply specific system ideas programmed into the machine. Production scheduling, however, seemed to be the only area in which you drew specific attention to requirements for decision rules. Are you concerned with that area which does not require decision rules; that

is, with "paper shuffling"? Or was your team successful in sur-
mounting the necessity for a large number of very complicated rules?
Or are we simply bypassing the need for decision rules and then lay-
ing ourselves open to all the problems that arise when the numerous
exceptions come up?

H. F. DICKIE: This integrated team dealt primarily with the logic
that the operating people used in arriving at their decisions. It is probably true that there is not a lot of major decision making done in an
area like requisition engineering, as an example. Here the primary
problem is how many turns of wire are needed in a coil, what is the
size of that wire, and what kind of insulation is required. In this experiment we tried to understand the logic that the requisition engineer follows in arriving at these decisions. We have mechanized the
bottom 70 or 80 per cent of the requisition engineering job, of the time
standards work, and the cost clerk's task. It isn't the cost analyst who
we have displaced; rather, it is the cost clerk. It isn't the industrial
engineer we have displaced; it is the man who does the routine planning of manufacturing operations.
I believe most of the discussion here about management decisions has
been a step or two above the particular level of decision making with
which the project was concerned. We did have to make some more
difficult decisions in the production control portion of the project. The
problems of scheduling both stock and special units, minimizing inventories, meeting promises, and keeping the men and machines busy
in the face of many perturbations required a whole set of decision
rules. We created a mathematical model of the shop in order to test
and refine these rules.

W. R. FAIR: Were you successful in formulating decision rules that
these people apparently followed in their current practices on some
levels?

H. F. DICKIE: We called it their functional logic. Yes, definitely.

A. O. MANN: You raised the question earlier, "Who takes over at
the higher level?" I imagine you meant bringing in other inputs, or
expanding the problem to cover the parameters of the total industrial
system. The answer appears to be research explicitly concerned with
total system development.

M. O. KAPPLER: Concerning the problem of successful planning for
logic and rearranging functions in a manual operating situation before
attempting mechanization, there is the consideration of whether to
adopt functions as they exist or to throw them out.
Our design work in military systems directed our interest into this

area. We were able to do some design in the SAGE military system; however, in the SACCS control system, the next important military system, we had an opportunity to start from the beginning and capitalize on the SAGE experience. In the SACCS control system we started with a small system analysis team that went to Omaha (SACCS headquarters) to determine basic functions and then look at how these could be automated.

The development of military systems essentially employs the method you outlined. I am surprised at what you have accomplished. It seems to me that you have gone a long way in the direction which we are taking in carrying over our military experience to business systems.

J. F. LUBIN: Was the selection of a "good" department really necessary for the ISP study or was it a political maneuver?

H. F. DICKIE: I feel we should generally select a well-run business in which to carry on our research. First, it makes it possible to direct our attention to advanced systems rather than merely cleaning up troubles. Second, our purpose is to sell our new developments to many of the company's business, and they consider improvements in a good department much more significant. Our current problem is the selection of a new systems research project. I feel strongly that to be outstandingly successful it must be as enthusiastically supported by all functions as this one was. The feedback problem seems to be the currently favored program. Certainly the potential for a sophisticated, multi-functional feedback system is exciting. Sometimes these technological advances must be joined with research on new organizational concepts, for it appears that the changes may be substantial, even revolutionary. Many of today's high functional paper curtains must surely fall.

M. O. KAPPLER: I imagine there might have been a tremendous political problem which would prevent selling the program, or achieving the amount of change needed. Based on what has been accomplished, my guess is that you will be working on top management problems soon—you have the courage.

J. E. FLANAGAN: How applicable are the principles that you have enunciated here for the main lines system to similar manufacturing systems?

H. F. DICKIE: We have surveyed the application of this system within General Electric and judge it to be generally applicable to the majority of the middle range of businesses. Certainly it is not directly useful in a pure flow shop like the flat iron business, or, at the other extreme, the purely developmental shop like the Flight Propulsion Laboratory.

Sylvania's data processing center: data processing— its role in administration

CHAPTER **B** by ROBERT H. GREGORY

Sylvania Electric is a decentralized company operating ten product divisions and one engineering division, with forty-five plants, twenty-two laboratories, thirty-two sales offices, and twenty-nine warehouses in seventy communities in more than thirty states. Their policy is to locate in small towns and, in some cases, being the only employer in a town, there is the added responsibility for employment stability. The products include a wide variety of lighting, electronic, metal, and photo products, with some product lines closely related— picture tubes and home electronics, and Semi-conductor and electronic systems—whereas others are essentially independent.

In view of the high degree of vertical integration, a large amount of communications between individual plant locations and divisions is required. This also poses some difficult problems for marketing and inventory control. An inventory control program for any one separate division in an integrated company is not suitable because the program spreads back to the point of origin—to the supplier, in effect—as well as forward to the consumer. This poses no great problem for sources of supply outside the company. However, internally the operation handles raw material through to the finished product, and many divisions are the sole supplier for certain products required by another division. A general manager can buy from an outside source if available, but such purchases further complicate the inventory control policies.

Since Sylvania is administratively decentralized and geograph-

ically dispersed, it is company policy that every decision affecting
the operation of the company must be made at the lowest level at which
sound judgment, based on all the facts, can be made. Decentralization
has proved a sound system of management, based on increases in
sales and net earnings.

Decentralized management and centralized data processing are apparently contradictory, but they need not be so in practice. Early in the
initial survey to set up a data-processing system, it became evident
that decentralized application of high-speed computers for record
keeping was impractical because of the high cost of having installations at numerous separate locations. The study further emphasized
the fact that existing methods did not supply operating people with the
facts in the proper format and at the right time for efficient decision
making. Managers were spending so much time compiling facts to get
the right information that they had no time for their primary responsibility of planning for optimum return on investment. These preliminary observations led to the following conclusions: that computers
were preferable to manual data processing so that people would have
more time for reflection; that decentralized record keeping was a
luxury; and that the philosophy of decentralized management and operation was indispensable.

THE COMMUNICATIONS SYSTEM

Sylvania was faced with three facts affecting systems design:
(1) geographically dispersed operations, (2) administrative policy of
retaining decentralized management, and (3) economic necessity for
centralized processing. Such a communications network has to handle
both administrative messages and the data required for accounting
purposes. In a well-balanced, integrated program, it is virtually impossible to delineate the boundary between a data-processing system
and a communications system. The communications system, in order
to function at peak efficiency, tends to lose its identity as a separate
unit and becomes, instead, an integral part of the input and output of
the data-processing unit itself.

The communications system, as it now stands, can be thought of as
an extension of the input and output of the data-processing system. In
its administrative role it is a separate and distinct unit established
to serve the administrative traffic requirements of the company as a
whole.

Certain requirements of the communications system are common
to both data-processing and administrative traffic transmissions.
Routing and classification of data is necessary to separate completely

the administrative and computer traffic at the Data Processing Center. Further classification is made by type of processing required—payroll data, and so forth—which are punched on tape at specified reperforator stations. In-line sorting of data-processing traffic is mandatory for transmitting administrative and data-processing traffic on a random basis.

The Sylvania communications system was designed to handle increasing work loads, with minimum modification and re-engineering, as more phases of the company were covered and people, becoming familiar with the communications system, used it intensively. The original network of 55 locations connected by 12,000 miles of circuit handling 40,000 words a day has grown to more than 20,000 miles of circuits between 94 stations handling 640,000 words a day.

Communications relay centers were set up at Salem and Williamsport to collect, schedule, and distribute information to either the Data Processing Center or any other Sylvania location. Due to a change in the traffic pattern brought about by the gradual consolidation of accounting activities at Camillus, the relay stations at Salem and Williamsport have since been replaced by a single relay station at Kansas City, Kansas. Switching procedures were kept flexible enough so that both administrative traffic and data-processing information could be handled by an operator following the same procedures. The use of identical operating procedures at every station in the network was imperative; otherwise we would need two separate and distinct sets of operating routines that operators would have to follow intermittently during the work day. Automatic sequential scanning of input devices for readiness-to-transmit permits an operator merely to insert tape in the transmitter gate, hit the circuit request button, and then prepare more messages or attend to other duties. The selector picks up the circuit and starts transmission at the right time.

The five-channel, paper tape, variable length messages used in the communications system raises some problems of compatibility with the seven-channel, magnetic tape, fixed length message format of the computer. The freedom of variable length messages had to be retained for efficient communications operations, to conserve circuit time, and to reduce the margin of error that arises when any decision for an element of programming is made outside the Data Processing Center. The scheme adopted was to convert the data from five-channel tape to punched cards and then to magnetic tape. Equipment for direct conversion from five-channel paper tape to seven-channel magnetic tape was considered desirable, but further study showed cost would be excessive.

A common language was established by means of a coding chart showing the code relationship among all pieces of tape-producing equipment throughout the company. This approach to uniform methods of reporting and use of functional codes throughout the company permits us to select control function communication codes.

A reconstruction procedure was set up to recover messages where descrepancies or inconsistencies were noted in the basic data while processing in the computer. Each individual data-processing message unit is identified by a sequential number to indicate where the message originated and the switching center through which it was relayed. Each message is logged at each stage so that checks on sequential arrangement of messages can, within minutes, detect the loss of a message and request retransmission of data from the reporting location. At the end of each day, each location sends an administrative message to the computer supervisor indicating the last message number so that the accounting for all messages can be completed. "Hash totals" on each data-processing message facilitates the detection of erroneous messages or faulty transmission.

THE DATA PROCESSING CENTER

After a solution to the communications problem was devised, it was possible to plan for a single facility to house the computer, communications equipment, supporting punched card equipment, Data Processing Center personnel, and part of the corporate accounting and budget personnel. There remained, of course, the proviso that decentralized management would buy the idea of a centralized service department for the entire company.

Location

It was necessary to locate the service center in an area where it could not be considered part of or even closely related to any other operation. The success of the educational campaign to convince a manager that he should give up his smoothly functioning record keeping operations on the chance that a remote center would do a better job varied almost directly with the degree of independence that could be assured for our data-processing activity. Locating the center at any division headquarters or even at corporate headquarters in New York would have implied a small degree of independence. The argument of Mr. Leon C. Guest, Jr., Sylvania Controller, was that if we were going to have decentralized data processing, we should make it truly decentralized so that no one in the Sylvania organization would be suspicious that the general manager of Division X had any control—even by reason of geographical proximity—over our data-processing system.

It was not economically feasible to locate a digital computer either at each division accounting headquarters, or at consolidated area departments. We could not afford, as part of a communications network, to put high-speed printers at all locations. Our problem was to choose a location that would be easily accessible from the great majority of plants to provide the optimum in communications service. Analysis covering a full year examined sales, by destination, of all company products; examined geographical location of all plants, laboratories, warehouses, and other facilities; and made an extensive study of transportation factors and mail routes. The geographical center was computed to be near Ithaca, New York, and after an extensive survey of the upstate area, we established our Data Processing Center in Camillus, near Syracuse.

The Service Center

The Center obtains pertinent data from all areas of the company, summarizes it, and presents it in the most usable form to the management responsible for the operation. The Center is strictly a service department with responsibility for gathering facts from operating divisions and sending information either by mail, private wire system, or by courier at the earliest possible moment and in the most useful form to the individual who must make the operating decisions. The Data Processing Center's management does not, in any case, make decisions in connection with the operations of any of our product divisions. The accountants responsible for the particular plant operation approve all entries affecting the records of any products division or plant. This approval comes through the transmission of source data from the plant or division office. It is, of course, important that this philosophy be understood by all accountants employed at the Data Processing Center as well as by all management personnel.

Organization

The original organization plan set up in January, 1956, had areas of responsibility on a functional basis for systems and procedures, communications, computer operations, and personnel. Programming was placed in the computer operations unit because of the liaison thought necessary between the operations group and programmers. The organization for data processing was shown to be inadequate after four months because of lack of liaison between the communications, systems and procedures, and operations units. A new viewpoint—focusing on information flow—was adopted, and the difficult area of information flow for sales records analyzed. The study showed that we needed to develop data at many points throughout the company in a format suitable for efficient handling at the Data Processing Center. Since the original structure contained no responsibility for any of the particular operations involved in the flow of data, the structure was reorganized.

Sylvania's program required the development of an entirely new organization. Personnel were selected from within the company where familiarity with company operations was important and from outside the company where a technical background in communications, programming, and computer operations was basic.

Fundamental to the development of an integrated system representing the latest techniques in data processing are:

- Coordination by an administrator who knows Sylvania's management philosophy, division operations, and policies at the corporate and division level.

- Close liaison between Data Processing Center management and division and plant management of operations, marketing, distribution, and engineering.

- Effective orientation on the basic aspects of program planning and on specific applications prior to conversion to new methods.

The Manager of Data Processing is responsible for communicating with top management, keeping abreast of their thinking, and acting as the general manager of the data-processing unit itself. Such status has helped greatly because, in effect, the Manager of Data Processing is a general manager and head of a division. In other words, data processing is no longer merely a service group, but is itself established as a division.

The supervisor of planning and development has groups responsible for the whole range from method surveys through programming and communications. This method of organization provides an effective approach by which any data-processing function can be, first, surveyed to find whether it should be put on the computer and, second, coordinated, if accepted, through all stages of new system development, installation, and programming. Close liaison is, of course, necessary between planning and development and Univac operations in order to integrate all system requirements and to provide efficient scheduling of the input-output, as well as control of processing costs by function.

Consider the work of one group, computer methods personnel. They analyze the information developed by the systems and procedures group operating in the traditional sense as information gatherers and system designers. However, such information is developed under the guidance of computer methods personnel, for they must develop formats that can be used later for programming. They determine that information is in suitable format for programming and also effect system changes throughout the company to achieve reporting uniformity.

Relations throughout the Company

An orientation program was set up to reach five levels of the organization: Officers, division general managers and controllers, division operating personnel, and clerical staff.

Annual presentations are made to the Executive Operations Planning Committee, consisting of the president, vice president, operating vice presidents, treasurer, controller, director of industrial relations, and division general managers. The general approach is that clerical costs can be reduced by increased automation much as is being done in the factory. Reviews have covered the application of computers in three major categories: simple cost reductions, improved data-processing methods and quicker reporting, and direct use of computers as an aid in making management decisions.

Annual and quarterly meetings are held at Camillus for division controllers to cover intensively the entire program including present and future planning. Many meetings at division headquarters are attended by the Data Processing Director to present the program and to answer questions about present and future plans.

All changes in procedures—either simple improvements over present methods or parts of the over-all systems conversion requirements for computer application—are reviewed in detail with local management in advance of the change. We want them to understand what is proposed, why it is proposed, how it will be accomplished, what the effect on local personnel will be, and what benefits will be derived— by location, by division, and for the company as a whole.

Actual orientation of clerical forces is necessary to carry out a successful conversion without disruption of location operations. Prior to the start of actual conversion a "dry run" prove-out of machines, forms, and procedures must be completed satisfactorily; and detailed operating procedures must be completed and tested. Explanation of the system and orientation of the clerical force must be handled by a crew of specialists familiar with all phases of the system. A system is not considered to be operating effectively for turnover to location personnel until it is completely debugged throughout all phases from original source to final output.

Program success requires full utilization of the combined talents of the executive, the operations analyst, and the electronic computer expert to find practical solutions to the many problems involved in gradual conversion to EDP. Close liaison is maintained with division controllers regarding present and future program plans; with division systems and procedures personnel for planning, system design, and eventual installation; and with key members of the operations group for initial planning and approval of the final system and to serve as check points to protect the interests of the division.

Information Analysis

An expeditious way to divide areas of responsibilities and assign them to specific groups was to select a particular computer application and analyze the information flow for that project from the time of recording source data until its ultimate computer processing.

Customer order entry was selected as a model since it involved three major elements: preliminary processing on tabulating equipment at local points, integrated data processing, and, finally, processing on the computer. The breakdown of responsibilities by groups falls into two general areas. The first area is the development of system and operating procedures, which includes initial planning, system and procedures installation, communications, and operating personnel at the division and corporate level. The second area is the more technical aspect of computer input conversion, programming, processing, and output.

The first phase of information flow—gathering, handling, and processing—was concerned with data flow at all divisional and field locations prior to transmission of data to the center. The study focused on certain factors common to information gathering:

- Peak and total volume.

- Format of presentation.

- Degree of mechanization and planned revision.

- Compatibility of existing methods of handling data with the uniform reporting requirements of Univac.

- Design of forms to meet computer input requirements.

- Existing operating routines covering machines, systems and procedures, and communications.

These activities were concerned with the point of document origination and required some participation by every group in data processing. A close community of interest became evident after the study was well along, and we concluded that a coordinated effort of all groups involved was required. It was impossible to determine where the responsibilities of the systems and procedures group let off and those of programming started.

The second stage of data flow was found to consist of computer information handling, computer information processing, and output finalization. These areas of concentration could be clearly established since the operations were technical in scope.

The third area of data flow was concerned with output feedback to the point of utilization. Computer requirements forced us to revise the format of certain reports, just as it was necessary to revise, in many instances, the format of input data. Furthermore, some changes in report scheduling required close liaison with all levels of management in order to gain optimum reporting efficiency. By reducing delay and changing reporting interval, it was possible materially to tighten the reporting procedures of the company as a whole.

APPLICATIONS

The first major project undertaken was the transfer of a 27,000 employee payroll to Univac. Source data at each location are recorded on a payroll summary sheet and are later punched into paper tape and typed on hard copy. Each location can, if it prefers, elect to report input data on an exception basis, i.e., no transmission for the employees who work the standard week of forty hours. Control totals are inserted and a source audit is performed to assure that both control totals and message format are correct. Upon automatic transmission, the data control system at the Center switches to one of three reperforators assigned to payroll. Tapes are converted to punched cards and finally to magnetic tape for computer audit and processing. The payroll program output includes detailed information for gross and net, checks, deductions, and labor distribution. Source information is obtained for tax, labor analysis, incentive computation, personnel administration, plant cost comparisons, and insurance statistics.

Payroll checks are printed on the high-speed printer and mailed, by the Payroll Department, back to the point of distribution. Payroll processing was picked up on a location-by-location basis and the whole company was covered by the middle of 1957.

The second major project transferred was customer order entry. Starting with the receipt of a customer order at a field or factory warehouse, an operator uses prepunched tabulating cards to originate combination customer, warehouse, and shipping documents. Five-channel tape is punched as a by-product with all significant details for invoicing. Later, these data are used to develop detailed and source data for nine basic types of accounting and analytical information.

All communication codes as well as 60 per cent of the constant data in the order are inserted automatically in tape from the prepunched cards via a cardatype and punched in two separate tapes for two product lines. Tapes are transmitted to the product billing centers at Salem, Massachusetts, for lighting products and at Williamsport, Pennsylvania, for electronic tubes.

After divisional processing, the data are sent to Camillus for processing to get detailed information for accounts receivable, credit and collection, sales accounting, sales statistics, inventory control and planning, warehouse scheduling, sales, and district office performance. Source information is obtained for company and division market research, division production planning, and sales forecasting and budgets.

Experience with payroll and order entry applications proved that certain rules must be followed in adopting any application to central processing in Sylvania:

- Accurate data requires source verification audits at all reporting locations.

- Control totals are required as an integral part of every message.

- Quick transmission of error corrections is necessary to continue computer operation without interruption since the computer only accepts audited data which meet criteria set up by division personnel. The computer will produce correct, although incomplete, reports if errors are not corrected immediately.

- Continual liaison is necessary between departments within the Data Processing group and operating personnel. Such liaison is facilitated by locating the corporate accounting function at the Data Processing Center. These people act as the division's representatives at the Center.

- Uniform reporting methods extend to format and communication functional codes at every location.

- System revision is necessary to conform with computer input, processing, and output requirements.

We have, as you might expect, found that machines have imposed format restrictions, for they are less flexible than people.

Present Status

Applications handled at Camillus on a consolidated and centralized basis for the company are payroll, accounts receivable, credit and collection, permanent property, accounts payable, taxes, and corporate accounting.

During the first two years of operation—mid-1956 to 1958—the payroll, accounts payable, and sales record for Lighting Division and Home Electronics were transferred to the computer. Corporate accounts receivable were handled jointly on the computer and tabulating equipment for about two years and were wholly transferred to the computer in early 1959. The computer was operating on a full two-shift basis in the fall of 1958 and reached a full three-shift basis by early 1959. The goal to have the Data Processing Center break even on a current basis within its first two years of operations was reached. Even more important gains are expected with the completion of our accounting consolidation program plan to concentrate on those report areas concerned with inventory control, stock replenishment, and production planning and control.

CONCLUSIONS

Our primary concern in evaluating data processing for Sylvania was the possible effect of a Data Processing Center on the company's policy of administrative decentralization and geographic dispersion. Communication channels between units in our vertically integrated organization had to be kept open.

To date, our experience clearly indicates that a Data Processing Center is purely a service center and does not affect the decision-making processes of management either on a corporate or divisional level. The primary responsibility is to act as a data-handling center and provide management with information concerning their day-to-day operations.

Further planning for data processing in Sylvania is based on the premise that the Data Processing Center will act as a service center charged with the responsibility of submitting timely, precise information to all levels of management in order to facilitate decision making. Two kinds of reports are involved: reports for action and reports for review. Data developed by the Center for action reports require immediate action by all levels of operating management and supervision. Our major goal in this area, which has been well defined for a long time, is to concentrate at the Center the responsibility for producing this information. This transfer will reduce delay in reporting and achieve, whenever possible, a higher level of uniformity.

Uniform reporting procedures will enable us to develop reports for top management for review so that they may coordinate the activities of the operating divisions and do long-range planning for the company. We can, through centralized data processing, consolidate the results of action reports and produce source information for developing reports not previously available to top management because of the difficulty of collecting timely information.

Our goal is to give management the reports already prepared and to develop new information that can assist all levels of management in carrying out day-to-day operations and also in planning future activities.

*P*reparation for logic—
an orderly approach
to automation

CHAPTER **C** by CHARLES K. SIMON

Much has been said and written about new tools for management controls. These tools—which include computers, systems, and special programs—have received a great deal of attention in the current modernization programs for corporate management.

"Operations Research" has been used in certain aspects of preparing for "new systems." On the other hand, management and supporting staff personnel have begun to feel that machines are being created that will completely solve business problems rather than provide aids to management.

However, little is heard about what is perhaps the single most important tool in this present surge to improve management controls. This tool is the "Preparation for Logic." It is the application of the "rule of exception" to the study of the internal business systems and organization of a corporation prior to the installation of computers. When done properly, the results, generally, are effective management controls and correct corporate structure.

Although the latest equipment is used, the operating cost of a management control might be exeedingly high. Where a system is working efficiently, modernizing is relatively easy. However, one of industry's biggest present-day difficulties is the obtaining of equipment for new management control systems before adequate preparation. This lack of planning has caused the downfall of many potential customers desiring modern management control systems.

169

TERMINOLOGY

For the sake of clarity, the two most important terms used in connection with "preparation for logic" are defined and discussed below.

Management Controls

Management controls are merely good management, set up in a clearly defined written and visual pattern, utilizing manpower to a realistic effectiveness and allowing for the performance of all required functions, from sales to invoicing.

Rule of Exception Technique

"Rule of exception" technique is management by predetermined planning wherein compliance is ignored and non-compliance is treated as an exception requiring decision and action. This is nothing new—it is a tested and useful business principle. When we describe a competent executive as one who surrounds himself with competent subordinates, delegating authority to them and handling only those problems that cannot be handled by his subordinates, we are describing true "rule of exception" technique.

This technique is more often described and discussed than applied. There is, however, a direct, positive relationship between the application of this technique and net profits.

Probably the main advantage of a computer controlled "rule of exception" technique system is that such a system, once operating successfully, forces compliance to the system. At the same time, it prevents individual personalities from contaminating the true logic of a good business control system.

Moreover, when a computer is used in connection with such a "rule of exception" management control system, extensions of the management control system to include additional studies, reports, controls, and efficiency checks does not overburden corporate overhead. Other controls, obtained manually, could cost a substantial part of the corporate gross profit. These same controls, when added to a computerized management control system, often cost no more than a few extra man hours. These additional controls produced by the computer usually pay for themselves right away. In fact, any control produced by a computer which does not pay for itself should be reviewed for application validity before being incorporated in the management control system.

GENERAL DISCUSSION

Why Is the Preparation for Logic Necessary Prior to the Installation of Computers?

Analysis of people, paper-work, responsibilities, and methods should result in establishing a truly logical flow of product and efficient use of man hours. Since computer functions are based upon logic, the use of a computer to operate a management control system is only as efficient as the system itself is logical. The computer is generally used to reduce the man hours required to run a system manually. It will not substitute for the "preparation for logic" required to correct the internal business system of any corporation.

Many of today's management control systems could be operated without a computer; however, it is generally more economical to use a computer. Industry does not always have the money in its budget, nor the trained personnel on its staff, to manually operate management control systems.

Good management, in today's business structure, is fast becoming a prerequisite for adequate net profits and healthy corporate growth. It is no longer adequate to merely exist with an assurance of satisfactory profit and growth. In view of the complexity that faces corporate management today (mergers, the need for outside capital to carry expanding inventories; and a public demand for improved distribution and service), it is little wonder that requirements are changing. In addition, technological and design improvements are forcing today's corporate management to go forward or be left behind. A "middle of the road" path can easily be the first step towards losing corporate control.

Improved management controls are not only desirable, they are necessary. It is not uncommon today to have a dollar of reduced inventory result in a quarter of a dollar increase in gross profit.

Another aspect of the control problem is that although an average executive can remember as many as a hundred factors of his business, and know their relationship to each other in logic and in time, he cannot work in detail on more than six or ten of these factors at any one time without disregarding the balance. Admitting that abilities vary, the executive still faces the following problem: the human brain is best at solving one problem at a time.

When the executive is confronted with more than one problem, he takes short cuts. Choosing what appear to be the most important facts (usually less than ten), he may then make a decision based upon an analysis of the reduced data. As an alternative, he may delegate such decisions to the submanagers and then correlate the findings of each submanager into his decision. Unless some mechanical system is used to record the relationships and interdependencies of the points of factors within his business enterprise, this latter approach is, unfortunately, more often theory than practice.

The Basis of Preparation for Logic

In discussing how "preparation for logic" in business must precede management controls, a simple analysis can be made by creating a hypothetical corporation.

The Model

Let us consider the size of the hypothetical corporation to be in the range of five hundred to five thousand employees. Management is guided by group thinking, administered by one executive, assisted by his staff, and guided by the board of directors.

In an IBM analysis of the potential market for the sale of RAMAC-type business control systems, the sales potential (based upon a model narrower than ours) was over 2,500,000,000 dollars.

The Supposition

Let us assume that we supplied the hypothetical corporation with the following tools of good management controls. Furthermore, assume that all charges for the cost of these tools were paid for in advance for ten years.

1. A random access memory type of computer of sufficient memory capacity to record all corporate functions and records in digit form. This computer would have adequate computing capacity for the corporation management control functions.

2. All necessary supporting equipment, including tabulating, printing, and other machinery.

3. An air conditioned facility in which to house the equipment.

4. Competent programmers.

5. An experienced computer engineer.

6. A good technician.

7. Sufficient supporting and operating personnel.

The Question

Given the above, what would happen in most cases?

The Answer

Nothing.

The Explanation

In many cases, management, disregarding "preparation for logic," would make an attempt to apply these tools to their present system. Confusion would follow with the equipment of "operations research" getting the blame.

The Reason

A good management control system is based upon logic. Such a system, operating with the use of a computer as its core, is completely based upon and dependent upon logic. The present management system that we find operating in our "model" represents logic contaminated by personalities. Because the traits and habits of people have already affected logic, a distorted pattern exists which is not applicable to the purely logical function of true "rule of exception" technique.

The Solution

Preparation for logic must precede good management control. The big job in our model corporation and in industry in general is this "preparation for logic." Once this is accomplished, the application of management control systems, using the latest mechanical equipment, may follow.

In considering the problem of building good management controls, we might apply a rule of thumb which uses three parts "preparation for logic" to one part "application of the system."

Examples

Proper and improper applications of management controls are discussed below. Only the corporate names are fictitious.

Case 1—Proper Application

The Jones Milling Corporation was an old line machine tool product company with an international reputation. Its stock paralleled the general market trend. The Corporation usually showed a net profit but lacked aggressiveness. It has limited expansion and diversification.

New management was brought into the Corporation after a change in ownership. This change resulted from the acquisition of funds required for a new plant and and new equipment.

In an effort to diversify the product line, an entirely different business was purchased and absorbed into the parent plant. This dual product operation was then installed in a brand-new plant with some old and new equipment. From the exterior, the company looked new. The new executive offices gave an appearance of complete modernization. Unfortunately, inside the building, the same people were operating with about the same system as before. Now, however, they operated with the added burden of paying off a new building and equipment loan. This demanded greater efficiency, which they could not produce.

Budget figures, adjusted to include new plant and equipment factors, just weren't being met. Management, however, continued to operate by "seat of the pants" methods.

Expansion, including new plant and equipment, required more planning. Management, which formerly depended on individual decision, had now grown too big for this approach. They now needed a "team" approach and yet were not organized for it. As sales increased, in-process and finished parts inventory went out of control because their system was unable to control inventory levels effectively. Inventory costs were reducing profits, and late deliveries were seriously affecting sales.

Corporate management contacted the local IBM sales office and an established management consulting firm. At this point, management became intrigued with the possibility of using a random access memory computer system to operate their management controls. This new system would memorize all of their business functions, digest their current data, and become a new tool in operating their business. However, management discovered that while IBM would give them the basic information on how to install this management control system, the actual installation of the system and the responsibility of its working was theirs alone. They then realized the fact that a management control system cannot operate satisfactorily without adequate "preparation for logic."

Analysis of the over-all problem by a consultant indicated that the company could benefit from a mechanized system, but that their internal controls were in no way prepared for the installation of such a system.

Examples of duplicate reports, lists, and other paper work were brought to light. As a result, a program of analysis, preparation for a logical system, and installation of a logical system was instituted.

A flow chart was developed showing the existent management controls system oriented with each and every piece of paper work in the organization. The responsibility for all management action was indicated on this flow chart. This chart pinpointed the actual duplication of effort, reports, and records. It also showed that over 30 per cent of those management decisions which were repetitious did not follow corporate policies. Numerous cases were brought to light wherein one supervisor handling two or more identical problems made completely contrary decisions.

The president was then convinced that he would have to put his house in order before installing and applying his ultramodern RAMAC management control system. The board, corporate top management, consultants, and IBM all accepted the logic of this recommended procedure.

Thus, management guided by the consultants, proceeded as follows:

1. An ideal flow chart was drawn up to depict what should finally replace the present, unacceptable, paper work system. The future plan to adapt the system to the RAMAC computer guided the developing of all forms and procedures.

2. One by one, the various departments were reorganized and their controls adapted or altered to comply with the new flow chart.

3. As a natural evolution of this reorganization, personnel changes occurred, job distributions were revised, and an incentive system was installed and accepted by the company and the union. Methods were improved, physical changes were made to equipment and buildings, and a new plant addition was designed and constructed. New products were designed. Industrial engineering and management control personnel were trained. A strike was avoided. Slowly and deliberately a completely revamped, manually operated management control system was emerging.

At this point, no tab, computer, or accessory equipment had been brought into the plant. The new system of management control that developed grew out of a "preparation for logic" necessary before the eventual installation of mechanized equipment.

What happened was as follows:

1. The resulting management controls system, although operating manually, was just as logical as if it were operating on a computer.
2. In contrast to a computer system, twenty-three extra people were required to manually record, compute, and operate sales, product, inventory, schedule, manufacturing, shipping, receiving, and controls. These twenty-three people represented about a 12,000 dollars per month extra expense. When compared with the additional expense planned for machine rental and operating cost for the computer system, this was rather insignificant.

3. Justification for the computer system still existed. The manual

system updated schedules and records only bi-weekly, while the computer could do this daily.

4. The manual system worked, and worked well.

5. In one division of the company employing approximately three hundred people the product output and sales rose over 30 per cent in a twelve-month period. This sharp increase was accomplished using four fewer employees.

6. This division changed from a "red figure" operation, supported by other profitable operations, into a position of being the "tail that wagged the dog." Profits were high, sales rose, and corporate bonuses to the staff of all three divisions resulted, mainly from the profits made by this one division. Moreover, in two years this division improved the quality and delivery of their product to such an extent that the line was fast becoming a leader in its field.

7. The corporate stock rose.

In line with the prearranged plan, the next step in the corporate program was the ordering of a RAMAC computer and adequate back-up equipment, followed by the mechanization of the management control system.

Mechanization improved the over-all efficiency of management and further reduced inventory. But, the economies and benefits experienced from mechanization were much less than those first realized from the original "preparation for logic."

Case 2—Improper Application

The Standard Time Corporation is a large old line manufacturer of watches and clocks. Their products have been universally accepted for over half a century.

Clock and watch capacity in the U.S. is well in excess of demand. With the increase in imported watches, U.S. manufacturers were forced to lower their prices and face a seriously shrinking market.

The company turned to reorganization and diversification. These efforts lowered overhead and improved over-all profits, but did not alter a large deficit in the watch and clock operation. Two major factors contributing to this situation were: an overexpanded and poorly controlled inventory and a high "return for repair" problem.

A newly revised corporate management reviewed the performance of competitors. One competitor was expanding its sales, maintaining competitive prices, working on a low "return for repair" percentage, carring low inventories, and making the only real profit in the industry.

This profitable operation was modern in its management techniques, and had what appeared to be an efficient, up-dated management controls system. A well-integrated management controls system seemed to be the key to profits.

Standard Time Corporation already had tab equipment, a small computer, and supporting equipment which they were using in connection with payroll, accounting, and standard cost installation.

They decided to set up a management controls system. Unfortunately, they were not thoroughly informed regarding the preplanning and effort that they should put into their "preparation for logic" prior to installing their system.

The staff tried to program their existing system into the computer model represented in a computer handbook. They were assisted by a sales engineer. The job was carried out by the same personnel who had created their existing unsatisfactory system. An excessive amount of money, time, and effort was spent on this project. The results were interlaced with confusion.

What they actually tried was to program a series of illogical, overlapping controls into a logical system. It just wouldn't work. They ended-up relying on the old system while they continued to ineffectively spend money and effort to improve the new system.

This was a case where the lack of "preparation for logic" was the key to a system's failure.

Case 3—Proper Application

The General Grinding Machine Company, manufacturers of a well-known line of machine tools and other machine equipment, had just bought out a well-known small tools company.

They had relied on their auditors (who were also consultants) to guide their installation of a computerized management controls system.

Adequate preparation for this system and a carefully worked-out installation resulted in a good, workable accounting, payroll and standard cost, statistical, production control, and production planning system.

In fact, this system worked so well that management instigated a carefully planned investigation regarding the possibility of extending the computer control to cover all scheduling, shop loading, shipping, and inventory control. The final result was a completely integrated computer management controls system.

A 305 RAMAC was ordered for use in the system. In reviewing the expenditure in 1957 (prior to the 305 RAMAC being received) the board of directors withdrew their approval of the computer. Their decision was based upon the theory that they were getting along all right with what they previously had and didn't want to incur any extra expense at that time. While this type of thinking sometimes restricts progress, in this case it permitted the "preparation for logic" based on the installation of a simplified tab 604 system that made for smoother corporate operation.

It is also interesting to note that even if they had obtained a 305 RAMAC computer, which could have handled this job, they would not have eliminated enough of their twelve IBM operating personnel to pay for the additional cost of the RAMAC. True, they could have changed General Grinding's weekly updating of schedules to a daily updating; however, there is serious doubt that this would have proved sufficiently advantageous.

This is a good example of how much can be accomplished with careful planning and a cautious equipment approach. Further note should be made that General Grinding's installation covered a two and a half year period.

The company obtained a duplicate set of equipment and installed it in their subsidiary tool company. Some of the twelve IBM operating personnel were transferred to this company as a training and installation crew. In a few months these trained people had straightened out the paper work within the subsidiary and had a management controls system in operation which was similar to that of the parent plant. This is further proof that people, not machines, are the key to good management controls and "preparation for logic."

General's experience with the installation of the original phase had shown them the need for adequate "preparation for logic." As a result, product lines and departments were incorporated into the system one at a time. A production control procedure was set up using an IBM 604 computer with two pieces of collating and duplicating equipment as a core. Five people were used to operate the card computing room. Duplications were eliminated and ground rules established.

The production control procedure set up on the 604 computer was backed up by punch card, collating, duplicate punching, and other standard equipment. This type of system required large quantities of punch cards and card storage equipment. The operation was set up under the comptroller's office with a total of twelve persons, including the five people operating the card computing room.

Estimated savings were 500,000 dollars per year for full system usage. The department cost was 8500 dollars per month, which included the salary of the twelve people. The rental of the 604 computer was only 400 dollars.

Even with this far from up-to-date equipment and excessive punch card handling, the following results were achieved:

General Savings on Personnel

Payroll	35 to	4
Statistics	20 to	5
Stock-Chasers	14 to	5
Production Planning	16 to	9
Timekeeping	17 to	9
IBM Operating Personnel	0 to	12
	102	44

People saved: 58, money saved: 500,000 dollars. It is interesting to note that this effort is almost five years old and was developed and programmed prior to the availability of 305 or RAMAC or equivalent.

Case 4—Proper Application

The case of Midwest Casting Corporation is unusual. It had three divisions; one supplied sand castings to industry, the second supplied permanent mold castings to fabricators; the third manufactured and sold its own branded line of cookware.

While this corporation was financially strong, with a large cash reserve, it had lost money for two successive years. Banking interests, after purchasing corporate control, installed a new president, board of directors, and top supporting staff.

New management informed each division that it would have to show a profit or be liquidated. The over-all structure and operation of each corporate division was examined by a management consultant, and a detailed report of recommendations was prepared.

The sand casting division was a modern, semi-automatic, mechanized foundry, as up to date as any in the U.S. Management and its internal control systems in this plant were notably efficient. The permanent mold foundry was operating in a much less efficient manner. Permanent molding methods and equipment were antiquated. For many years management had felt that their methods were superior to competition. They had been secretive regarding their operations to the extent that they were not fully aware of savings that could come from new machines, processes, and controls. The permanent molding division sold basic cookware castings to the cookware division at a price which reflected their inefficiencies.

The cookware division then fabricated their complete line of finished pots and pans. Labor efficiency was extremely low, and for some some years this division had faced a serious union-labor situation. Constant union-labor problems had led to walkouts and other serious disturbances. Their productive labor rates, when compared to com-

petitive rates, were completely out of line. In fact, poor labor efficiency and high permanent molding and manpower costs were prime
reasons for lack of profits in this division.

The initial attitude of management was to solve the problem of low
profits by increasing sales and improving management controls. In
this manner they intended to eliminate sufficient overhead to make a
unit profit on all sales, and in time, by building up sales, create a
substantial over-all gross and net profit.

Analysis by a management consultant, however, resulted in the following recommendations, which were successfully carried out:

1. Due to a declining sand casting market in the country and the fact
   that customers were beginning to obtain cheaper substitute products, it was recommended that the sand casting division be liquidated. Liquidating this division did a great deal towards further
   strengthening the financial situation.

2. Limited modernization and streamlining of operations of the
   permanent molding plant was carried out. This was coupled with a
   systematic reorganization of all production controls. A deadline
   was established for the plant to show a definite minimum profit.
   A maximum effort was to be expended in "preparation for logic."
   Acquisition of any new major business equipment was to be held
   in abeyance until management was convinced that profits in the
   division, and the division itself, were there to stay.

In the cookware division, sales expense represented over 50 per
cent of the cost of goods sold. Products were sold directly to the
consumer. The paper work controls covering the sales operation
were over complicated. Their inefficient tie-in with production and
inventory control had resulted in a top-heavy inventory.

Fortunately, styles in cookware do not change rapidly and the corporation had the cash to carry this burdensome inventory. It was
pointed out, however, that the carrying charges that might be saved
by reducing inventory could be a major step towards showing a profit
in the division.

An analysis of the manufacturing cost of cookware indicated that
the finished products could be purchased from outside vendors at less
than the division's own manufacturing costs. A program was developed to do this. All production was subcontracted and cookware facilities were reduced to only those needed for office, warehouse, and
repairs. Based upon the action above, the cost of goods sold was first
reduced by 17 per cent and then finally by 27 per cent. Moreover, this
action almost completely solved the labor problem in the closing and
subsequent liquidation of the plant.

A vendor control was incorporated into the inventory control system, and the over-all system was improved within the limits of manual operation. An analysis of applying a modernized computer controlled inventory system was evaluated. It was found that at the proper time a RAMAC controlled sales, scheduling, inventory, vendor, repair, accounting, and invoicing system could be advantageous. Necessary preliminary investigation and planning was carried out, including coordination with IBM regarding the required equipment, people, and programming. At this point the project was held in abeyance. It was decided that the proper time to apply the more modern mechanical system would be when net sales and net profit of the division had remained above a certain minimum for a stated period of months.

Within two years this division was sold to another, larger corporation that already had what they considered an adequate mechanized management controls system. Since the new owner had already completed "preparation for logic," this would permit an early integration into the business controls system.

Looking at the three divisional situations and the respective action taken in each case, we see how the proper use of "preparation for logic" as a prerequisite for improved management control avoided a great deal of misplaced effort and expense. In the sand casting division, good management controls were not enough to solve the problem. In the permanent mold plant the immediate cost of modernized mechanized controls made them too much of a risk at that time although they were desirable. In the cookware plant, although improved controls were needed, savings from these controls would be secondary to savings more promptly experienced from subcontracting. Moreover, subcontracting took no investment.

Case 5—Proper Application

As a participating member of the Navy's PERT (Program Evaluation and Review Technique) program, this writer has found that the PERT technique provides an effective management control tool.

PERT is the Special Project Office of the Navy's new method of using a computer system to keep track of an over-all technical effort. It is now being applied to the POLARIS Fleet Ballistic Missile effort.

A technique applied to a technical effort must, to be realistic and effective, require accurate schedule dates based upon accurate standard data and elapsed time estimates. There are few standards in the highly technical research and development missile effort, and accurate elapsed time estimates are difficult to obtain. To arrive at as accurate an estimate as possible, reporting personnel are required to make three time estimates: "optimistic," "pessimistic," and "most likely." All three estimates are evaluated statistically into a probable time.

The accuracy of these estimates is the foundation of the PERT system. Only by a "preparation for logic" within each and every company, project, department, and section involved with PERT can a company improve the reliability of time estimates.

Corporations in the PERT network are beginning to emphasize their efforts involving "preparation for logic" as a prerequisite to reporting efforts. This approach is beginning to show up in the improved quality and value of the system.

CONCLUSION

Is there anything basically new in this approach? Not really, for as long as one piece of paper exists in a business enterprise, it represents management controls.

Then what is new in this discussion? It is the degree of compliance and timing of compliance in applying management controls to achieve maximum effectiveness. It also includes the application of the "rule of exception" technique, with a computer and supporting mechanical equipment, backed up by a random access memory capable of storing large amounts of information.

While the idea is not new, its use and application with a computer is new and revolutionary within U.S. industry today.

Every case of well-prepared, updated new management controls, installed properly, is a boost to the current management revolution; while every poorly prepared case resulting in management dissatisfaction is a strike against it. Careful "preparation for logic" is a prerequisite for assurance of successfully installed management controls.

DISCUSSION   (Following Mr. Simon's presentation of his paper)

J. E. FLANAGAN: Over the years, we have accumulated considerable information about production control. We know quite a bit about forecasting techniques, and material explosion. We know about assembly floor scheduling, a little less about machine floor scheduling. We know about inventory control. But, to my knowledge, we have not yet evolved a theory of production that brings all of these things together and relates one to another. Do you feel that a theory of production is a necessary antecedent to on-line production control; and, do you think we have evolved a theory of production?

C. K. SIMON: The answer to your first question is, "yes, there must be a theory." If we must build a new theory for each new corporation, we will not accomplish our objective. Therefore, we must depend upon standards or standardization. The answer to the second question is that a theory of production exists. The parts list itself is the foundation and start of the production control theory. The parts list describes the total product and shows what it is made from. It then shows what each successive product level is made from. Therefore, each phase or area in control of production must be geared to the parts list as a core of the theory. This is the core information that we visualize must be in the computer. Everything relates back to the parts list and comes out of the parts list numerically.

J. E. FLANAGAN: Do you feel that our lack of knowledge of how various forecasting techniques affect parts inventory would be an obstacle in using on-line production control?

C. K. SIMON: It is an obstacle. All such interference factors have an effect upon on-line production controls. As an example, an application of forecasting failed when developed along with an existing production control system. While the production control was successful, it was probably less effective because of the failure of the forecasting technique. In this case, there might have been one hundred extra parts in inventory because there wasn't a good forecasting technique; however, the production control system kept the one hundred excess parts from growing to the one thousand excess parts which had been previously carried in inventory. With the new system, unpredictable sales fluctuation peaks could be met with a maximum of one hundred extra parts.

NEW APPROACHES—
FUTURE POSSIBILITIES
IN MANAGEMENT CONTROL
AND INFORMATION SYSTEMS

SECTION **V**

Exploring the military analogy—real-time management control

CHAPTER **A** by DONALD G. MALCOLM

Many writers have described the era of "information technology" our society is now entering as one wherein the capability to formulate decision criteria precisely and to process information electronically will create markedly new patterns in management. Prognostications include a trend toward recentralization of many management functions, toward semi-automated management, and toward an organizational philosophy formed around the precise information and communication needs of the activity.

This chapter explores how far we have come in learning to "design" optimum management controls, and presents the thesis that the prototypes of integrated and automated management functions are perhaps first being experienced in the current development of such real-time military control systems as SAGE and SACCS. A study of approaches and solutions to the design problems of these military systems offers some valuable parallels to the design problems in business management controls. In the following pages, some of the problems that faced the designers of the SAGE system will be examined, along with some of the solutions now embodied in the system. Finally, a plan to bring experience in military control systems to bear on research at SDC in business management control systems will be discussed.

However, before turning to this task, it is necessary to establish some points of reference in regard to current uses of electronic computers in the management domain.

USES OF ELECTRONIC COMPUTERS

In the rush to apply computers to the automation of existing information systems, the task of redesigning a given system so as to be consistent with an integrated total company information-communication need is generally not undertaken. Rather, an application is made in one component of the organization with little attention given to the total company system beyond a compatibility check. While this approach may be justified on grounds that improvements of this size and scope must start modestly and build gradually and surely, there is a growing recognition of some of the suboptimal results that can occur. Thus, electronic computers are not being used in ways that tap even one-tenth of their ultimate potential in the management process—particularly in industry. The situation will become a matter of greater concern to the users of computers as the nature of this potential and the means of achieving it become better recognized. In short, the situation will appear to get worse before effective long-range programs are designed and under way.

An examination of the four major uses of computers in the management process will help to elaborate on the above statement. The major uses of computers are:

- As a data-processing tool in the automation of the information, in communication, and in reporting and control systems.

- As a design tool in problem solving in the research and design of management control systems, in policy determination, and in planning studies.

- As a training tool in presenting training exercises.

- As a controlling device in decision making—an ''on-line'' controlling device.

For the purpose of this discussion, a management control system is defined as a set of policies, procedures, and information processing which is designed to give direction to activities by clearly establishing goals, by measuring progress toward these goals, and by indicating or initiating corrective action. Over the years, management has developed several approaches for providing control. Typical methods have included organization, planning, scheduling, inventory, quality, cost, and manpower controls. It is significant to note that each of these is a component or function of the establishment and that the concept of integrated total system control still remains virtually unexploited.

A Data-Processing Tool

Since the first installation of a large-scale electronic computer strictly for business use in 1954, at General Electric in Louisville, there has been a mushroom-like growth in the application of computers to the routine automation of existing information, communication, personnel, and data reporting systems, such as payroll, inventory position and control, production release, and invoicing systems. Of the over 650 million dollars worth of computers installed by mid-1959 and the 600 million dollars worth of equipment on order, it has been estimated that up to 90 per cent of machine time will be used for applications in these areas.

It should be pointed out that most of the systems being automated are not evaluated for the purpose of determining whether or not they best perform the function for which they were initially designed. The majority of such computer installations are undertaken for the purpose of reducing time in report preparation or in an attempt to effect clerical savings.

A Design Tool

The computer is being used increasingly as the vehicle for research in the design of management control systems and for policy determination. Another important use is in operations research studies, where complex analyses can only be performed efficiently and in a timely manner on the computer. These studies can, therefore, be categorized into two broad approaches—complete analytical formulation of a complex problem, and computer simulations to solve problems experimentally.

Analytical formulations of problems using approaches such as linear programming have in many cases been built into the on-going control of operations. In a like manner, the simulation approach has been useful as indicated by the considerable number of projects undertaken in systems design and evaluation, systems research, and planning and training.[1] The use of analyses of this type will be necessary for on-line management controls to provide the predictive capabilities desired by management.

A Training Tool

There is a growing utilization of computers in the area of education and training. Simulation exercises are proving to be a most effective way of posing realistic, fast reacting system problems to business studies, managers, and executives. The "automated case history" approach provides the immediacy and realism needed to obtain real involvement and the motivation on the part of the trainee. It

is evident that system training in large, new systems will necessitate
appropriate computer simulation training exercises in order to assure effective introduction of these systems.

A Controlling Device

At present, only exploratory work is underway in using the computer directly in management decision making. In this category of usage the computer may be viewed as an "on-line" or "in-line"
controller—operating on the information received concerning sales,
production, changes in environment, etc. to make decisions on personnel requirements, schedules for production, inventory pricing, etc.
on an up-to-date basis. Such usage, to be effective, involves having
adequate decision-making criteria in a computer model of the company. The challenge facing the would-be designer of a truly integrated
on-line control system is:

• To utilize the computer and associated input-output equipment as
  an on-line device.

• To make the computer an effective instrument for experimenting
  with and evaluating the effectiveness of proposed changes in policies, procedures, and plans.

The only significant strides currently being made are in some of
the components and subfunctions of the business.

REAL-TIME CONTROL, REAL-TIME COMMUNICATION, AND REAL-TIME INFORMATION SYSTEMS

In using a computer as an integral on-line controlling device, the
"real-time control, communication, and information system" has
evolved as a system design concept. By this is meant that the information is transmitted instantaneously, without conversion, into a
centralized computer which processes it, compares it with predetermined decision criteria, and issues instructions to men and/or machines for corrective or purposeful action. This may be thought of as
"real-time control." Further, the computer by means of direct outputs informs affected parties of this information as it is developed.
This is "real-time communication." Lastly, suitable condensations
of the above information are prepared, transmitted, and displayed to
higher levels of management for broader system decisions. This is
"real-time management information."

The meaning of the word "real-time" lies in the fact that information is used as it develops and that elements in the system are

controlled by the processed information immediately, not after the
fact or by making periodic forecasts of the expected future state of
the system. The best-known examples of systems of this type are currently to be found in the military. It is in these applications that we
may find some guidance in the way of design approaches that may be
useful in evolving better on-line management control systems.

MILITARY OPERATING AND COMMAND CONTROL SYSTEMS

In recent years the application of electronic computers to military
operating and command control systems has proceeded at an increasing rate. In the Air Force these are referred to as electronic support
systems. As an indication of the extent of interest in such systems,
the Air Force is currently spending more than a billion dollars per
year on them. However, this expenditure includes equipment in addition to the computers. In many of these systems, the computer complex is the central nervous system which processes, integrates, and
analyzes the various information inputs, makes and communicates appropriate decisions, and develops the display information required by
the ultimate human decision makers. A few examples of such centralized, real-time, computer-controlled systems are:

- SACCS (Strategic Air Command Control System)—a system which
  is designed to keep the SAC Commander continuously posted on
  the up-to-the-minute status of every SAC bomber and missile.
  There are several echelons of management control to be tied together in this system, involving a network of computers for information and control purposes.

- SAGE (Semi-Automatic Ground Environment)—a continental air
  command and warning system. SAGE is a system designed to maintain a complete, up-to-date picture of the air and ground situation
  in the continental United States and other parts of North America,
  to control modern air defense weapons rapidly and accurately, and
  to present appropriately filtered pictures of the air and weapons
  situation to Air Force personnel who conduct the air battle.

Several similar control systems such as one for processing intelligence information and one for weather information are under development.

SAGE—A DESCRIPTION OF ITS FUNCTION[2]

From the preceding discussion it is evident that real-time control
systems differ significantly from current business and logistic man-

agement control systems. To better illustrate the nature and scope of
such real-time activity, a brief description of the SAGE system may
prove useful.

The Semi-Automatic Ground Environment (SAGE) system is a vast
interconnected network of air defense direction centers which receive
information from many sources, process the information rapidly on
AN/FSQ-7 Military Computers, display pertinent information to human decision makers, and generate battle orders to jet interceptors
and other weapons in the air defense system. SAGE centralizes the
air defense system for the handling of information and direction of
weapons.

The air defense system requires monitoring of all aircraft flights
in the United States and around its perimeter to determine whether
the aircraft are friendly or hostile. Since there are close to 50,000
scheduled flights in the United States every day (and many more that
are not scheduled), it is necessary that SAGE operate on the "exception principle." The approach is to keep track of flights until they
can be identified by several means, then reject further consideration.

Air Defense Requirements

What are the management-like system requirements for integrated
control of weapons defending a country from airborne attack? The
various weapons and input sources involved are operated by the three
military services; they are developed and improved by many different companies. As a result, control information requirements are
diverse and non-standardized. The general requirements for an air
defense control system may be stated approximately as follows:

- Provide positive recognition of an air attack.

- Provide up-to-the-minute status of defense capability.

- Be capable of issuing immediate defense instructions.

- Be operable immediately upon installation, at high efficiency.

- Operate on a continuous basis with high reliability.

- Be adaptable to a growing air defense capability.

A brief discussion of each of these points will bring out some of the
problems faced by the system designers and implementers.

Provide Positive Recognition of an Air Attack

In order to recognize an air attack and its changing character during a battle, the following system capabilities are required:

1. Disseminate decisions and orders without delay to those who will take the necessary action.

2. Direct, using rapid communication media, the various weapons to specific targets and control each to the degree required by the weapon design.

3. Display the defense-in-action on suitable consoles for management decision making.

4. Coordinate among all operating personnel, the various echelons, the military services, and civilian agencies involved.

5. Human factors must be taken into account in the entire operation.

Be Operable, as a Man-Machine System, at High Efficiency, Immediately

The system must function effectively the first time an attack occurs and under conditions of high turnover of diversely skilled personnel. A means for the following must be provided:

1. Continual training of personnel in individual and team skills.

2. Operate the system with simulated inputs to obtain experience in operation during an attack. A high degree of realism is necessary to properly exercise the system and bring it to a high level of preparedness.

Be Operable with High Reliability on a Continuous Basis

To operate continuously, a high order of reliability and maintainability is required. This involves a set of duplicate computers as well as duplicates of other equipment and alternate communication lines. This factor accounts for a large portion of the expense of the system. The following functions must be performed:

1. Surveillance of the airspace in which air flights of hostile intent may occur. Detection of all aircraft movement.

2. Monitoring of all flights which enter, or could enter, the airspace. This means most of the flights in the country.

3. Identification of all flights monitored by matching and correlating with flight plans or other identifying information. When necessary, initiate direct means of identification by Air Force aircraft.

4. Communicate and coordinate information on a country-wide basis, with emphasis on adjoining areas and the next-higher headquarters. This description of the air situation is necessary to determine whether an attack is present or immenent.

Provide Up-to-the-Minute Status of Defense Capability

To perform this function, the system must:

1. Keep all echelons informed as to the status of all the various weapons available.

2. Provide all echelons information on the immediate situation, both as to individual weapons and as to the air and battle situation. This information must be suitably filtered, summarized, and communicated for higher echelons.

3. Provide display and/or built-in decision-making means to permit rapid and accurate evaluation of alternatives in allocation, assignment, and commitment of weapons.

Issue Immediate and Appropriate Defense Instructions

In order to provide immediate response and to effect control, the system must:

Be Adaptable to Growing Air Defense Weapons Capability

In order for the system to grow and adapt to ever-changing weapons technology, the system must have the following attributes:

1. The computer program must be modified to integrate new weapons that are continually being added to the defense. This necessitates the use of a general purpose, internally programmed, large storage capacity computer.

2. Changes in existing weapons, their control apparatus, etc. must be handled without undue delay and rearrangement of the whole system.

3. As a corollary to this, new characterization of attack configurations must be able to be added to the system.

The SAGE System

How were the complex and diverse requirements for an integrated air defense control system met? As one might expect from his experience in the automation of a portion of a business enterprise, the techniques and procedures in use which were developed over a long period of experience were not scrapped, but rather consideration of their automation was used as a starting point in the design of the new system. In all, development of the system involved the cooperation of thousands of individuals and the combined efforts of a large number of scientific, business, and military organizations.

In order to meet the requirements listed above, provision had to be made for the automation or semi-automation of the following:

- Collection of information and data and elimination of noise therefrom.

- Sorting, correlating, and further processing of the information.

- Generation of displays to permit human monitoring, decision making, and intervention.

- Displays must include a presentation of the air situation and be kept current.

- Means for identifying individual aircraft in the air situation.

- Filtered and summarized displays to permit high echelons to make general decisions about the situation.

- Transmission of information and data to all points where it is needed.

- Means for deciding about the use of weapons and for directing them against the attack.

- Means for computing control information and transmitting it to the various weapons.

- Means for system training.

These many functions point up the size of the task and the need for a uniform description of the system design. SAGE was therefore designed as a network of interconnected direction centers as shown in Figure V-A-1. Here are shown twenty-six SAGE Sectors organized into seven SAGE Divisions. There is a direction center in each sector which receives information and data from many sources in its area—from radars about present positions of aircraft, from air traffic control centers about flight plans, from weapons bases about weapons status, etc. The direction center's data and information sources are shown in Figure V-A-2. At each division level there is a combat center which has essentially the same functions and equipment as the direction center.

At each direction center, the man-machine operation is conducted in four principal places. These are: the Manual Data Input Room, where information arriving by telephone or teletype is entered into the computer; an Air Surveillance Section, where the machine make-up of the air situation is monitored and assisted; an Identification Section, where the aircraft "tracks" shown in the air situation are identified by matching them with known flight plans and other known

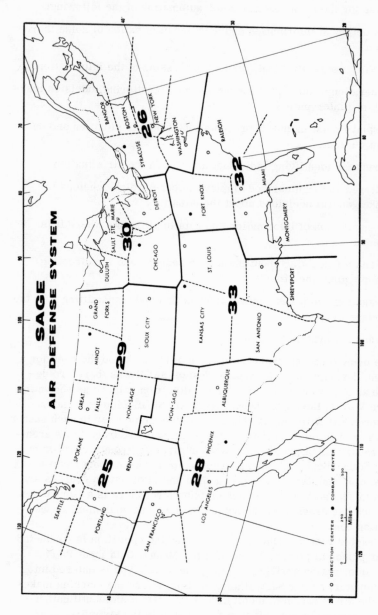

Figure V-A-1. Map Showing Air Defense Sectors.

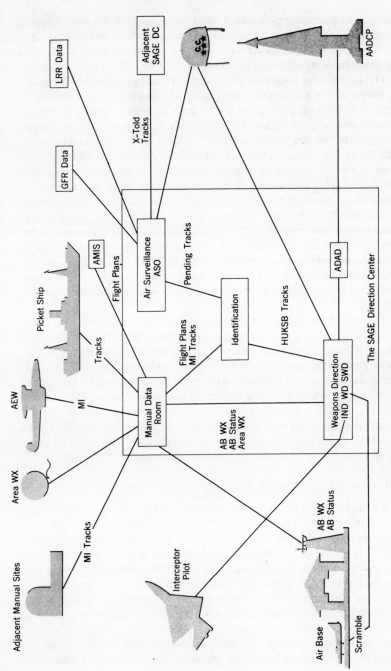

Figure V-A-2. SAGE Operations Inputs.

or requested information; and a Weapons Direction Section, where the
individual interceptions of hostile aircraft are directed and monitored.
In all, over one hundred display consoles and some sixty-five military
and civilian contractor personnel work in a SAGE Direction Center.

The network of long-range and gap-filling radars which formed
the basis of our air defense system before and during the development of SAGE are now connected to their direction center by means
of automated digital data links. Similar links connect adjacent direction centers for the "cross-telling" of pertinent radar and other
data. Real-time data on present aircraft positions are also relayed
from "manual" direction centers (areas where SAGE is not operational) and from extensions to the radar net on ships and aircraft
which range outward from our perimeter, by telephone and teletype.
This information is inserted into the computer by card punch entry
equipment in the manual data room. Other items of information, entered in a like manner, are civil and military flight plans, weather
information, and weapons status, although some of the last is by
automatic data link direct to the computer input system, as are the
radar and cross-tell data. Extensive voice communications are also
available.

The direction center transmits output data by an automatic digital
data link directly from the computer output system to certain weapons, to adjacent direction centers, to combat centers (higher headquarters), and to radar sites for requesting height information. Information is also fed automatically from the computer to teletype
circuits, to certain weapons systems, to adjacent manual direction
centers, to higher headquarters, etc. Associated with one of the
direction centers in each SAGE Division is a Combat Center, where
the next-higher echelon or organization operates with filtered and
summarized data from the direction centers under its command.

A Review of SAGE Design Features

The Direction Center is the smallest self-sufficient component in
the SAGE system. The Direction Center is a man-machine data-
processing and on-line control complex, at the heart of which is a
pair of large, high-speed, general-purpose digital computers generally referred to as the Q-7 Military Computer. Associated with the
computers are the necessary input and output systems and other
auxiliary equipment. Two computers are "duplex" to provide the
necessary reliability and maintainability. If one computer should fail,
the second can take over immediately. The magnitude of the SAGE
task may be best realized perhaps by the fact that the operating computer program, which has to be designed to include every function of

air defense in which the computer is involved, consists of approximately 100,000 individual instructions and that these programs, together with programs involved in system training and in the production of the programs themselves, involve on the order of a half-million instructions.

In Figure V-A-3 the system design of SAGE is depicted in block form. Here the manner in which the human and automated decision-making activities are made, the closed loop feedback of control and monitoring information, and the central role of the computer are illustrated. Features of the SAGE system design include:

On-Line Control Features

1. Automated and semi-automated real-time assemblage of information from many sources.

2. High-speed communication of assembled information to the computer through input systems that provide for some monitoring and noise elimination, for sorting, temporary storage, and buffering between real-time and computer processing cycles.

3. Use of the above-mentioned automatic transmittal features for communication with many and various types of agencies and equipments including weapons systems, individual weapons, other computers, higher headquarters, height finders (requests for inputs), etc.

Decision-Making Features

1. Use of an on-line, man-computer, sample-data system for control purposes.

2. Use of an extensive, multi-informational, dynamic display system to permit human monitoring, intervention, and decision making.

3. Use of on-line, low-level decision making by the computer.

4. Automatic display in real time of decision alternatives by the computer.

5. Man assistance of and intervention in machine information processing by real-time monitoring.

Display Features

1. Use of approximately 4000 data selection buttons, 130 action buttons, and 64 light guns for direct communication between the operators and the computer.

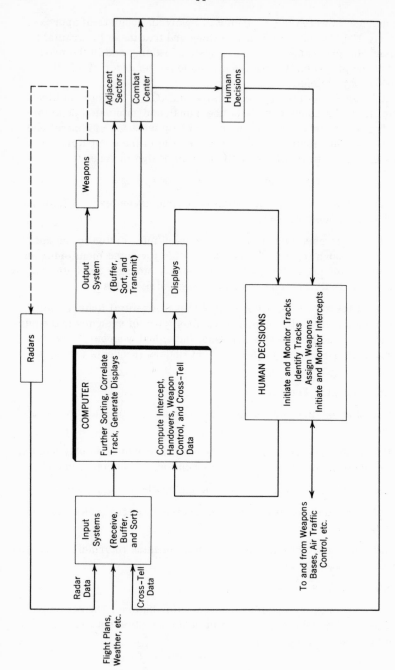

Figure V-A-3. Conceptual System Design of SAGE.

Provision for Simulation

1. Built-in simulation and recording equipment and programming for system training.

Error Correction Features

1. Use of duplicate equipments and self-diagnostic and self-error-detecting maintenance procedures to achieve very high reliability in operation.

Data-Processing Features

1. Use of a general-purpose information processing and computing device with large and readily available information storage capacity and with very-high-speed computing capability.

2. Automatic real-time transmittal of control and other operational information in digital form through a versatile output system that sorts information according to destination and acts as a buffer between computing cycles and transmitting equipment.

3. Use of a large integrated computer program of some 100,000 instructions which includes and ties together 100 subprograms and handles thousands of types and varieties of information, controls the sequence of operations of all subsystems, performs all information handling and computing tasks, and assists in evaluation of alternatives and in decision making.

A comparison of the SAGE computer itself with some of the modern scientific commercially available computers may be of interest. The SAGE computer was designed in the period 1951 to 1954. Since the computer is produced by the International Business Machines Company, who, together with Massachusetts Institute of Technology's Lincoln Laboratory, also created the design, it is most appropriate to make a few simple comparisons with the latest of IBM's computers. Table V-A-1 compares the SAGE computer (two of which are in each direction center) with the IBM 704, 709, 7090, and the Q-7A employed in the combat center.

APPLICATION OF SAGE EXPERIENCE TO THE DESIGN OF MANAGEMENT CONTROL SYSTEMS

The SAGE experiences can be appraised from several standpoints: the hardware, the air defense characteristics, and the computer programming are a few. The purpose here is to explore the experience from the point of view of the manager who must initiate effective

Table V-A-1. Comparison of Computer Characteristics

Characteristics	AN/FSQ-7 (SAGE Computer)	IBM 704	IBM 709	IBM 7090	AN/FSQ-7A (Improved SAGE)
Word Length (bits)	32	36	36	36	48
Min. Computation Cycle (μsecs.)	12	24	24	4.8	2.5
Max. Random Access Storage Capacity (bits)	2,228,224	1,179,648	1,179,648	1,179,648	3,932,160
Random Access Storage Time (μsecs.)	6	12	12	2.4	<2.5
Max. Drum Storage Capacity (bits)	4,765,592	294,912	294,912	None	13,369,344
Total Maximum Internal Storage (bits)	6,993,816	1,474,560	1,474,560	1,179,648	17,301,504
Max. Number of Tape Units	6	10	48	64	16
Card Readers or Entry Punches	4	1	3	8 each	1
Output Printers	1	1	3	8	1
Live Input-Output Features	Yes	Not included in design			Yes
Tubes (approx.)	58,000	5,000	10,000	(Transistorized)	(Transistorized)

programs, provide sufficient resources, and develop a proper organization for the system. The following may offer guidance to managers who desire to develop a real-time management control system.

Systems Analysis Approach

In reviewing the development of SAGE one is impressed, first, with the fact that several years were taken in its design. Further, as has been pointed out, in designing a system of this magnitude the primary focus was on determining precise system requirements. Thus, in many respects SAGE has evolved from answering the question "What must we have in the way of a system?" to asking "What can we do to improve or automate existing practices?" As we look over the current process of creating new management control systems in either the military or in industry, it becomes obvious that the latter approach is often the easiest to justify and has therefore been the traditional route.

The design process stemming from asking the former question, which in essence becomes "What is the best system?", is often called the systems analysis or systems engineering approach to the problem. Thus, one principle in creating a new system involves a careful look at the requirements of the system via the systems engineering approach. A list of steps involved in this approach follows:

Establish criteria for management information needs.

- Determine current information, decision, display, and report practices, using a graphical flow form.

Make preliminary system design.

- Develop a preliminary statement of system requirements; i.e., specify reporting frequencies, types and routings of reports, type of equipments, displays, etc.

- Determine what to automate or computer program and what to leave as currently performed.

Evaluate preliminary design.

- Determine hardware cost, training implications.

- Assess the nature of the improvement to be gained.

Develop a revised model of the proposed system.

- Test the design, using the systems analysis approach.

- Use an approach involving simulation or gaming to obtain the participation of the ultimate users.

Develop system specifications.

Install, debug, modify, extend the system.

Systems Training Approach

In providing a major resynthesis such as the SAGE system, it has been found necessary to train people in the new methodology. Training in SAGE involves elaborate computer simulations of a predicted attack environment. This requirement represents a new concept to the management world. Basically, the justification for elaborate training stems from the fact that there is no other way to adequately prepare people for the acts that they would have to perform under a real attack situation.

An important additional value in this approach is the proficiency obtained by operating the system as a whole, involving the communications and interrelations of many people and machines. The proficiency of individuals, then, is properly judged by measures in the total system context. One would not want, for example, to emphasize performance in one part of the system that would act to the detriment of the total system. To adequately demonstrate proper performance in such a broad system, a comprehensive means of training using simulated exercises has been provided. In short, one wants to train each person to act in an optimal way from the total system point of view. Thus, whether the environment is real or hypothetical (as in SAGE) is not the only factor in determining the need for simulation in training.

Thus, if a drastically new concept of management control is to be developed, it appears quite likely that the installation time, the acceptance, and therefore even the ultimate efficiency attainable by the system will be considerably enhanced by appropriately designed simulation exercises along with proper criteria for measuring individual performance in relation to total system performance.

Organizational Dynamics

In the design and implementation of SAGE, the ability to centralize many activities has been made possible. As the Air Force perceived the comprehensive changes in the Air Defense Command structure required to support these concepts, it organized the air defense function more centrally, using the control system as the guiding structure. Further, in developing the over-all SAGE system itself, it was found necessary to create a proper management organization to guide the process of design and implementation. The concept of a system manager, or ESSPO (Electronic Support Systems Project Office), has come into being with the mission to properly manage the joint efforts of system analysis, system design, computer manufacturer, computer programming, and system training activities.

While the following is a very broad generalization, it would appear that the quickest route to effective development of a truly integrated management control system involves proper points of view on the part of management in regard to the possible effects on organization; that is, the possibility of recentralization and elimination of certain functions must be within the system designer's scope. In addition, it appears necessary that the organization to perform the system analysis have proper organizational status itself and that top management plan for the necessary lead time for this activity. While quite evident, the thought should be emphasized that top management support and participation is vital in order to obtain results.

Advances in Management Techniques

On-Line Control—A Technical Achievement

The SAGE system has proven that an on-line, direct read-in-read-out, integrated computer operation is possible. This is an important technical achievement that can have significant implications in the management controls area. The feasibility of utilizing this feature can best be determined by a systems analysis bringing out the cost and effectiveness of the application.

Management-by-Exception[3]

The large data-processing capacity available in SAGE made possible a centralized operation with large masses of data carefully sorted by built-in criteria. The outputs presented to the decision maker are only the exceptions requiring attention. This feature could be extended in current management control systems on a centralized basis.

Interrogation, or Fast-Simulation, Possibilities

The ability for the human monitor to ask the computer certain questions like "What would happen if I issued this order?" has been also demonstrated on SAGE. This interrogation feature, utilizing "fast simulation," requires the building of analytic models for desired predictive purposes. Using appropriate models, this capability can be applied on an on-line basis in management control systems.

Precise Formulation of Objectives for Computer Programming

In utilizing computer based systems it has become quite evident that there is need for precise formulation of what is to be done by the

computer program and precise, as well as concise, computer programming languages. In this regard considerable activity is required: first, to develop precise statements of objectives, translate
them into appropriate analytic models of the problem and thence into
operational instructions, for the computer programming task; secondly, to recognize and participate in the development of appropriate
computer languages to facilitate the large labor involved in computer
programming; and thirdly, to develop and test adequate decision-
making criteria required in the formulation of those functions to be
automated. This field of computer programming development requires considerable augmenting in building total system management
controls.

To perform the computer programming task—perhaps the most
complex, difficult, and time-consuming task—has been the increasing
refinement and coverage expected of SAGE as new weapons are added.
The computer program must be comprehensive enough to handle a
wide variety of possible situations and must include precise rules
(or formulas) for handling these situations. Specifying these rules—
making certain they are the right ones, are efficient, etc.—is a task
referred to as formulation. Once the situation to be controlled is
recognized and the rules are determined, the task of designing the
program can be done.

The point of these remarks is to stress the need for continued research in the area of computer programming techniques in view of
the fact that it is a very rapidly changing technology. It appears
likely that any approach to systems design will involve a team of
many skilled people, including engineers, mathematicians, psychol-
ogists, statisticians, computer specialists, management, and system
specialists.

BUSINESS MANAGEMENT CONTROL SYSTEMS RESEARCH

The remarks of Leavitt and Whisler in their provocative article
"Management in the 1980's" are appropriate at this point.[4] Perhaps
the way of Management Control Evolution may be epitomized by
their observation concerning the growing "information technology":

"... the upshot of Taylorism (Scientific Management, Industrial
Engineering Approaches) seems to have been the separating of
the hourly worker from the rest of the organization, and the
acceptance by both management and the worker of the idea that
the worker need not plan and create. Whether it is psychologi-
cally or socially justifiable or not, his creativity and ingenuity

are left largely to be acted out off the job in his home or his community. One reason, then, that we can expect top acceptance of information technology (automatic decision making in effect) is its implicit promise to allow the top to control the middle just as Taylorism allowed the middle to control the bottom."

It has not been the purpose of this discussion to assert positively that the approach in military real-time control systems, which has been quite effective in the military application, is either necessary or practical cost-wise in the management control domain. While the concept appears quite promising, these are questions that can only be resolved by further study. The possibility of developing a comprehensive, integrated, total company on-line controlling concept is worth serious study. If the lead time can be reduced in arriving at the desiderata of truly designed information-communication systems, a significant contribution to the management field would be made.

To explore the nature of the research, a project in Business Management Control Systems Research has been established. This research project[5] is aimed at developing a generalized computer model of a business, one which will permit experimentation with certain policies, procedures, and organization. Hopefully, this research will lead to some answers to questions concerning cost and effectiveness of various management control system approaches. The results may some day permit us to truly design management control systems that are more nearly optimum from all points of view.

REFERENCES

1. D. G. Malcolm, "The Use of Simulation in Management Analysis—A Survey and Bibliography," Operations Research, Vol. 8, No. 2 (1960).
2. Acknowledgment is made to R. C. Hopkins for his assistance in preparation of this material. A more detailed discussion of many points contained herein is included in his paper Significance of SAGE to the Feasibility of Semi-Automated Management, SP-87, System Development Corporation, 1959.
3. Examples of this feature are found in certain military management controls. For example, the PERT system in the Navy Polaris program permits all of the planned activities in that program to be monitored centrally by the exception principle. See: D. G. Malcolm, "Application of a Technique for R and D Program Evaluation," Operations Research, Vol. 7, No. 5 (September-October, 1959).
4. H. J. Leavitt and T. L. Whisler, "Management in the 1980's," Harvard Business Review, November-December, 1958.
5. See Section VI, Chapter B.

DISCUSSION   (Following Mr. Malcolm's presentation of his paper)

M. G. HOLMEN: I would like to add a word about the SAGE battle staff; it consists of the director of operations, the director of material, and others who don't regularly operate the system. Don Malcolm has described the operating system which functions with a senior director and crew who can vary from 20 to 120 men depending on the work load. The battle staff has a normal administrative peacetime function; they probably devote 90 per cent of their time to seeing that materials are requisitioned, etc. As a result, they never become as familiar with the operation of the system as the people who work with it full time. They aren't as skilled in the day-to-day operation and interpretation of data.

In the design of the SAGE system, the battle staff function was designed to make the maximum use of the staff personnel without letting them interfere in the day-to-day operation. The battle staff has available to them all kinds of information pertaining to the system operation. They do not direct the computer or the machine system to do anything without going through the man part of the man-machine channel. This is a significant point for any industrial control system. It is to the credit of the designers of the SAGE system that they foresaw the need for the man part of the system.

M. O. KAPPLER: The SAGE training program has anticipated this requirement and has made provision for simulating battle conditions. In a simulated war situation there are periodic opportunities which cause people to think and to operate the way they would under wartime conditions—peacetime hats are shed and the commander does assume an active function.

A. J. ROWE: In this sense, business games are similar to SAGE exercises.

*I*mplications of computer programming research for management controls

CHAPTER *B* by ROBERT BOSAK

An ever-increasing amount of research and development work in data processing is being carried on at the System Development Corporation and at other companies involved in large-scale programming. Some of this work has direct implications for management control systems and warrants serious consideration.

The area in which the most effort is being expended is that of programming languages, that is, the language that a human being would use in communicating with a digital computer. A general-purpose computer is potentially capable of solving a wide variety of problems at what appears to be fantastic speeds when compared to human solution. The word "potential" is used because while the capability exists, the computer must have human aid in the form of a program in order to perform useful work.

THE AREA OF COMPUTER LANGUAGE

A program is a list of minutely detailed instructions for a computer which delineates every step the computer must take in solution of the problem, allowing for all possible variations and exceptions. What makes programming so difficult is the basic incompatibility of the human programmer and the subhuman machine. One cannot tell the computer "Turn to page 10 of a book." Instead one says:

- Pick up the book.

- Open it.

- Is this page 10?

- If it is, stop.

- If not, turn the page.

- Return to Step 3.

The human being is unaccustomed to thinking in this seemingly trivial detail. His mind jumps ahead, makes simplifying assumptions, classifies and generalizes. He tends to become bored with intricate and infinitesimal clerical details. People who think logically enough to solve problems and at the same time give great attention to clerical detail are somewhat rare. The reason for our problem is that human beings and computers do not speak the same language.

Computer language is the language of electronic pulses which are on or off, whereas the human being thinks in terms of concepts and generalizations. A great deal of progress has been made in solving this problem of matching the computer to the human. The solution has consisted of the development of languages which more closely resemble the language of the human being, and the development of automatic translators to translate from these languages to the language of the machine. These automatic translators are really other computer programs and are generally called compilers. Two of the characteristics that such artificial languages must have are:

- They must be complete; that is, any problem in the area for which the language was designed must be expressible in terms of the language.

- They must be non-ambiguous; that is, a statement made in the language must have only one interpretation.

All languages used by humans, even those in the more precise sciences, are incomplete and highly ambiguous. The language of mathematics, however, comes closest to the ideal. The initial attempts to devise problem oriented languages were limited to those problems that could be expressed in algebraic form. In fact the first successful compiler is called FORTRAN, which is a contraction of Formula Translator.

These efforts to develop an algebra-like language have culminated in the recent adoption of an international algebraic language developed by a group of representatives from American and European computing societies which met in 1958 in Zurich, Switzerland. There are several groups at work both in this country and abroad in programming the compilers necessary to translate from this language to a variety of machines.

The development of compilers for business and management problems has not advanced nearly as rapidly. Whereas for scientific and engineering computing, algebraic language could be used to express every problem, no such language exists in the business area. The few programming languages that have been developed for business data processing are a long way from a language which is natural to the business community. As the language of business becomes more precise, we will be able to provide programming languages that more nearly approach the one normally used.

THE AREA OF INFORMATION PROCESSING

The next area in which a considerable amount of research is being undertaken is the improvement and development of information processing techniques. The major effort in this area has been concerned with the problems of storage and retrieval of large masses of data. An ideal system would be one which would: first, receive any data, correlate it with information already stored, and store the data; and secondly, have the ability if asked any question, to pull out information relevant to the question, organize and analyze this information, and give an answer to the question. All of this should be done, of course, very rapidly.

The present state of the art is a long way from this ideal, and there is considerable doubt as to whether it is completely achievable. Present systems will only accept data in a fixed format (the number of types of data is severely restricted), do little or no correlation with other stored data, and can be asked only a very limited number of types of questions. Research and development in this area is proceeding on many fronts. Some of these are:

- The development of large-size, high-speed storage units.

- New concepts of storage organization. One example is the concept of associative memory. Under this concept a storage cell contains not only stored information but the locations of other data that are related to it in some way.

- New concepts of organization of data. An example of this is the work being carried on in the automatic abstracting and indexing of documents.

SELF-LEARNING AND SELF-ORGANIZING SYSTEMS

Research in the area of cognitive machines is done under a number of names, all more or less synonymous. Some of these names are Automata, Thinking Machines, Machine Learning and Self-Organizing Systems. People who have any knowledge of computers have in the past taken a rather dim view of references to giant brains or electronic brains or any other term which implies that computers think. In the last few years there have been results of several experimental studies which indicate that it may be possible to program a digital computer or construct a digital device to carry on functions which closely resemble the thought processes in the human mind. Present-day computers do exactly what they are instructed to do, if they are operating properly. If the computer is instructed to remember something, it will do so perfectly, and if instructed to forget, it will do so completely. When instructed to process information, it will do so exactly as instructed with no deviation whatsoever. To sum it up in a phrase, the action of a computer is completely predictable. A thinking machine must to some degree be unpredictable; in fact, the more unpredictable the better.

One interesting experiment that is being conducted is the perceptron under development at Cornell Aeronautical Laboratory and reported in the July-August, 1958, edition of Datamation. This represents the first attempt to construct a "brain model." A system consisting of a large number of small electronic units similar in function to the association cells in the brain respond to visual input signals. The association system acts primarily as a relay station, changing the connections between input and output units by strengthening the signals in some channels and weakening the signals in other channels. The system connections are largely random. The association system "remembers" preferred connections statistically or probabilistically.

Some experiments on a more modest scale have also been carried on in developing computer programs that learn to solve simple problems. In these experiments the computer is not told how to solve a problem but merely given a succession of problems and each time told whether it has achieved a successful solution or not.

IMPLICATIONS FOR MANAGEMENT CONTROL SYSTEMS

Progress in all of these areas of research have important implications for management control systems. In the area of progamming language, developments will make it possible for programs to be

written and modified more efficiently both from the standpoints of
man hours and elapsed time required. It will also make it possible for
less highly trained personnel to program the computer. The ultimate
is to remove the programmer entirely from the process of writing
operational programs. In effect the manager would write and modify
his own programs.

The second area discussed, that of improvement of information
processing techniques, clearly is important to management control
systems. A management control system is vitally dependent on the
ability of the system to rapidly digest information and the ability to
give the manager timely and accurate information on which to base
decisions. It might also be said that unless breakthroughs are made
in certain problem areas of information processing techniques, an
automated management control system of any significant size and
complexity will be impossible. The area of cognitive machines is
clearly blue sky and is regarded by many as something straight out
of science fiction—but atomic power and space travel were in the
same catagory twenty years ago. The obvious effect of significant
progress in this area would of course be to remove the human entirely
from the system.

DISCUSSION (Following Mr. Bosak's presentation of his paper)

H. O. DAVIDSON: I believe I heard a statement to the effect that it
appears possible to program a computer to work very much like the
human mind works. Should we not say "works like we think the human
mind works"?

R. BOSAK: The computer programs that I mentioned learn by being
told whether their solution to the problem was right or wrong and not
by being told how to solve it. They are not attempts to simulate the
action of the human brain.

A. R. BROWN: Perhaps, instead of taking our present idea of the human brain as a model, we might seek a way to teach computers to
learn without trying to have an a priori idea of that this way must be.

A. H. ROWE: We have talked about modeling business systems; however, we probably really don't know enough about modeling system
behavior. But as we model we shall learn more about the modeling
process.

M. O. KAPPLER: Although research in this area is complex, it is an
important attempt to advance the state of computer programming. In
the past, one of the most time-consuming activities in obtaining a

satisfactory computer program was the testing after it was written. The work that Will Karush is doing here at SDC on a mathematical analysis of computer program testing technique, to minimize the effort that goes into it and yet insure a good product, is very worthwhile. In the SAGE computer programs almost half of the total effort is spent on testing. A tremendous contribution would be made to the writing of computer programs if testing were more efficient.

J. FLANAGAN: At IBM we are working on an application program for generating computer simulations. Based on past experience, writing tailor-made simulations has been a tedious and time-consuming task. We investigated the feasibility of using the generative approach for a significant class of simulation studies. As a result of this investigation, we are convinced that a generative program can be written and will have utility.

R. L. SISSON: How far along is this effort?

J. FLANAGAN: It is far enough along that we can begin programming. The language and logic of the program are well defined.

Some human factors considerations

CHAPTER **C** by MILTON G. HOLMEN

USE OF SIMULATION IN TRAINING AND TESTING OF COMPLEX SYSTEMS

The use of simulation for development and training is not new. Military units have conducted war games since the days of Hannibal and Alexander. The junior varsity simulates each prospective opponent throughout the football season to develop and train the varsity in how to deal with the specific opponent to be faced the coming Saturday.

The "electronic look" in simulation is identical in purpose, but quite different in operation. In the days before electronic warfare and electronic management controls, the most complex simulation did not go beyond one group of men pretending to be another, or a piece of stovepipe being used to simulate a cannon. Men and machines as individuals and as large systems may now be simulated in an electronic system with such realism that the operators themselves are unable to tell whether or not their training mission is "live."

A simulated fighter plane may miss its intercept against a simulated bomber, leaving it free to drop its simulated bombs, which kill simulated people. From this simulated disaster, live people can learn how to prevent real mass destruction and the death of people as real as our own wives and children.

Simulation has its biggest payoff in the development and implementation of complex systems in which large computers are major components. In the implementation of a new computerized system, simu-

215

lation of the environment within which the system operates and simulation of some aspects of the operation itself are needed in order to
develop the standard operating procedures (SOP's) needed to make the
system work smoothly.

The SAGE System Training Program (SSTP) has been used as a
vehicle for the development and shakedown of the detailed SOP's for
the SAGE system of air defense. A recapitulation of the operational
problems identified through SSTP during its first year of operation
required forty pages of concisely worded, single-spaced typing.

It seems like reciting a truism to say that the development of
SOP's necessarily precedes training in their use. But this particular
"truism" is far from true. In a system as complex as SAGE, which
requires rapid and close interaction of men and complex machines,
the development and training often proceed together and are frequently the same process. The procedures appropriate for one team
may not work for another because of the different distributions of
talent on the two teams.

Standardization of all possible procedures is desirable so that all
crews may operate with identical methods, but this is usually difficult
to accomplish. Team members interacting with each other develop
subtle shorthand methods of communicating. These shorthand signals
are not always consciously used by all parties concerned, so they cannot readily be formalized for use by other crews.

As one part of a crew increases in skill, other parts of it must
change their methods of working in order to raise the proficiency
level of the whole system. A crew can reach maximum efficiency only
if kept relatively intact over a sufficient time period for all crew actions to be tried out until perfected. The crew in a complex system
should have enough members to guarantee that vacations, sick leave,
and other causes of absenteeism will not require frequent substitution
of outsiders. If replacing one man in a twenty-man crew requires a
week of training to reach previous operating standards, the replacement of six or seven will probably require no more than two weeks of
training. Replacements should be infrequent, even at the cost of making them larger when they do occur. The replacement of one or two
men in a simple system makes almost no perceptible difference, especially if the crew is large enough to operate without all members
physically present and working. In a more complex system, however,
or in one where every crew member must work efficiently every moment of the operation, it may be most effective to replace one-third
of the crew at a time, and to place that crew on training status in a
simulated environment until the newcomers are trained and absorbed.

DESIGNING MANAGEMENT CONTROL AND TRAINING CAPABILITY INTO THE SYSTEM

Some principles to be used in designing complex computerized systems will be suggested in this section. The first principle is that anything desired in the system must be designed into the system. A corollary statement is that only detailed plans are completed plans. Any element left to chance is a threat to the operation of the whole system.

Also very important, but often overlooked, is the necessity for carefully designing the operator's role in the system. Some systems are designed to eliminate to the greatest possible extent the need for men in the system. This is often a worthwhile goal but it should not lead to providing only monotonous jobs for the operators, jobs which produce and maintain a high state of tension in the operator, or any job requiring a combination of skills seldom found in one man.

Human engineering utilizes knowledge developed in behavioral sciences for the design of optimal man-machine systems. Human engineering approaches increase the probability that the men and machines are properly matched in the system. There seems to be a tendency on the part of not-so-human engineers to look upon each man in the system as something comparable to a mechanical or electronic component which will do what it can do. If the mechanical or electronic "black box" breaks down, the design engineer specifies a better one next time—larger, better insulated, harder alloys, or something of the sort. He doesn't often change the rest of the system to adapt to the one black box.

If the system being designed has a very difficult job for a man to do, the design engineer can specify a requirement for a better man—more pay, more motivation, more intelligence, etc. But better men aren't being designed. Those available do not always do what they can do. They become tired and inattentive, irritable or irresponsible, or they just walk off the job. The human engineer, or human factors scientist, can help insure that the people included in the system have jobs that can be performed by different people day after day without undue strain on their minds or bodies. This may require changing other components more subject to design change, but should result in a system which works smoothly.

It is not safe for system designers to assume that that which is visible will be seen, that which is seen will be correctly interpreted, that which is correctly interpreted will be understood, or that which is understood in small units will also be understood when it is immersed in a larger mass of data. As an example consider the altimeter: any child can read it but many skilled pilots have died because it was read incorrectly or interpreted incorrectly on a crowded instrument panel.

Several kinds of capacities must be designed into the system at the time its major components are designed. One of these is the capacity for training, usually involving simulation. It is also necessary to design the management controls on which successful operation of the system will depend.

It is perhaps surprising to include in this list the necessity for designing the capacity for change. A static system has a built-in immediate and guaranteed obsolescence. A system in which the capacity for change has not been designed either must soon be junked or must have its operations suspended while changes are made to it. A large, complex system is slow to build and must operate at a high rate of efficiency to justify its existence. The environment in which it operates, the precise task which it is to perform, and the means for performing it will change during the time the system itself is being built. Since an expensive system cannot tolerate inefficient operation, means for adapting must be built in.

The means for testing the system must also be designed along with its other elements. Perhaps the appropriate principle here is "System tests should be designed with the echoes of salesmen's promises." Both the acceptance tests and the routine "confidence checks" must be designed to discover whether the system is accomplishing its purpose, not merely whether its various parts work independently.

Every aspect of the system must be evaluated against the operational requirement for the whole system; otherwise, new features will be added to the system which do not contribute to its principal mission but which may actually compete with more mission-contributing aspects for the same funds, time, space, and manpower.

It is important to remember that every additional part and function of an automated system that increases reliability will generally decrease flexibility. In a non-automated system, the boss knows what his men are doing while he is watching them but he doesn't necessarily know what they are doing when he is not watching them. In a highly automated system changes are so difficult to make that management can have real assurance that the system operates all the time in the manner in which they see it operate a small fraction of the time. They can be sure of this sameness of operation day after day whether they or their workers want this sameness or not. Overautomation tends to reduce adaptability, so each automated feature must be examined to determine whether its cost in flexibility (as well as in money) justifies its inclusion.

In any management control system, members of management get information from regular reports or by asking for special items of

information. The information needed may be machine prepared, but it
is ordinarily checked or presented by people. Decisions by management may be announced orally or in writing, but are addressed only
to people. In an automated system, the means for implementation of
decisions by management should be available to management only
through people who regularly deal with inputs to and outputs from the
machines. Otherwise, their instructions may be presented in a format
or at a time which will interfere with correct operation of the system.
In other words, outputs from the automated portions of the system
may reach management directly (through computer displays or print-
outs) or indirectly (through machine operators). Inputs should follow
only the indirect channel; management should enter the system only
through the people in it.

Another principle is to schedule conservatively so that all parts
can be integrated into the system in the proper sequence, especially
when scheduling retrofits and changes. The man who is ripping out
the old equipment ordinarily can do his work in time, because it is the
first part of the job. The man who is replacing it with some other
equipment, however, has long lead times and many other activities
which precede the installation of the replacement equipment. It is not
merely an application of the facetious Gumperson's law that the man
whose function is installing something critical is more likely to be
behind schedule than the man who removes its predecessor.

Another rather obvious injunction is to depend wherever possible
on general-purpose modular equipment. This is one of the best means
of designing a system for change.

TRAINING IN DETAILED OPERATING PROCEDURES

At the time a computerized system becomes operational, it must
be turned over to someone for operation. The persons who are selected to operate any large system are accustomed to having a task
to do, some physical facilities with which to work, and a working force
of trained personnel. They look upon all of these elements of the system as relatively unchangeable in any short period of time.

They are also accustomed to working with a set of operational procedures over which they have considerable control, and which they can
change at least as fast as they can convince their co-workers of the
need for such changes. When they begin to operate a large computerized system, they find the usual buildings, personnel, and processing
equipment (including the computer), all of which they consider fairly
fixed parts of the system. They usually find a rough outline of the
operational procedures by which the system is to be run.

The first time they try to impose a procedural change upon the system, however, they are likely to run into a new phenomenon, that of the relatively inflexible computer program. They can't see the instruction in the program because it exists on a memory drum, in a plugboard, on a piece of magnetic tape, or in a core memory somewhere. Changing any one aspect of the system requires considerable study in order to avoid interfering with the effective operation of other aspects of the system. This is a problem to which managers of such systems may become accustomed, but it is important to warn them that the flexibility of a computer program is roughly comparable with the flexibility of their union contracts, and about equally subject to their unilateral control. Computer programs, like union contracts, are subject to small regular revision by agreement among the persons directly concerned. Larger changes involve more time, more people, and more negotiation through formal channels.

In operation of the SAGE air defense system, the operations in the computer are not visible, while those in the manual direction center can be seen and readily understood by participants and observers. Interactions by telephone or data link between radar sites and SAGE computers and among several computers are invisible. Many of these can be made visible retroactively by use of recording programs in the computers which can later be summarized and printed.

Research by Kepner and Tregoe has indicated that the invisible functions are learned much slower than those which are available to regular observation, particularly if that observation is by more than one person. Further, the invisible functions are often operated with considerable amounts of error, or considerably below their possible capacity without anyone in the system, even those directly concerned, realizing the degradation involved. Men developing procedures and training personnel must pay particular attention to making the invisible functions become visible at some time for system development, testing, and training. After they are operating close to their capacity, they may be permitted to become invisible again, but they must be tested periodically against the standards which they should meet.

As a system becomes more complex, the training and development requirements for the human operator change completely. In a complex system each individual may be responsible for the functioning of a quarter million to a million dollars worth of equipment. Since his cost is quite low in comparison to the value of the hardware he operates and the cost of his over-all operation, management can afford to pay him well and cater to his whims; i.e., the individual becomes a king within the complex system.

The individual operator probably knows the system with which he individually is concerned better than anyone else; therefore, his opinion about the system must be considered seriously and must generally be solicited in order for the system to operate smoothly and achieve reasonable efficiency.

In the SAGE System Training Program this is accomplished through the debriefings following each training mission. Every console operator who takes any action or provides information used in solving a problem must be consulted in order to determine the most appropriate method of carrying out the operation and in order to determine whether the prescribed methods are actually being used.

The precise determination of training requirements at the time a system is designed is probably impossible. However, the best possible estimate of the training requirements should be obtained, and facilities developed for meeting these requirements. When the training program in a complex system gets under way, it is necessarily concerned at first with minor details, which later make up the total system. As soon as the various components of the system manage to operate at a fairly simple level, however, it is necessary to shift the focus of training from molecular details to larger-scale problems. Thereafter the training should be almost entirely problem oriented.

An example of this kind of training can be drawn from the SAGE System Training Program. One of the most effective ways of using this program involves a multiple problem orientation for every training exercise. During operational missions, test missions, and other training exercises, the crew members record any aspects of the system operation they do not understand, cannot control to their satisfaction, or that do not meet the specifications of the system as they perceive them. The training staff then develops a critical incident in the next training exercise for each of these problems.

Before the training mission begins, the crew being trained is briefed with respect to the general nature of the critical incident to be presented, and is provided with a standard operating procedure for use when this incident is presented; the implications of the SOP for all crew members are then discussed. A typical training mission will contain four or five such critical incidents.

The training observation team pays particular attention to the actions of the crew when these incidents occur. At the end of the training exercise the incidents are discussed with the crew members responsible for dealing with these problems and with the crew members with whom they interact. The good and bad aspects of the proposed SOP are then discussed and changes are proposed where these seem desirable. An SOP for dealing with each of these critical incidents becomes standard for the direction center only after all crews have tried out the SOP and have found a way to make it work to their satisfaction.

HOW INFORMATION IS DISPLAYED TO AID IN DECISION MAKING

In the design of a computerized system it is important to distinguish between the two principal functions of the system or each major part of it. One function of such system is pure data processing, as in the automation of timekeeping and payroll procedures, or in a control system for finishing engine blocks or assembling refrigerators. The requirements of such a data-processing system are quite different from those which are human-decision oriented. The latter invariably involve some data-processing steps, but also have a component of complex data presentation to the decision makers. Further, they require means by which the decision makers may communicate with the computer and frequently with each other as well.

In dealing with the problem of how to display information which is to be used in decision making, one must consider three classes of information. The first of these is operations information—what is happening in the system with which I am working or over which I have control? The second has to do with the status of the facilities available for operating the system. The third consists of those items relating to the environment within which the system operates. Operations information ordinarily changes the most frequently of these three, that relating to the status of facilities is intermediate with respect to change, while that relating to the environment is ordinarily the most stable.

All information presented for decision making should contain some explicit or implicit time tag. Ordinarily, operations information is regularly updated by the computer every few seconds or minutes so no explicit time tag is needed. Information relating to the status of facilities and to the environment, on the other hand, is usually changed less frequently and often only when a change in the facilities or environment occurs. A time tag, therefore, should be attached to such information, indicating the latest time at which the accuracy of the information was checked.

There also is another continuum on which these classes of information may be distributed. Information relating to operations must ordinarily be presented with very little summarizing. This information must be displayed exactly as received, or with only first-order transformation. Ordinarily some summarizing relating to the status of facilities is possible, or attention signals may be attached to facilities ordinarily available which are for some reason not available at the moment. Information relating to the system environment is ordinarily summarized to the maximum possible extent.

Since a computer has no consciousness to be distracted, no subconscious to mislead it, and no unconscious to guide it, it doesn't care how the information with which it works is coded. A human being, however, is easier to confuse or mislead. Information presented to him for decision making should be presented in one of two forms in order to avoid delays and errors. Homologous coding is the first of these forms. Such coding is familiar to all of us in television weather broadcasts. Pictures of clouds are used to indicate cloudy weather. Pictures of rain indicate rainy weather. Dotted falling lines indicate snowy weather. Storm front lines, wind arrows, and stylized pictures of the sun can be understood without any translation on the part of the viewer. Counterparts for these can be found in any system operation.

The second possible type of coding, which is intended particularly to increase the speed of decision making, is the summarizing of information into decision categories. To use the weather example again, a SAGE display to be used by a weapons director in deciding what air base to use for landing an airplane can contain a weather display indicating the ceiling, visibility, wind velocity and direction, temperature, icing conditions, and other factors which could bear on his decision (if he had plenty of time to interpret them). Or, a presentation could be made which shows an X over a base at which the weather is not sufficiently good to land aircraft within the next fifteen minutes and a circle around those bases at which particularly good weather conditions prevail. Thus the machine is in the position of recommending a decision or presenting possibilities to be considered and other possibilities to be rejected. No translation is required in these cases.

Decision makers interacting with each other often need to know what information their colleagues used in making certain decisions. It is not enough, however, to know merely what information they could have used if they had wished, for the actual material displayed before them at the time of making a decision may be pertinent information to a supervisor, subordinate, or co-worker. Under such conditions a closed circuit television arrangement or the use of master and slave consoles may be desirable and may be available at far less cost than regular communication through the computer.

CONCLUSION

There has been no attempt to imply that each of the areas discussed is the exclusive province of persons trained in human factors science. But these are problems which have been identified, clarified, or solved by a human factors approach. At all stages in the design, development, and implementation of complex computerized systems, a team made up of men of many different skills is needed. It is not necessary to define in great detail how each professional group is to be used. It is not, in fact, even desirable. This is a new technological area being developed, and the present personnel and professional categories are not very meaningful.

If all appropriate skills are represented, and leadership of the team tries to give each man a chance to work on the problems that man finds most pressing, rapid development of the technology will go hand in hand with getting a good job done by people enjoying challenging work.

DISCUSSION   (Following Mr. Holmen's presentation of his paper)

C. K. SIMON: Have you found any difference between the training of uniformed personnel and civilian personnel?

M. G. HOLMEN: We have trained Aircraft Control and Warning crews consisting of both civilian and military personnel, and we have not noted differences in the rate at which these people learn. The training environment we create promotes original thinking, and military and civilian crews have about the same number of good ideas. We have, however, noted differences in motivation.

C. K. SIMON: How does the individual's resistance to guidance by the machine vary his own decision making?

M. G. HOLMEN: Again, there is no difference between civilian and military. But we have learned that the men who don't know about manual control of an interceptor learn to use the computer rapidly. They cannot fall back on manual methods to control aircraft because they don't know manual methods. On the other hand, men who know how to control manually tend to fall back on those methods and don't learn SAGE quickly.

A. O. MANN: Donald Malcolm indicated a continuing effort to apply more automation to the system and you have dwelt mainly on human factors. Is there any prospect of building libraries of computer simulation runs with the computer system? Thus, when major problems arise in the physical system operation, might we automate the comparison of actual inputs (parameters, variables, etc.) against the stored simulations to determine whether we have already experienced the problem by simulation and established optimal decisions accordingly? Might the computer thus automatically actuate decision output where reasonable match is made and, in the absence of match, turn the problem back to the person for manual decision? Is there any prospect you know of for thus automating more major decision-making functions?

M. G. HOLMEN: I don't know of any with that specific goal in mind. There are efforts to improve simulation through training and to use simulation in adapting system changes.

A. J. ROWE: I think what Alan Mann is suggesting is a set of rules or principles. This presumes there is an underlying pattern or some underlying philosophy which can be put in terms of quite precise rules, principles, or formulas.

A. O. MANN: What I am thinking of is the possibility of developing history in advance and storing it in a computer, the computer later picking the closest model to the new actuals and, thereby, the already determined best decision.

M. G. HOLMEN: In our SAGE training exercise, we use a tape recording system which indicates what has happened during the exercise. An appropriate data analysis is used which summarizes and prints the action. Thus it is possible within an hour (or, of course, as long as a year later) to find out what actually was done and to determine whether or not the action taken was the best. We have used these action records for operations analysis at SDC and in connection with running nation-wide system training exercises. So, we do have a simulation library which corresponds in some sense to the one you have in mind.

J. D. GALLAGHER: You touched on a point that many of us in the industry have had many difficulties with. You mentioned that as the manager moves from one place to another he tends to take along operating reports with which he is familiar. Can we, with some certain restraints, establish formal requirements for given jobs?

M. G. HOLMEN: I am sure you can by first considering the decisions the man has to make and then by providing the information he needs to make them.

R. L. SISSON: To what extent is your kind of training dependent on systems with computers?

M. G. HOLMEN: Our training methods are used with both manual and computer systems. We do use a computer for the production of our training materials. We recently produced a nation-wide training exercise which simulated an aerial attack on the whole world, although we concerned ourselves only with the radar sets in Continental United States and Canada. The IBM 704's we used in producing training materials for this exercise ran through some 31 billion calculations, indicating aircraft positions in three dimensions, in time, and covering 6 million square miles of material. This exercise probably involved

more computation than was required for all of the artillery fired in
World War II, and it was done in about 250 hours. We need the computer to provide the materials for really sophisticated simulation,
but it is not required as a part of the training.

The next step
in management controls

CHAPTER **D** by WILLIAM R. FAIR

"The Next Step in Management Controls" is not a prediction
of things to come, but an argument for what things should come. More
specifically, it is a prescription for a short-range goal for management control system designers.

CLIMATIC CONDITIONS FOR MANAGEMENT CONTROLS

There are normally "climatic conditions" outside immediate
control which limit not only what we can do but even what we need
think about. These conditions in the problem at hand are quite real
but considerably more subtle than in many other areas and hence de-
serving of specific attention. Prime among these "climatic conditions" is the fact that almost every management control system designer will find himself in the unhappy position of working within one
frame of reference but communicating with a large number of people
whose frames of reference are quite different. The mere existence
of this communication problem puts the burden on the would-be designer of having a very deep and complete knowledge of his subject.

Depth and completeness in this context mean not only a grasp at
the level of solving the technical problems to the satisfaction of other
technicians but having that extra insight which allows one to translate the essential ideas into language meaningful to non-technicians.
Without it, failure is virtually inevitable. The purse strings are often

227

under the control of non-technicians who must be sold continuously on
the value of the investment they are asked to make in any effort aimed
at change. In an area of this kind, executives are not prone to buy a
pig in a poke; therefore, ability to make the values meaningful to them
is mandatory, which has the corollary of requiring deep insight and a
high level of understanding. The influence of this insistent demand for
value demonstration then is to steer one into relatively more modest
goals at any particular time horizon than if one were designing a
physical system which could, in effect, be its own demonstration of
worthwhileness.

Another "climatic condition" that limits the extent of a desirable
goal is the fact that after any change from an existing control system, even if rudimentary, a considerable time must elapse before
the actual "payoff" emerges and even then the basis of evaluation is
necessarily vague. Both points tend to influence a manager to be con-
servative, almost independent of the apparent merit of a suggested
change or a proposed research program. This suggests that what he
is asked to approve be limited in its horizon time, meaning the time
till the evaluation is complete, to something consistent with the horizon time of other projects which are contestants for the same resources. It is probably impossible to state an exact horizon limit but
something of the order of two to three years appears appropriate. It
cannot be emphasized too greatly that any proposal for a new control
system will be regarded in a very basic way (though perhaps not ver-
balized) as simply one more investment opportunity. This means there
is inevitably a competitive atmosphere within which any proposal will
be evaluated, and success can be insured only by anticipating and
preparing to meet the competition.

To summarize the net effect of the "climatic conditions" as interpreted here, we will consider that they imply boundaries on our course
of action consistent with a goal which:

- Has a high probability of being achieved in the sense of solving the
  associated technical problems (a corollary of "deep and complete"
  knowledge).

- Can be made clear to a management group in terms of its own
  frame of reference.

- Permits an evaluation of its contribution in less than three years.

An examination of influences with less sweeping impact on what
can and should be done is shown later in a specific proposal. In the
section immediately following, an examination is made of the status
quo in business management control systems. Following this a set of
proposed changes is developed. The third section is devoted to the

process of actually making the changes. The fourth and final sections cover respectively a review of the implications of the proposal and a summary and defense of the position taken.

ASSESSMENT OF THE STATUS QUO

Any attempt to characterize the state of the art, or perhaps better the state of affairs, of a broad subject such as management control systems must necessarily be limited to the highlights or dominating aspects. The points to follow are far from exhaustive in coverage but are relevant to the central question at issue, namely, How should the status quo be altered?

The Breakthrough in Technology of Handling Information

The technical aspects of this point are now so well understood that there is no need for further elaboration here. The most important point for our purposes is that the cost of communicating, transcribing, and conducting logical operations on information has now been radically altered. This is perhaps best understood as a permissive influence in that we are now encouraged to think in terms which in the past would have been patently uneconomic to the point of being completely academic. The consequence of the extremely rapid rate in technological advance is, of course, that we find ourselves in a position of severe imbalance between our capacity to work with sophisticated concepts and the actual development and communication of the concepts themselves.

Acceptance of Conventional Accounting as a Model of the Business

To the vast majority of business people, accounting as practiced today provides the only model. In addition there are a number of people who consider the model as reality. The importance of this fact to those who would change management control systems cannot be overemphasized, simply because it makes the achievement of a real change immeasurably harder. Very few people in business have had the opportunity to reflect on the way in which the accounting model developed, particularly on how an instrument well adapted to detect fraud and measure tax liability has gradually been used as a general-purpose information source. Having become accustomed to information presented in this form, business people have adapted their concepts and patterns of thought and communication to it rather than adapting the information to the job or person. When one suggests the reverse process, as now seems not only logical but well within economic limits, he must expect a real reluctance to abandon a pattern of behavior that has a long history of working apparently quite well.   .

The Controllership Function in a Business Organization

The increasing importance of maintaining a communications system in organizations as they grow larger and more complex has quite naturally increased the stature of those responsible for its maintenance. In other words, the position of the information handler has increased vis-à-vis the production or sales manager and recognition has been made of this fact. It seems, however, that there are some very essential questions to be asked as to where the provision for information stops and the exercise of control begins. Or perhaps, to be more specific, Where should the exercise of control be located? Most non-controllers would answer that they felt the control function was theirs since the responsibility is theirs, yet we have a title which implies the contrary. The conclusion to be drawn is, of course, that the meaning of the term and, as a matter of fact, actual practice varies widely from company to company. Given this situation, it behooves the control system designer to understand the nature of these relationships in the company whose system he proposes to "improve." Positions are at stake and this fact cannot be ignored.

Types of Information Handled

To many, if not most, management control system designers the analogy of a servomechanism and the problem at hand is quite familiar. We can define a servomechanism as a device which measures the deviation of a varying quantity from a goal (which may vary with time) and uses the deviation information to instigate corrective action aimed at making the deviation zero. The essential point for our purpose is that there are two separate and distinct types of information brought to bear in the total operation. One type determines the goal, i.e., what we would like to achieve. The other type of information relates to the determination of actual achievement.

In a business system, as in any other, a goal is of necessity meaningful only in terms of the future, not the past. Actual achievement on the other hand is only meaningful with respect to the past. We can thus identify one set of information with planning and another with control. However, if one looks at the sales and financial reports circulated internally in many corporations, he will see that no attempt is made to make such a separation. A typical report will include data on "last month," which is wholly appropriate to control, and categories such as "year to date" or "this month last year," which in general are not. The latter two can be of considerable help in extrapolating experience to find a reasonable new goal, but they are of no help whatsoever in deciding whether there has been a deviation from the previously chosen goal.

It is probably better to say that there is an absence of formal or detail planning which negates the possibility of determining whether the goal was reached or not. Undoubtedly there are many variants to the situation described, some of which either match or come quite close to appropriate segregation of information for planning and control. The moral for the control system innovator is that he should not expect to find concepts in general use that may appear to be self-evident.

Risk Involved in Large Changes

To explain this facet of the status quo we need first to define the term "large changes." A "large change" is taken to mean a recombination of structural elements that cannot be reached along a well-defined path, i.e., a "quantum jump" from an existing situation. It is true in the design of management control systems as in the design of physical systems that certain problems arise which are combinatorial in nature. In these cases, there are alternatives whose behavior can not be predicted by extrapolation from experience, but rather require drastic regroupings, reassignments of duties, change of the location of certain activities, etc. In such cases an atmosphere of reluctance is almost certain to prevail. Experience with other attempts at quantum jumps may have shown a surprising difficulty in being carried out. Management therefore is inclined to an evolutionary pattern, if it is at all possible. On the other hand there is the potential dilemma that the same management which prefers an evolutionary pattern of development will want to see the kind of startling results that are unachievable except with drastic recombinations. There seems no answer other than to point out that, in this sphere as in most others, high gains come only with high risks.

The Problem of Transients

Many efforts have suffered from a lack of appreciation of the difficulties encountered in actually putting changes into effect. One possible explanation for this phenomenon is that there is too much effort on making the design of the new system have every last desirable characteristic possible. It is therefore quite easy to underestimate or even ignore the problems of the transient state which must exist between the time that the old system has been superceded and the time that the new one is operating smoothly and efficiently.

There is almost surely an interaction between this tendency and the attitude of management which emphasizes the desirability of the evolutionary approach. Perhaps we may look forward to the time when the experimental attitude is more prevalent in business generally, but for the moment at least, disturbances to equilibrium are not viewed with favor. This aspect of the situation reinforces the point mentioned earlier that the designer must have a very deep and clear understanding of his problem so as to make the transition smooth. If he is not in a position virtually to guarantee this, he should cut his goal down to the size which permits him to do so.

A PROPOSED COURSE OF ACTION

The course of action to be developed here relies heavily on work done by a number of people, among the most important of which is Jacob Marschak. His work on the role of information transfer in determining the effectiveness of teams lies close to the core of the model around which this proposal is formed. We cannot do justice here to all the thought and careful presentation (in somewhat formal mathematical terms) revealed by his writings, but can only acknowledge a debt and recount some ideas that he has either suggested or or stimulated.

The Team as a Model of a Business Organization

A team as conceived by Marschak is a crude model of a business organization in that by definition its members share a common goal. One can certainly point out many cases of conflicting goals among members of an organization, and to the extent that these are dominant, the team model is of little use. However, observation of existing businesses leads us to believe that either conflicting components of organization members' goals are not dominant in many cases or the natural dominance has been vitiated by some means outside our immediate purview, e.g., a wage incentive system. In any case it can be accepted that the mutuality of interest among the members of a business organization is sufficiently high to permit us to characterize it as a team without a fatal loss of realism. We will further characterize an individual member as having the capacities to:

- Observe his environment, i.e., acquire information about changes in his surroundings.

- Communicate information to other members of the organization.

- Make decisions according to a policy, i.e., receive information, operate on it according to a prescribed rule, and deduce a conclusion.

• Take action affecting some element of the environment—do something.

Confining attention to the simplest possible organization, i.e., a two-man team, we define one to be the superior and the other the subordinate. We are then in a position to address attention to the manner in which the team, as a team, can make decisions. Since, by definition, the superior is the originator of policy, one option is for him to delegate the job of reaching a certain kind of decision to the subordinate. But to do so he must transmit information to the subordinate, revealing the policy to be followed. The subordinate is then in a position to combine the policy with his own observed information to reach a decision. The other principal option available to the superior is to have the subordinate relay his observations to the superior, who then personally goes through the process of combining policy and observed information to reach a conclusion. In either case we encounter the phenomenon of information transfer. This leads readily to the concept of an information transfer system, meaning the mechanism for conveying the intelligence, with information flow being the movement of the intelligence itself.

This example also suggests the concept of delegation, meaning the passing of authority from the superior to the subordinate to conduct certain activities on behalf of the team, and responsibility, meaning the acceptance of an agreement by both parties that the subordinate will act in certain prescribed ways in the interest of the team. With the aid of these concepts we are finally in a position to raise (though not to answer immediately) the central question, namely, What do we mean by a management control system and what would we have it accomplish? It is clear even from the rudimentary example above that the price of assigning interacting tasks to more than one individual is the transfer of information. And if we are satisfied for our purposes to characterize an organizational structure as an assignment of the total necessary set of tasks to a given set of people, we can say that the required information flow is a function of the organization structure chosen. Further, reasoning that economy dictates fitting an information transfer system to a specific movement pattern of information, it follows that an economical information transfer system is dependent on the organization structure. There is no reason not to consider the converse, i.e., that of adapting the organization structure to an existing information transfer system, but it seems meaningless to attempt to discuss one without taking the other as given.

From the foregoing discussion it seems reasonable to assert that one of the desired aims of the whole complex of organization structure-information flow-information transfer system is to insure that all tasks necessary to achieve the organization goal are carried out and that each person receives the information necessary to the accomplishment of his own set of tasks (or perhaps it is better to say the conduct of his own activities). We are thus led to the postulate that an effective information system, which we define to be the combination of a specified pattern of intelligence movement and an information transfer system, will be so designed that each individual receives all the information pertinent to his responsibilities. We must then specify what is meant by an individual's responsibility in terms of how it affects the information he needs.

Characterizing the Responsibilities of an Individual

At this point we draw on another well-established model, that of input-output as described by many economists, in order to characterize the responsibility of an individual. Responsibility can thus be defined in terms of what is called an activity vector. This vector specifies the inputs he receives, e.g., money, services from other organization members, material, etc. In turn, he is expected to deliver certain outputs, e.g., manufactured product, transported product, services of a specified nature, etc. It should be noted that this kind of specification of responsibility leaves a wide latitude for the degree of authority delegation intended. To the extent that the components of the activity vector are few and highly aggregated, a large amount of authority is passed on as to the manner in which the inputs will be used to attain the outputs. As more and more detailed specification is made, less and less latitude is left to the discretion of the subordinate whose responsibility is being defined.

It can be seen that a simple listing of inputs and outputs that specify a job responsibility gives no clue by itself as to any functional relationships that may exist between input amounts and output amounts. We may often infer that the more output expected, the more input required, but given the complexity of most jobs, i.e., complexity in the sense of both multi-component inputs and multi-component outputs, it is reasonable to expect that functional relationships would emerge only after long study and perhaps experiment. At least, however, the data for a rudimentary model of a job (meaning an individual's responsibility) become available over time as actual performance is recorded in these terms. It may be hoped that this will help solve the operations analyst's perennial problem of lack of pertinent data.

The Interaction of Components

Turning to the question of how responsibility and the need for information interact, it is helpful to introduce an example. Normally, the responsibility of a production unit is to make some specified number of output units "as efficiently as possible." It is clear that, within the framework of this example, output from production is specified by the sales organization. However, to be effective, production clearly needs the information contained in the sales organization's goal. In the absence of this information, production has no recourse but to make its own forecast, which is necessarily a poorer vantage point than that of the sales group. The point of this example is that the whole set of outputs for a production unit are normally specified outside the domain of that unit and that the input-output model focuses attention on that characteristic. The converse is true in most sales activities in that the output vector (sales of various products) is unspecified by internal requirements but the amount of inputs to the sales activity, e.g., products to sell, many for advertising, etc., is very definitely limited by internal constraints.

The argument being presented can be summarized as:

- An effective management control system requires an information system which delivers to each person that intelligence necessary to carry out his assigned set of tasks.

- This implies that information (reports) be grouped according to individual responsibilities rather than by similarity of content (e.g., all sales information), by geographical association, or other.

- Individual responsibilities can be defined to a highly explicit degree in terms of an activity vector which specifies input quantities and dimensions and output quantities and dimensions.

- Given the activity vector for each job, the required flow of information becomes almost obvious, and one can then design the transfer system to meet the need.

Defining Planning and Control

Up to this point the nature of "control" has remained somewhat in the background to allow the introduction of other useful concepts. We now turn to the question of how planning and control can be defined in terms of these other entities. As indicated earlier, the concept of control is associated with events which have occurred in the past in the sense that one measures the deviation of actual performance from planned performance. But such a determination presupposes the existence of a formal plan, which, within the model being developed here, means a statement of the activity vectors for each job as they are planned over some future time period. Clearly a plan cannot be adapted once and for all but rather must be modified from time to time as new information becomes available. This suggests the adoption of a regular planning and control cycle consisting of the following sequence of events:

- Determination of a plan having activity levels in each job which cover the interval to some specific time horizon.

- Reporting of actual performance versus planned performance in terms of the same activity vectors, emphasizing deviations.

- At the beginning of a new planning cycle each manager should review the performance of his subordinates compared to plan, to determine reasons for deviations. The exercise of control then comes about in that any of several actions can be taken to close the gap between plan and performance. These might include changing a physical facility, educating the subordinate, arranging to give him additional information, replacing him, etc..

- Adopting a revised plan extending to a new time horizon which reflects the new information gathered during the interval since the last plan revision.

This process can be seen to be a continual one in which there is a regular repetition of the revise plan-observe-control-revise plan cycle. It seems impossible to generalize on what the time interval between plan revisions should be since this is dependent on the dynamics of the environment, but it does turn out to be useful to select the plan horizon so that it is nearly constant. For example, if the interval between plan revisions is a month, the horizon might be six months. This permits the planner to think of changes to the previously set goal.

Relating the Organizational Model to Accounting

At this point it is worthwhile to compare the model as it stands with conventional accounting to point up the difference. Accounting data have been used to record the time sequence of events, and are not often organized along responsibility lines. Job descriptions exist which define the individual's responsibility to a considerable degree of explicitness; hence the activity vector idea is really an extension of an existing entity. But at present, the principle measure of performance is a single dimensional measure of utility, namely profit; not only for the organization as a whole but for subunits. In the model

proposed here, there is no attempt to reduce measures of effectiveness of an individual's performance to a single dimension. Since this
is a departure not only from existing practice but also from conventional utility theory of classical economics, it should be given careful
consideration. According to utility theory an individual does (or can)
make decisions on what action to take on the basis of maximizing his
utility. Given the existence of a utility function or some operational
process for finding it, this is a very satisfying method for characterizing behavior. However, when one faces the problem of determining
the utility function of a specific job, the obstacles are prohibitive. At
present there seems to be no satisfactory way to determine such a
function.

The Model of Control in an Organization

As noted earlier, the basis for exercising control within the model
proposed here is the component by component comparison of goal and
performance. In other words attention is devoted to whether or not
the goal was reached in all of its many dimensions rather than directing attention to a single measure which supposedly subsumes the whole
set. Obviously, such a comparison tells nothing about whether the goal
was worthwhile in the context of the organization's over-all interest,
but it does have the virtue of revealing that the job was either accomplished as agreed or not. The question of relevance of the local goal
to the broader organization goal thus is made a part of the planning
process. At first glance this may appear to be nothing more than a
shift of emphasis or mere semantic difference, but there is a very
real value attached. It forces an understanding before the fact of what
the local goal is to be. The subordinate is thus protected from being
judged by criteria other than those he pursued. Making the goal explicit at an earlier point in time by no means eases the problem of
relating the local goal at one level to the one at the next level up in
the hierarchy, but it does place the whole problem into focus and
demonstrates where further work is needed.

There remains still another question, namely, the basis on which
an individual is supposed to pursue a multi-component goal. If he
can no longer maximize utility, what is he to do? The answer is that
he can maximize the probability of attaining at least the required
amount of each output while not exceeding the amount of each input
allocated to him in the statement of his activity vector goal. This is
the meaning of the phrase used earlier, "as efficiently as possible,"
and the implications of adopting this point of view are of great importance.

Considerations of a Multi-Component Goal

A virtue of the proposed system is that it ties together flows of non-dollar quantities like material, products, and services as well as dollar flows which are kept track of via double entry bookkeeping. In this sense the model can be regarded as the multi-dimensional extension of a single dimensional model. This development can be expected, providing there are drastically reduced costs of processing information. It should be noted, however, that what is being proposed is a genuine integration of dollar and non-dollar measures. Thus, rather than dollar measures, there would be "statistical reports." Once single measures of effectiveness are abandoned, the need for "allocating costs" (meaning dividing dollar costs incurred in a discrete unit into subunit "costs") would not be required. What the subunit actually receives is some good or service made possible by the dollar expenditure. The dollar expense should not be divided into any unit smaller than that which receives all of the benefit of the expenditure.

A similar problem is the practice of arriving at "transfer prices" to account for movement of a product between organizational subunits, e.g., production to sales. Unless there is real freedom for one unit "not to do business" with the other and actually go outside the company for the service performed, it seems clear that the "price" is an artificiality, with only questionable benefit. This division of company profit into pieces is a constant source of disagreement among executives, whose performance is liable to gross misassessment merely through the change of a single number whose basis of choice is at best hazy. If, on the other hand, multi-dimensional measures are accepted, the need for "transfer prices" and "subunit profits" disappears. The production chief's responsibility can be stated in terms of quantity of a given product made, labor cost, etc., and similarly for the sales executive, without the need for refereeing the question of who is to get how much "profit."

To make the proposal developed here truly operational, one requires a concrete situation within which to describe all of the facets. However, in the spirit of at least trying to remain operational we will attempt to summarize the essential features of what is held to be a reasonable short-time goal for a management control system designer working in a given company:

- To clarify the implications of the new computer and information-handling technology in the minds of non-technicians.

- To introduce the concept of multi-component measures and at least begin the process of educating members of the organization to a new pattern of thinking.

- To redesign the information flow so that it is disseminated in units (collections of data) directly applicable to the spheres of responsibility of specific jobs.

- To introduce at least some modern information-handling machinery, e.g., a computer, if it is not already in being.

- To bring into full use and appreciation the regular cyclic process of revise plan-observe-control-revise plan with an appropriately chosen report frequency and planning horizon. This specifically includes abandoning the annual budget idea, which has inherently a decreasing horizon time as the year goes on.

IMPLEMENTING THE CHANGE

Of all the dictums that might be brought forth under the subject of bringing about change, the most important is that it be evolutionary in appearance if not in fact. This statement is not based on an exhaustive study of the personal psychological implications of rapid change or a lack of confidence in ability to solve technical problems but rather on the observation that an organization of any size has a built-in inertia that militates against any rapid change. For example, even though an executive group might be completely convinced of the value of a change, it must (or at least does) insist on taking enough time to get the understanding and cooperation of the people affected. If one appeals only to a set of values which exclude the personal interests of the organization members, the action might well be different, but experience seems to indicate that as a matter of fact these values are not ignored. When a choice must be made between taking time for education and taking the rougher "sink or swim" attitude, the former seems to prevail, particularly if there is even a small lingering doubt about the consequences of the change. In other words there is a problem of re-education that cannot be avoided, and the path which takes this into account will lead to the destination faster than the one that attempts to circumvent it.

Without attempting to pursue the subject at any depth, it should also be noted that there are vested interests associated with any way of doing things. A surprising number of purely technical problems such as brewing beer, blending grease, and making paper are still carried on largely as arts rather than sciences. Part of this clinging to the artisan pattern is in accord with genuine technical problems which have not yet been solved to the point where the solutions are teachable, but part lies in the fact that the artisan feels that he is apt to suffer if his special monopoly of knowledge is broken.

Consequently any attempt to reduce the artistic content of the operation is apt to meet with opposition. The vested interests exist, though hopefully to a significantly lower degree, in present management controls. It may be somewhat unpalatable, but the fact that the group who may react this way has control of the existing information transfer system must be recognized. Their position of control means that change must be sought through the group, not in spite of it.

There appear to have been few major technological changes in the past which have not introduced some local differences as their aftermath, and there seems no reason to expect an exception in this case. But armed with an anticipation of the possibility of opposition, one hopefully can avoid most of it. In the long run it seems as if the information handler will continue to rise in his importance to an organization. Persons controlling existing communications should be encouraged to broaden their personal horizons, adopt new concepts as their own, and fill the expanded role. It is bound, however, to take time to create the attitude required, and the evolutionary pattern is the one which is most easily assimilable.

Where control has been very loose, a second dictum on implementing a change in the management control system is to couch the new scheme in terms of "presenting more information." The state of control in certain parts of industrial organizations is poor as seen from the standpoint of the technician who knows (or thinks he knows) how things can be by proper use of the newest techniques. In some cases there is complete reliance on the statement, "It's good because Joe says it's good." To introduce a tight control system "all at once" in this kind of situation is to invite the reaction that the person whose activities are now going to be watched more closely has somehow failed. Even if this is actually true (and in most cases it won't be), it is doubtful that there is anything to be gained by generating such a reaction. An innovation can be started by gathering additional information without reporting it back immediately. After the system is well established, the reports can be expanded and can gradually lead to the exercise of control in the manner described earlier.

If the executive (superior) is viewed as analogous to the actuator of a servomechanism, it is quite possible to create a closed system without actually closing the loop. That is, arrangements are made to supply the executive with all the necessary information to exert contorl; however, he can decide on the basis of interpersonal reactions when and how fast actually to start controlling.

Turning from general comments about procedures worth following in implementing a new management control system, we come to the specific steps required to reach the goal outlined earlier:

- Sell the underlying principles to the executive group who will operate as crucial parts of the new system. Particular emphasis should be placed on enlisting the support of the operator of the existing information transfer system.

- Select a unit of the company suitable for a pilot test which will serve both to "debug" technical difficulties and allow the management group to reach a position where they can make an informed evaluation with only moderate cost and risk.

- Make a preliminary determination of the responsibility vectors of all jobs above the level where direct personal supervision makes most written communication unnecessary, e.g., the foreman level.

- Start reporting on the basis of activity vectors, augmenting existing data collection where necessary. Regardless of the level of detail selected initially, at least some non-dollar measures should be included to start the education process. Starting of reporting in this fashion need not await the completion of all additional data gathering procedures to provide complete reports.

- Extend and improve activity vector descriptions based on the report recipient's reactions. Normally the initial activity vector categories will represent a staff person's idea of what is important, e.g., how aggregate the measures should be, etc. Eventually, however, the categories must represent the thinking of line personnel who are actually delegating the authority and responsibility defined by the activity vector.

- Introduce formal planning with a constant time horizon (more correctly, almost constant) as described earlier. The plan is, of course, expressed in precisely the same terms as the reports.

This above list is certainly an oversimplification of the actual process of implementing a new system. It may be worthwhile therefore to merely mention some of the omissions from the above list. In particular nothing has been said about:

- The method of making and approving formal plans.

- The method of exerting control.

- The technical design of the information transfer system, which has as major subsections the role of computers and the problem of event coding systems.

- The utilization of activity vectors in model building to reveal relationships among components of the vector.

- The impact of the proposal on present accounting and recording system capabilities.

Undoubtedly a discerning reader could make this list of omissions substantially longer, but if the point is accepted that no major stumbling blocks are foreseen, the case can be rested without additional comment.

IMPLICATIONS OF MULTI-COMPONENT ACTIVITY MEASURES

As mentioned earlier, the introduction of multi-dimensional activity measures in lieu of classical utility theory is held to be a crucial change. Without an adequate theoretical underpinning, the kind of understanding held to be essential would be missing. On this basis we will take up a more complete description of the behavior model on which many of the arguments rendered above must rest.

In the model, which is in large part due to Herbert Simon and stated more fully in his "Models of Man,"[1] it is assumed that, at any time, we can characterize the psychological state of a person in terms of a set of "aspiration levels" and a set of alternative courses of action known and available to him. (This is oversimplified but will serve for the purposes here.) The "aspiration levels" are stated in terms of boundaries such that on one side of a boundary satisfaction is attained—i.e., this goal component is reached—while on the other it is not. It is presumed further, as was introduced earlier, that a person seeks a course of action which gives him high assurance of reaching his goal in all its components. (A "maximizing" course of action was suggested earlier to avoid a long digression, but this is unnecessary.) Then, at any point in time, a course of action which is satisfying is either available or not. If it is available, it presumably is pursued. If not, however, a search process ensues which is designed to reveal a satisfactory alternative if one exists. One possibility is that a good alternative is found and again is presumably pursued. Another possibility is that after some period the search fails to reveal a satisfying alternative; the person then begins to revise his aspiration levels in the direction of making them more easily attainable. Further search ensues, and the process continues until the goal and at least one course of action are compatible. Still another result may take place in the form of neurotic behavior due to frustration. This happens in the business world but need not concern us here.

Since it is clear that both searching for and pursuing a chosen course of action take time, aspiration levels are necessarily constant over some interval of time. In our terminology, goals do not change as a continuous function of time but rather at discrete (though not necessarily regular) intervals. In the proposed model for management control the revise plan-observe-control-revise plan cycle has been regularized, but primarily for reason of economy in information transfer. In any case the important point is that there is a close analogy between the process described and Simon's model.

Both the accounting model and utility theory in economics have the virtue of allowing relatively simple manipulation, i.e., the simplicity of scalers versus vectors; and both seemingly have a strong intuitive appeal through the medium of presuming that a business "maximizes profit" or at least maximizes something. This so nearly fits the facts in some cases that there are people who think it will serve all purposes. However, this often leads to contradictory statements such as wanting "maximum sales at minimum cost."

Perhaps the situation in management controls will begin to change, with theory leading the way, but the enormity of the task cannot be overestimated. It is perhaps repetitious to point out the vast number of people who confuse a model with reality, but this fact means that there is the needed step of eliminating this confusion before a new and better-fitting model can be evolved and brought into general use.

An important problem worth discussing is the development of a rationale for an appropriate classification of events. The problem of designing systems of records seems to be done largely on an intuitive basis, and developing a rationale for this process alone would seem to be a non-simple task. If we accept the idea of a multi-dimensional goal, however, the problem becomes more difficult as well as more pressing. For example, we may very well want to identify an event on the basis of time, place, person responsible, dimension of the good or service transferred, name of the product, dollar cost, etc., or of any subset of these characteristics. For an operation of any size and complexity the characteristic space of classification is very large. Coding problems become complex and the cost of information transfer can become prohibitive. This problem has yet to be attacked at a level commensurate with its importance within the new technology.

SUMMARY AND CONCLUSIONS

At the risk of being overbrief, the argument presented herein can be stated in the form of four points, as follows:

- The concepts of Marchak's model on teams are very valuable to a management control system designer and they lend themselves to direct application.

- Simon's model of multi-dimensional utility is potentially revolutionary and should be pursued immediately in the sense of changing existing systems of reporting.

- The state of knowledge on the part of both technicians and those who will or won't support technicians is such that the progress rate will be maximized by attempting small steps in a clearly evolutionary manner.

- The power of those who control present information transfer systems is so great that change must be sought through them rather than by challenging them, even when existing ways are defended because of vested interest.

As a final defense of the position taken, the course of action proposed has the following desirable characteristics:

- It provides individuals information tailored to their individual needs.

- It enhances the position of those who must carry it out, hence should be well received.

- It has good odds of salability because it is neither too expensive to test nor too risky.

- It can be made understandable in the language and frame of reference of a businessman.

- Most important of all, it has the kind of structure that permits expansion to accommodate advances and new knowledge.

REFERENCES

1. Herbet A. Simon, <u>Models of Man: Social and Rational</u>, John Wiley and Sons, New York, 1957, p. 287.

A publicly regulated system of management control services

CHAPTER **E** by ALAN O. MANN

INTRODUCTION

During only the last two and a half decades there have been technological developments which have produced major and most significant contributions to the formulation of the concept which we are now
beginning to call the management control system. It was in the mid-
thirties that initial business applications of automatically switched
tele-typewriter networks began to appear. Electronic computers for
data processing, and the computational techniques of Operations Research appeared in the mid-forties; and in the early fifties, efforts
were begun toward coupling the communications and processors into
integrated management control system. Thus, it is really only within
the latter portion of the fifties that forward-looking leaders in management and science have begun seriously to attempt correlation of
electronic machines and human beings into a unified system of control, based on pyramiding demands in our social organizations for
correlation between our physical activities and our information concerning them.

While the needs have been felt over a much longer period of time,
and many partial efforts have been made to satisfy them by the development of the telephone, telegraph, and facsimile, by Taylor's
and Shannon's work, by primitive contributions in automation, by a
multitude of office machine developments—punched cards, calcula-
tors, bookkeeping machines, and the like—very little significant

work was done on a truly integrated basis. As a matter of fact, it wasn't until quite recently that there began to come into being, lucid and apparently valid definitions of most basic elements of the organizational problems within our accelerating and expanding economy.

For instance, it was in February, 1954, that the American Management Association and United States Steel came out with their coinage of the terms Integrated Data Processing and Common Language, which gave new emphasis to the concept of integration and impetus to the task of integration.

In two books issued in 1947 and 1950, Norbert Wiener, besides the presentation of his concept of Cybernetics, did much to clarify the system problem simply by defining certain terms that were taking on new meanings in the light of the changing state of the technology. Thus he clarified the word "information," defining it as "a name for the content of what's exchanged with the outer world as we adjust to it, and make our adjustment felt upon it. The process of receiving and of using information is the process of our adjusting to the outer environment, and of our living effectively under that environment. The needs and complexities of modern life make greater demands on this process of information than ever before.... To live effectively is to live with adequate information."[1]

And of control Wiener said, "Control...is nothing but the sending of messages which effectively change the behavior of the recipient[2].... Where a man's word goes, and where his power of perception goes, to that point his control and in a sense his physical existence is extended."[3]

Then, further, to round out basic definitions required but not hitherto provided, Wiener said of communications, "Society can only be understood through a study of the messages and the communications facilities which belong to it: and...in the future development of these messages and communications facilities, messages between man and machines, between machine and man, and between machine and machine are destined to play an ever-increasing role."[4]

Yet, to date, insufficient work has been done to obtain a clear indication of what a fully integrated system for all data processing in a large organization should be like. Even the few large and leading organizations that have been doing work in this area are feeling their way toward integration and seem unable or unwilling to spend the needed effort and money required for constructing an over-all system. Instead, they are making piecemeal approaches unilaterally in separate parts of the organization, either with or without some sort of overall coordinative guidance. In the majority of cases where some coordinative leadership does exist, it is provided not by objective, impartial, and broadly experienced personnel but by specialized

representation whose background, training, experience, tempera-
ment, and skills all point project thinking and action in the direction
of only one division of the organization with all its past concepts and
techniques. Past concepts and techniques have of necessity, due to
hardware limitations, been based on the breaking down of operations,
functions, responsibility, and authority into echelons of bits and
pieces, and of time itself into periodic bits and pieces. Hence, the
work on applications of new equipments is broken down into corresponding echelons of bits and pieces, providing a less than suitable
climate in which to develop an over-all integration.

The significant feature in this situation is that, while the people
are still not clearly working on an integrated basis, the characteristics of the electronic techniques now available are inherently, completely, and unquestionably integrative in nature. The multiplicities
and speeds of their functioning are so great that they can perform
great numbers of tasks on great numbers of inputs involving great
numbers of varying factors to provide great numbers of outputs with
so near a simultaneity that, from the human standpoint of evaluation,
we can call them simultaneous. The former segregations of information by barriers of time and space have been removed, the prime
requisite for integration. We therefore might conclude that current
unilateral and non-integrated approaches to the data-processing
problem of organization are circumstantially interim and temporary,
not truly representative of the future. As knowledge, experience, and
understanding increase, both of the enormous applicative problems
and the technological abilities of the equipments, the nature of the
major electronic equipments themselves will certainly contribute to
forcing general business applications into the integrated system concept of management control. It would seem inevitable that the hardware will consist of three major elements: communications network,
automatic switching and control centers, and electronic data processors, all working together in unity for the extension of "man's word
and power of perception." Trends during the last two and a half decades would certainly indicate this to be the case.

Within this outlook there are at least four features of major moment that should have important influence on the nature of future system development:

- The size of investment required for any individual system.

- The potential overlapping and duplication of system elements as
  more and more individual systems come into being.

- The inherent characteristic in the electronic art, of diminishing
  unit processing costs with increases in system speed, capacity,
  and power.

- Increasing problems of <u>utilization</u> within each individual system.

We know that in our present non-integrated stage there are only a relatively limited number of organizations in the economy that believe they can afford the large-scale equipments to obtain minimum unit processing costs and, at the same time, the full utilization that makes the minimized cost realizable. As equipment power, and hence, gross costs, continue to rise, even the present limited number of potential users would tend to dwindle. The remaining growing body of organizations would increasingly be forced to turn to, or remain with, smaller and less integrative equipments which operate at greater than minimal unit costs—largely because of the problem of utilization.

Of course there are still a number of open questions yet to be resolved. How many smaller organizations are there which, even now with non-integrated applications, could actually afford the present large-scale equipment but do not know it? How much further down in organization size can we go for actual economic justification of large-scale systems? How much larger would the body of potential users become if we were actually to bring into being, fully integrated control systems? What will be the impact of present upward growth trends in corporate size and corporate numbers? What will be the impact of known tendencies for equipment costs to go down as production volumes go up—will there be sufficient and significant enough total growth in the user body to increase appreciably the equipment production volumes?

Certainly answers to these questions are in the process of gradually evolving, while not perhaps in crystal clarity, yet nevertheless in forms that begin to take on some ordered shape and meaning. It is here that we pick up the main theme of this paper as we briefly analyze past and present indicators in an attempt to locate the elements, and synthesize the framework, of such ordered shape and meaning.

For there does seem to be a growing uniformity of pattern developing from among the myriad efforts of the users and manufacturers as they work their way through a web of conceptual haze, unforseen obstacles, and conflicting purposes. The pattern is one primarily of seeking means for reconciling minimum unit processing costs of large-scale equipment with less than favorable utilization—through expanded applications, efforts of integration, cooperative endeavors, and shared facilities. The pattern becomes increasingly similar to that which has applied historically in the development of the electric power, telephone, telegraph, and similar industries. The pattern appears to have the characteristics of a public business in the sale of services, pointing in the direction of the <u>public utility</u> concept.

THE PUBLIC UTILITY

But, we might ask, what is the public utility concept? In general there seem to be several basic contributory factors which characterize a business as public utility rather than unregulated free enterprise, as follows:

- It stresses maximum use and minimum profits, consistent with the continuous and efficient conduct of the business.

- "The public's concern about... [the] business...[is] so pervasive and varied as to require constant detailed supervision and a very high degree of regulation...although it is privately owned.... The business is 'affected with a public interest.' "[5]

- The business is expected to serve all comers, at a reasonable rate and without discrimination. (Therefore, its rates, services, finances, accounting, and other activities usually regarded as private are carefully regulated.)

- The process by which it has acquired public utility status is the political process by which a felt public need is satisfied through government action.

- There is a centralized supply of services.

But besides these inherent characteristics and the public attitude, there are also involved in the development of a public utility, policy contributions made by the management of the business. Where management begins to establish the following pattern of policies, they are contributing another element which can lead to the development of a publicly regulated operation:

- Stress on the need for creating customer satisfaction.

- Initiation of radical innovations in business policy.

- Constant indoctrination of all employees in dedication to service.

- Public relations stress on service.

- Emphasis on research and technological leadership.

- Establishment of financial policy which assumes that service has to be given wherever demanded and that management's job is to find needed capital and earn a return on it.

In 1922, Chief Justice Taft divided into three classes the businesses clothed with a public interest justifying some public regulation:

- "Those which are carried on under the authority of a public grant

of privileges which either expressly or impliedly imposes the
affirmative duty of rendering a public service demanded by any
member of the public. Such are the railroads, other common carriers, and public utilities.

- "Certain occupations, regarded as exceptional, [with] the public
  interest attaching.... Such are those of the keepers of inns, cabs
  and grist mills.

- "Businesses which, though not public at their inception, may be
  fairly said to have risen to be such and have become subject in
  consequence to some government regulation. They have come to
  hold such a peculiar relation to the public that this is super−
  imposed upon them.... The owner, by devoting his business to a
  public use, in effect, grants the public an interest in that use, and
  subjects himself to public regulation to the extent of that interest,
  although the property continues to belong to its private owner, and
  to be entitled to protection accordingly."[6]

The third class above is, of course, the only one that might possibly apply in the case of the computer business, but Chief Justice
Taft's statement still does not explain the nature of the public utility.
However, it is now generally recognized that the Supreme Court applies certain tests in identifying public utilities—five tests which all
have monopoly as a common factor, and another which applies to certain competitive businesses which are not monopolistic. The six categories of test are as follows:

- "Utilities that enjoy a natural monopoly—that is, where there are
  natural limitations on the source of supply essential to that business, thus preventing effective competition (water, natural gas,
  etc.).

- "Geographical location of an activity may give to that activity the
  character of a natural monopoly (grain elevator 'taking toll' from
  all who pass, union stations, terminal facilities, stockyards).

- "The character of the service may give to an enterprise monopoly
  advantage.... If the product is such that it can have only a local
  distribution, the possibility of outside competition is remote and a
  factor of monopoly is present.... Oil, coal, lamps, and candles may
  be shipped in the channels of trade to compete in every market,
  whereas gas and electricity must come from one or a very few
  local companies (Even ice plants in the South.).

- "The immediacy of the patron's needs. Where the patron's need
  is immediate, the enterprise enjoys what amounts to monopoly

advantage. This test, together with their other monopolistic characteristics, was powerfully persuasive in fixing the public character of the telegraph and the telephone. When the patron's needs
are urgent, he is compelled to deal with the concern close at hand.
There is no real alternative to furnish him protection.

● "The cost of the plant and the large scale upon which the business
   is conducted, as well as other economic factors either singly or
   in combination, may destroy effective competition and create
   monopoly advantage. The business may have grown to such proportions that such vast sums would be involved in constructing a
   competing plant that no one would care to take the risk for fear of
   failure. If these facts exist, we have a clear case of actual monopoly.

● "There are other situations, however, where competition exists in
   a business essential to the public, but where competition does not
   prove to work to the public advantage. In other words, the interest
   of the people dictates that competitive conditions should be supplanted by monopolistic. The bus industry is a case in point....''[7]

THE COMPUTER SYSTEM AS A PUBLIC UTILITY—PRO

While it may still be somewhat early to decide the exact nature of
the computer system business, each of the last three tests above may
apply to some extent within the near future. There seems but little
disagreement that electronic data processing is becoming more and
more of an economic necessity, that there are increasing volumes of
clerical, computational, and decision-making tasks that cannot be
done either actually or practicably by any techniques other than electronic. There is developing an increased urgency of the patron's needs
that may compel him increasingly to deal with the concern close at
hand. The local computer service bureau that is equipped with a small
computer may not be able to handle his need for a problem solution
at all or with as satisfactory speed or with as economic costs as a
distant bureau that is equipped with a large computer. But he may
find it necessary either to deal with the local bureau or abandon his
hope of solution.

The computer companies are fully aware of this situation and are
each endeavoring to provide more flexible and more powerful facilities in strategic locations for serving the patron's needs. However,
the cost of the plant and the problem of maintaining satisfactory
utilization gives major advantage to the first company that places a
truly modern, high-powered facility in a given metropolitan area.
The cost of the plant is such that this company immediately acquires

a definite advantage, other companies not caring to take the risk of installing a competing facility that may have difficulty developing enough business to be economic. Even though the first system in such an area may not be the best in existence, local users may be forced to deal with this system close at hand.

Furthermore, once a customer has paid for the programming of his particular problems on a given computer he is apt to be forced by economic necessity to continue his processing on that machine even though more efficient and less costly facilities may become available to him. For programming costs are high and programs are not to any practicable degree interchangeable between different makes and models of computer systems. Where translation techniques have been developed for the use of one computer's programs on another's, it has been done generally at a considerable sacrifice in the second machine's efficiency of operation. In addition, the supplier of a computer system necessarily becomes directly and very closely as-sociated with the user in many areas of services—system analysis, systems and procedures design, programming, operating, and main-tenance. In the process, the manufacturer becomes thoroughly familiar with the inner workings and intimate details of the user's business. If the manufacturer's services are of even reasonably re-spectable quality, the user develops a growing conviction that he is dependent upon that supplier and that one alone. He becomes in-creasingly unwilling to gamble that the manufacturer of a better set of equipment might offer an even better quality of service. He feels that the time and cost required for teaching and working with a new supplier may not be worth the gamble.

Thus it would appear not only that the first computer to enter a community acquires a distinct advantage but that every single cus-tomer that uses its services becomes almost inextricably wedded to it alone and adds in this way to its already established advantage.

Under such conditions there is considerable room for question as to whether competition would be good for the users' interests or whether competitive conditions should be supplanted by monopolistic. As a matter of fact there is a real question as to whether conditions may be so inherently monopolistic that there can be no room for continued development of free competition in the future.

There is another inherent characteristic of a public utility that is possessed by the computer business, namely an extremely low rate of capital turnover. In a public utility, capital usually has a turnover once in every four or five years. On the other hand, capital may turn over once in two or three years in a steel plant, annually in auto-mobile manufacture, or as many as eight times per year in a chain store business. The computer system appears to more nearly resemble the public utility than other types of enterprise, in this regard.

In the public utility there is not only a very large fixed capital outlay, with large fixed investment and maintenance costs as well, but also a major portion of operating costs are fixed. Thus the costs per unit of output tend to become substantially lower as usage approaches system capacity. This seems correspondingly true of the computer business.

Also, in the utility, unit costs of output decrease as the size of plant increases, despite the fact that distribution costs tend to increase meanwhile. While little known work has been done on the communications or distribution costs of computer system outputs to varying numbers of recipients, there is assuredly a strong tendency within the main system itself for output costs to decrease as the size and power of the system increases. Thus, just as a doubling of the capacity of a power plant involves considerably less than double the investment or operating cost, so it is with an expanding computer system. The fact that unit processing costs become lower with larger systems tends to make them more efficient for the users.

In a public utility such as electric power, the telephone, and the telegraph, there is a duty to supply demands for service at the time wanted by the user—without delay. Thus, in order to provide for these demands, these variable loads, it is necessary for the utility to provide capacity which exceeds the greatest demand of the customer body. Similarly, there must be provided reserve capacity to provide continuity of service insofar as possible in emergencies, as well as to provide for possible growth in load. Demands change from hour to hour within the day, and from day to day due to seasonal and other factors. But throughout, the utility must provide sufficient capacity to maintain satisfactory continuity of service to its customers.

While developments of full-fledged demand patterns on existing computer systems are still in their early stages, it is quite evident that the future pattern will be very much that just described for the public utilities. It will show up increasingly as more and more individual users reach the point where they are operating fully integrated systems on computers, or where service bureaus and cooperative organizations have acquired large and fairly constant loads from more stabilized bodies of users. The needs for availabilities of immediate reserve or stand-by computer capacity have been amply illustrated in the two recent computer fires in the United States Treasury Department and the Air Force case in the Pentagon. The emergency actions required in those two cases bore strong resemblance to public utility actions taken at times of hurricanes, floods, and similar catastrophes. Once a user organization becomes dependent on a computer system for its operations, it must have the same kind of service guarantees it gets from the utilities. It demands heavily then on the services of the supplier.

Also characteristic of the utility's economies is the need for development and maintenance of high load factors and high utilization factors by day, month, and year as means of attaining most economic productivity. The drive is to maintain a high ratio of average load to the peak demand during any given period of time. The drive is likewise to maintain a high ratio of average load to the rated capacity of the plant. Thus efforts are constantly made to fill the depressions in the load curves by various kinds of supplementary utilization as a means of obtaining lower unit costs. Similar efforts can be readily seen in the more advanced computer operations that are being well managed.

There is also at work in a public utility what is known as a diversity factor, the ratio of the sum of the maximum demands of the parts of a system to the maximum demand of either the entire system or any selected part of the system, measured at the point of supply. Because of diversity in the timing and amount of power required by the customers of separate power plants, it is quite possible to establish a joint plant that will serve them all with a smaller over-all capacity. (The smaller the total system capacity, the larger the diversity factor and the smaller the maximum coincident demand at a given time.)

Thus, in the power industry, diversity between customers permits the joint use of smaller transformers than if they had their own systems. Because of the diversity between transformers, there can be reductions made in the capacity of their joint substation. And because of diversity between substations, they can then be served by a common power station of lesser capacity. And the concept continues then to the point where even these common power stations become interconnected by transmission lines into a major, unified power system.

Here again, while there seem to be no published analyses of diversity factors in computer systems, it would certainly appear that they exist very much as they do in the power industry and may militate strongly in the future development of joint and cooperative usages.

But in the public utilities, both load and diversity factors apply equally to large and small plants, irrespective of the scale of their operations. However, there is a scale factor that favors expansion of the business and increases in the sizes of the plants. These would increase efficiencies and reduce costs further through greater specialization in both labor and managerial operations, and through additional economies in buying, selling, financing, and technological development. The importance of expanding scale arises from the fact mentioned earlier that larger units of facilities cost less per unit of capacity. And so it would seem to be with the computer business.

A further feature of the public utility business lies in economies inherent in joint cost—where it is cheaper to turn out two or more services from one single process or element of the system than to produce them separately. Examples are the development of a single water source into irrigation, urban water supply, and production of hydraulic power—or the production of gas and petroleum from a mining operation.

It would appear that as the integration of data-processing applications progresses, there will develop new by-products from the central processing that will come well within this category of economies of joint cost. As a matter of fact, it is the implied availabilities of such economies that are sparking some of the leading efforts towards fully integrated data processing in some of our leading organizations. Furthermore, the shared programs of organizations such as TUG, SHARE, and other computer users' groups are solid efforts to realize some of the economies of joint cost. The trend toward consolidation of a scientific computers and business data processors into single general-purpose systems is also pointed in the direction of joint cost economies by producing transactional documents, performing data manipulations, and handling the computations of decision making from a single production source. And there is in prospect another likelihood of tying to this same system the further elements now known under terms such as process control and production automation. Similarly there are efforts being made between different firms to standardize the transaction forms and language that flow between them so that the output from one can automatically become the input of the other and vice versa—another joint cost economy.

Besides these inherent similarities between the characteristics of the computer business and the public utilities, there are some historical and general features that appear analogous and might therefore bear more detailed and careful analysis than the mere outline below:

1. Many of our established public utilities had their beginnings in much the same pattern as that displayed by the computer business to date:

   - Organization of increasing numbers of joint ventures and co-operatives such as SPAN, users' groups, and service bureaus.

   - Sale of excess capacities and services by business concerns

not chartered for such but that found it an economic way of obtaining their own portions of service from a high-priced facility. Such are the insurance companies, educational institutions,
industrial concerns, and others who are selling time on their
computers to outside customers.

- Increased demands by users for wants not provided as
  quickly or as adequately as they wished—demands for what
  they wanted when they wanted it. All these early demands
  that led to the establishment of the utilities as such are well
  known. In the computer business there are analogous demands
  being made increasingly for faster speeds, greater storage
  capacities, better input—output devices, common language
  and simplified programming, fewer computer model changes
  and relief from their companion excessive reprogramming
  costs, data transmission links at lower cost with greater reliability and radically greater speeds, provision of stand-bys
  and emergency facilities and services, and reducing prices
  throughout.

- Growing numbers of mergers and acquisitions by larger companies of competing systems, as a means of attempting to solve
  some of the competitive problems mentioned previously. This
  pattern is apparent in the increasing numbers of mergers in
  the electronic data-processing field, among them Thompson-
  Ramo Wooldridge, GE-NCR, Litton-Monroe, Marchant-Smith
  Corona-Kleihschmidt, Burroughs-Electrodata, Friden-
  Commercial Controls, etc.

2. There is unquestionably a rising trend toward the coupling of
   computer systems with communications networks, slow in starting but now fast rising in acknowledgment of the fact that a substantial portion of all data processing consists of data communication. Thus, increasingly, common carriers are providing data
   transmission links as elements of integrated data-processing
   systems. Unquestionably this trend will continue upward at a faster
   tempo as the diversity, scale, and joint cost factors make themselves more felt. The common carriers which will provide this
   substantial portion of the over-all data-processing service are
   already public utilities—under public regulation.

3. Current practice in the computer business is becoming increasingly one of equipment rental rather than equipment sale, with accompanying provision of maintenance, spare parts, training,
   back-up facilities, and numerous services included in the rental

rates charged. This is another significant historical characteristic
of the public utility business.

THE COMPUTER SYSTEM AS A PUBLIC UTILITY—CON

While there appear to be many features in the computer business
that would indicate its possible evolution into a publicly regulated utility, there also appear to be some features that might be interpreted
to indicate otherwise. The following are some of these more salient
features.

Earlier, we quoted Justice Brandeis' statement on the public's
"varied and pervasive concern" with any public utility—that the business must be "affected with a public interest." It is noteworthy that
through our statement of the PRO's, we referred only to corporate
users—commercial and industrial concerns, organized enterprises
and not individual members of the public at large. At the moment, it
is difficult to envision any prospect for the individual person, the
householder, or the head of family, acquiring any pervasive concern
as a user of a large-scale computer system. None of the individual
day-to-day demands on him for data processing, information handling, or information retrieval would seem to warrant his rental of
even a microsecond of computer time. So it may well be that no
varied and pervasive public concern will ever develop to bring the
business under public regulation.

On the other hand, there are trends that may gradually bulk the
householder's or family's data-processing tasks in centralized computer systems, provide them with unasked-for services, and con-
front them with charges they would have to pay. Among these trends
come developments on comprehensively automated credit control
systems, standardization of bank checks for transit operations,
permanent registrations for voters, automobile licenses, etc. Some
rather extreme schemes are being advocated for the assignment of
permanent identification cards to individuals (similar to those now
used by Sweden), automatic deposits of their income payments to
their permanent bank accounts, automatic transferrals of their regular utility payments to their creditors by the bank, recording of
charges on interim purchases by the bank on the basis of their identification cards, automatic payment of such charges by the bank,
preparation of income tax declarations by the bank, etc. Review of
the new and additional services being offered by the banks seem
rather to point in the direction of their increasing involvement as
paid comptrollers for the individual. It is thus conceivable that the
data-processing needs of the individual, due to the needs for simpli-

fication and cost reduction by the corporations and government agencies which serve them, may increasingly be consolidated and bulked to an extent where large, centralized processors will be performing basic data processing for the majority of householders. The public may develop an interest not only in potential costs but also in threats to some elements of their financial liberties, before the over-all control system has been fully developed. The trends alone may work to develop a truly public interest and spark the legal and political actions that establish public utilities.

Noticeable in the PRO section of this paper is an underlying assumption that computer system usage will generally turn into large, powerful, high-speed centers serving large numbers of customers on joint, or shared, bases. Contrariwise, there has been the assumption that sales of smaller-scale independent processors to individual users will dwindle. While some primary reasoning has been given in support of these assumptions, it is conceivable that a technological breakthrough might so increase the power while reducing the costs of integrated data processors that past and present standards of economic justification for shared usage might be displaced. On the other hand, increasing complexities of interrelationships and communications needs between organizational groupings would indicate otherwise. It may be that there would develop within the field of computer usage the same variety of practices that exists within the electric power and telephone businesses—some user organizations procuring and operating their own systems but at the same time using portions of the utility facilities, some very small organizations electing to do completely without certain of the utility services, numerous utility firms in the one field of business but segregated geographically or otherwise by regulatory decisions, etc. partially due to entry into the field by new companies of new systems at seemingly lower prices than usual. This development may be good for the users, sharpen the producers, and indicate a continuation of the free competitive enterprise system in computer marketing for a good many years to come. But it may also repeat business histories in other fields, rapidly eliminate the smaller and weaker firms and establish a relative handful of large concerns in control of the total business.

There is a technological consideration that may be the strongest point against the utility concept. There is a tremendous amount of developmental work yet to be done in determining our ability to design and economically operate massive communications-computer complexes for satisfactorily servicing the varied and random needs of very large bodies of users. The required high-speed, high-reliability communications techniques have not yet been developed. There is as yet no appreciable degree of standardization among the equipments

that will be operating during the next few years. Even the earliest
and largest companies in the field have shown remarkably little skill
in the establishment of standardization throughout their own prolific
streams of model releases. And the newer entries in the field have
certainly done nothing but aggravate the situation. Such wide variations in concept and logic provide an extremely complicated base on
which to build an integrated, public-service, all-inclusive data-
processing system. The variations in facilities, plus the variations
in their associated programming, plus the variations in the data-
processing needs among all types, sizes, and conditions of users
seem to present an almost insurmountable problem of unification,
integration, and coordination into the single-system concept of a public service.

But despite the enormity of the problem it is being tackled in major
degree by and for the military, Federal Government, and giant user
corporations. There are many new signs of developing standardization ahead—organized efforts to establish a common language and
more truly automatic programming, joint efforts by competing companies on gigantic system developments, natural attrition among the
more obviously unsound equipment concepts, and many inherent aspects of computer economics that will drive remaining suppliers in
the direction of the single best answers on system concept, system
logic, and hence, system design.

CONCLUSIONS

In the absence of more detailed and thorough analysis, or of more
than a single viewpoint, it would be unwise to draw a positive conclusion that electronic data processing will become a public utility or
that it will not. However, the present considerations in favor of a
public utility seem to overweigh contrary considerations—at least
sufficiently to warrant concentrated attention to the possibilities. If
public regulation appears right and proper, we should move toward it
in a planned and ordered rather than haphazard fashion.

It might be well to summarize the possible effects if the computer
business should become a public utility. What might the effects be?

EFFECTS RESULTING FROM A PUBLIC UTILITY

Computer Facilities or Installations

Organization

Emphasis would be on rendering services and the use of utility
owned facilities on rental bases. Thus the organization would shift

from an industrial orientation to a commercial. Manufacturing's output would be absorbed by the company itself, with diminished portions sold to outside concerns. Increased emphasis would be placed on the research and development end of the business, more in a drive for improvements that can be passed to the total body of consumers than for the development of new products.

Personnel policies and practices would be apt gradually to shift from the high-salary, high-turnover patterns of today's electronic industry to the lower-salary, security-slanted, long-service patterns of the utilities. Over-all organizational emphasis would be on continuity of public minded services to a relatively permanent body of year-in year-out customers, rather than on special sales deals, occasional years of unprecedented growth in dollars gross, and occasional golden years of high net profit. Personnel satisfactions would have to come increasingly in the form of rewards for services rendered to old established customers and decreasingly as rewards for conquests of new customers.

The financial and accounting organization would gradually change its complexion somewhat from the profit and loss orientation of competition to the equable rate-setting and revenue accounting of the publicly regulated business.

Cost and Price

Equable spreads of costs across the total user body would become of greater importance than establishment of maximum attainable profit margins. The business would become more cost oriented than profit oriented. Capital outlay would be directed towards the improvement of services to existing customers and the extension of services for anticipated new demands rather then for maximum dollar returns from new risks undertaken.

Standard rate structures would supersede price lists, and company operated facilities would constantly expand as profit margins decreased. The story of the American Telephone Company's financing by the Morgan interests when Vail took over the presidency may well be the financial pattern that will be followed sooner or later in the computer business. Vail set the policy and publicly declared it with his simple statement, "Our business is service." That policy revolved primarily around the assumption that the company had to give service wherever there was a demand and that management's prime job was to find the needed capital and earn a reasonable return on it.

Marketing and Services

Marketing would shift decidedly from the sales emphasis of the

competitive enterprise to the public relations, service conscious
types of consumer contacts. Marketing pressures would be more for
the improvement and expansion of services rendered than for the
sales volumes required to maintain manufacturing levels and goals.

It may be significant that the practices already established in the
computer industry have placed both sales and services under the
marketing manager, and that as sales increase, the service operations expand in greater proportion, so that gradually the service element of the business may naturally gain ascendancy over the sales.
The establishment of computer system rental policies has of course
contributed to this and thus moved the business a step closer to the
utility structure.

Equipment Design

Communications and Data Processing

Earlier, the statement was made that it seems inevitable that the
hardware of the integrated system concept will consist of three major
elements: communications network, automatic switching and control
centers, and electronic data processors. As yet, neither a major
computer manufacturer nor a major communications company has indicated an intent or policy of attempting thoroughly to solve such a
total system integration. Until a single company does so, there would
seem to be as yet no leading candidate for becoming the first EDP
utility. Surely electronic information handling becomes about an equal
admixture of communication and data processing. Perhaps the utilities concluded they should not engage in the portion that was free enterprise, and the computer companies that they should not intrude
upon the precincts that were under public regulation. But if our preliminary conclusion is correct or even approximately so, some company must certainly rise to the challenge soon.

Even stranger is the fact that the users in the military and larger
corporations have been making increasingly stronger demands for
such fully integrated systems. Many military system contracts have
been placed with teams of two or more firms, forced together from
these two fields and given the assigned tasks of constructing the total
system in its three elements. But still no single concern tackles the
assignment of satisfying the burgeoning, unsatisfied demand that will
be covered most adequately only by such singular effort.

It would appear that the design would require the maximum speed,
capacity, and power of computer equipment; major breakthrough in
broadband communications via microwave and coaxial cable; and
switching equipment with the speeds and capacities of the computer
itself. There should be major reductions in the amount of electro-

mechanical equipment required for the system functions, and reductions in the volumes of paper media used—printed or typed documents,
punched tapes, punched cards. Character-reading devices and visual
displays should be developed to utilize the maximum speed capabilities inherent in the electronic art. All of these needs revolve around
the primary importance of the scale factor in the development of the
public utility structure.

Standardization versus Language Compatibility

There are at present efforts being made to establish a common
language, simple to learn and employ, that will make it possible for
all of a variety of computers to operate from identical common language instructions. It is hoped that the computer companies will all accept such a common language and design compilers for their own
computer models which will effectively translate the common language into their own machine languages. It can be foreseen that in the
early development of such practices, some machines will operate
much less efficiently than others. It would accordingly seem likely
that this situation will lead gradually toward an increasing standardization of equipment design as all companies strive for maximizing
their equipment efficiencies under the newly accepted standards of
language. Such developments would be consistent with the public
utility concept.

Users

It would be anticipated that the effect of the public utility concept
on the users would be all to the good. Under the concept all types and
sizes of customers would have to be handled as equably as possible.
Standardization of equipment concepts would develop, and much of
the haze, misunderstandings, and conflicting concepts within the electronic data-processing art would necessarily be resolved. Consumer
costs would come down and service emphasis would increase. Not
only would the user body acquire a greater understanding of the benefits to be received from the modern processing techniques, but they
would also be in a better position to register their demands and have
them satisfied.

SUMMARY

As we have indicated earlier, the possible evolution of an electronic data-processing utility provides an interesting and challenging
opportunity for research, first to reject or confirm its likelihood.

Assuming confirmation as a very real likelihood, then there is much research to be done in analyzing and evaluating the coming effects—on equipment design, on organization and policy, on users, and on the over-all developments in the management control system. It would seem that the greatest single impetus that could be given to the development of the unified or integrated management control system might come from the evolution of the computer business into a publicly regulated electronic data-processing utility.

REFERENCES

1. Norbert Wiener, The Human Use of Human Beings, Houghton Mifflin, Boston, 1950, p. 124.
2. Ibid. p. 8.
3. Ibid. p. 104.
4. Ibid. p. 9.
5. Justice Brandeis' dissent in New State Ice Co. vs. Liebmann (1931).
6. Chief Justice Taft, Wolff Packing Co. vs. Govt. of Industrial Relations (1922).
7. William E. Mosher and Tinla G. Crawford, Public Utility Regulation, Harper and Brothers, New York, 1933, pp. 7-9.

RESEARCH IN MANAGEMENT CONTROL SYSTEM DESIGN

SECTION **VI**

Some basic questions

CHAPTER **A** by JOHN F. LUBIN

A periodic reappraisal of new techniques such as management science, operations research, mathematics in management, and system development appears necessary to avoid rapid, haphazard growth. Often, those who have been trained traditionally, fear technological unemployment if such notions are accepted. Nevertheless, imaginative research can be built on many foundations; and it does seem reasonable to take an occasional look at the assumptions on which proposed structures are to be built. It is too easy for those doing creative work to reject this kind of activity as unnecessary and view it as a pursuit of generalization. But a most useful function of review is the statement of objective and the appraisal of premises proposed.

Perhaps the best method for providing a constructive review of management controls is to pose a series of probing questions:

- Is system development in its modern sense any fundamental improvement over the well-known concept of managerial planning and control?

- Is not system development synonomous with management?

- In what way have those in operations research and system development contributed to better management controls?

- Is the computer an essential element in modern system development?

- Would it be productive to study successful managers and their methods to gain insights on system design?

- Has there been overemphasis of the formal and logical approach and neglect of the informal and intuitive?

- What response should be made to those who maintain that a good manager is one who knows when to avoid the system?

- Who plays the major role in system design: the system developer or the system operator?

- Should systems be designed to prevent or encourage modifications of the system by the managers during operation?

- Are research programs designed to utilize available techniques and hardware as well as to discover fundamental knowledge?

- Should research emphasize the development of theories of system design?

- What are the appropriate premises for those doing system development?

It is possible that serious consideration of these questions would lead to an appropriate basis for research in management control systems. Further, perhaps the research could be conducted in actual business firms by observation of operations in addition to computer simulation. Perhaps this research should concentrate first on the fundamentals of system development, especially an analysis of premises, and not overextend itself by establishing a too ambitious program in general management control systems.

It would appear that a common language has developed in management thought in the last fifty years. This is in part due to the efforts of Fred Winslow Taylor in developing a system which was so acceptable that his terminology became the standard. Thus, the system itself created the common language. In recent years, it has been usual to form teams and committees to standardize terminology, which may be a sterile approach. Indeed, while operational systems work cannot be independent of application, it may very well be true that the research and the formulation of theory should be.

DISCUSSION   (Following Mr. Lubin's presentation of his paper)

M. G. HOLMEN: One of SDC's contributions was to demonstrate that there is no best way which is independent of the people involved in the particular system, unless it is an extremely simple system.

W. E. ALBERTS: It has been my experience that work in the field of management controls and systems has contributed real results by helping people meet real objectives.

J. F. LUBIN: With regard to basic research in systems, results or "payoff" should not be the criterion. In particular, it should not be the basis for establishing a research program on this subject.

R. L. SISSON: A key point in regard to systems work is that you must start with sharp people. It does not matter what their backgrounds are, so long as they think about management. They should question everything you are doing. What is management and what criteria do they use as related to the researcher's criteria? An excellent example is the project Ford Dickie undertook. The team questioned everything from the manufacturing process to the forms, and the words, and the fields. I believe that is why the project was successful. Therefore, I think it would be a mistake to orient our thinking away from basic research. There should be a separate effort to implement the research.

J. F. LUBIN: I do not think that commercial enterprises such as General Electric Company or United Air Lines should do basic systems research. Research as such must be done outside of the control by operating persons.

R. L. SISSON: I agree that basic research should be separated from operations. A manager desiring a system analysis has vague requirements because he does not know how to measure his own desires. Improvements in this situation tend to depend on experience and intuition for system design. The only way to overcome this is to provide the opportunity to do basic research without the requirement for solving specific problems.

A. J. ROWE: An interesting point, however, is that research does not necessarily have to be done in the corner. There is a wealth of information in the people who happen to be working on specific jobs. The fact that they are working on jobs instead of research is often just a happenstance. The point is that interaction with the real world will possibly produce thinking of value to research. In some sense a man who every day solves problems and is a thoughtful individual may really be doing experimentation or research. I think this is as much research as somebody off in a corner thinking about problems. I don't think you can simply go off in a corner and never interact with the real problems. Even Newton watched the apple fall.

M. G. HOLMEN: Concerning the question of system design, flexibility is a key factor in that overautomation tends to reduce adaptability; so, every automated feature must be considered in terms of its flexibility as well as in terms of cost. Thus, a static system has a built-in, immediate, and guaranteed obsolescence. Likewise, a system in which the capacity for change has not been designed must either soon be junked or must have its operations suspended while changes are made to it. However, the building of a large complex system is slow and must operate at a high rate of efficiency to justify its existence. The environment in which it operates, the precise task which it is to perform, and the means for performing it will change during the time the system itself is being built. Since an expensive system cannot tolerate inefficient operation, means for adapting or flexibility must be built in.

My point is that you don't change a system or a computer program by unilateral decisions. A division head who doesn't like the way the accounting system is operating doesn't change it by going to the accountant. He changes it by going to people who designed the system and by talking to the people who have the knowledge and capability of changing it. We have to make systems users aware of this requirement of flexibility and teach them how to get the flexibility by going outside of their operations and outside of those they don't control.

A. J. ROWE: In order to properly design large-scale, complex systems, considerably more knowledge is needed. In the design of a bridge, knowledge about elasticity, strength of materials, and vibration is used. In the design of business systems, no comparable knowledge exists. Little is known about how the system will behave under changing conditions. In addition, there are no experimental means of doing research in the actual operations in order to discover fundamental laws. This, undoubtedly, is one of the basic problems of research in this area. What is needed is fundamental research where one can test hypotheses through experimentation. Further, I can't see how this experimentation can be done in the real world.

M. O. KAPPLER: A somewhat different kind of research is through the technological advances based on trying something new. For example, RCA designed a new vacuum tube that had both elements in the same envelope. Although this is a very simple example, it illustrates that what is new today is not merely what we happen to know about. Simply looking at the possible application of management control principles would be a worthy effort.

For example, the application of computers to management controls may yield some useful results. Computers provide two things that couldn't be provided otherwise: larger volume storage, and error-free information. In the past, management and command activities have not had suitable storage available that provided the assurance of getting the right information in an accurate form.

Another related use of computers is the ability to optimize through the solution of mathematical equations. For example, problems about paying for storage floor space or paying for transportation have fairly well-known applications. Such applications are done extensively because of speed computations. The exploration of how to solve problems in similar ways at higher levels of management would be a worthy project. Another possible area of exploration is the use of computers as aids in an actual system through simulation technology. We have had experience in both of these areas as a result of our military contract work.

J. F. LUBIN: Simulation and operational gaming have become important techniques in recent years partially because we do lack a suitable theory.

A. SCHULTZ: There are other reasons why simulation is important. Together with certain statistical techniques, it furnishes us with a new means of investigating complex problems such as management control systems. Considerable work still remains in applying this new tool in conjunction with the mathematics and statistics, and in defining the problem. This is what Warren Alberts and others who are faced with the responsibility of designing the business management system have in their minds when they state that much of this work is going on in a vacuum.

W. R. FAIR: The time frame of reference for research seems to be wide. One could think big and spend ten years in an ivory tower environment. Another possible option is to select a time frame of reference—a time interval—in which a research group has to come up with something that demonstrates the money was worth spending in the first place—six months to several years. This question must be answered before other issues can be properly considered.

J. F. LUBIN: System Development Corporation should not "think small" on this matter of its proper role in research. They have a great opportunity.

H. F. DICKIE: I would like to summarize a few of the statements made in this discussion—since there appears to be a number of different viewpoints. One statement made was that there is a question as to whether current system work made things better. Another suggested that a ten-year research project would be desirable. A third generalized that mechanized information systems are inflexible and changes are extremely difficult to make. A fourth expressed thankfulness that his mechanized systems project did not have cost reduction as its objective.

I want to comment briefly on these points. A typical mechanized systems project at General Electric may have had some suboptimization; however, there were substantial reductions in inventories, manufacturing cycle time, operator and machine lost time, indirect labor expense, and a marked improvement in meeting scheduled completion dates. To me these seem like most worthwhile and valuable steps forward. Next, in reply to the statement that mechanized systems are inflexible, I want to point out that we have at least demonstrated to our own satisfaction that this obstacle can now be overcome and that changes can be made quite easily. Are we wrong in moving ahead today to what we believe is greater efficiency rather than waiting ten years for some greater understanding of management's objectives? To me it seems essential for survival in today's competitive international economy.

The results of the integrated systems project at General Electric have demonstrated a substantial percentage of potential improvement in total company profits. This fact alone was enough to stop a meeting of the top executives of the company. Evidence of what can be done is illustrated by tangible results such as the fact that manufacturing cycles reduced indirect labor expense by some 80 per cent and that better service was given to the customer by meeting delivery promises.

Further, in the computerized system we can make changes far easier than we could under a manual system, and we can see much more clearly and precisely what the effects will be. Certainly there are many great opportunities and urgent needs for management control systems research; but I would like to suggest smaller, cleaner projects. Among other things, the motivation is greater, the results more quickly useful and the ideas more easily conveyed to operating management. What's wrong with carrying on research and development today which has as its objective greater efficiency in time, cost, and accuracy?

J. D. GALLAGHER: This is fine if it is in conjunction with a given program. In Sylvania's case it was not the only reason for engineering the program. If it were, then the program would not have been successful because it didn't result in a material decrease in the over-all labor force of the company.

A research approach in management controls

CHAPTER **B** by ALAN J. ROWE

INTRODUCTION

An important challenge awaits the business manager of the future. In spite of expert advice on business operations and the availability of computers, management decision making and control are still extremely difficult and complex tasks, and with the inevitable shift of emphasis from intuition and judgment to management skills, the role of managers will become increasingly important.

To conduct research in management controls, however, a number of formidable obstacles must be overcome. Unlike engineering or the physical sciences, there are no convenient laboratories for testing new ideas and methods. Experimentation directly in an actual plant presents numerous difficulties; and the introduction of repeated changes in an existing system would cause resentment as well as unreliable results. System modification, repetition, or control of experiments may be virtually impossible in real-life situations. The required time and cost of testing new methods is often prohibitive. Computer simulation, on the other hand, provides an effective and rapid means for examining complex system problems, since the computer is capable of examining a year of simulated activity in a matter of minutes. In addition, data on system performance can be obtained which are unavailable in actual situations. Because of the above considerations, the computer appears to provide suitable laboratory for conducting research into new management control methods and ideas.

BACKGROUND OF THE PROBLEM

Although management control is widely discussed, little has been done to formulate a body of principles for use in business system design. It is interesting to note that the system aspect of control has not been widely applied in industry. Although the servo concept of control in management was described by Simon,[1] it has been only recently that the use of integrated controls or the systems approach has been expounded.[2] A natural extension of the systems approach is to include optimization in the design aspect of the problem. That is, a system should be "designed" to meet specific requirements before establishing controls. Based on this consideration, we can say that management control is concerned with integrated systems of men, material, facilities, and funds, to specify, predict, and assure the results desired from such systems.

An important problem related to management control is the decision-making process. In carrying out their daily activities, managers are confronted with discovering possible alternative courses of action and their consequences. Ultimately, what is required is a suitable basis for choosing among these alternatives. Where problems are well formulated, mathematical or logical decision rules can be applied which help achieve control. However, the majority of management decisions involve interdependencies among a number of activities. The joint optimization of many factors causes the complexity in solving the problem of decision making.

In addition to the difficulty of evaluating the effect of a given decision on the numerous activities within a business, there is the problem of variability of system inputs and system performance. The stochastic behavior of events is characteristic of the majority of problems in management controls and, in part, accounts for the difficulty in predicting system performance. A better understanding of the statistical aspects of system behavior will greatly aid in achieving correct design of management control systems.

RESEARCH PROBLEMS IN MANAGEMENT CONTROLS

Research in management controls should consider the behavior of the system as a whole. This research approach poses the following problems:

1. Relationship of system design to control.

2. Suboptimization as a result of component control.

3. Formalizing of system objectives.

4. Measurement of system performance.

5. Design considerations in management controls.

6. Relationship of formalized decision rules to control.

Relationship of System Design to Control

An important consideration in establishing management controls
is to relate system requirements to the control methodology. Thus,
research in the development of improved controls will be based
on the assumption that system design precedes design of management controls. However, the design of complex systems to meet
specified requirements often requires experimentation. Where an
actual system exists, it could be used as the basis for modeling in
order to conduct simulation experiments. However, as is often the
case, when a new system is being designed it has an entirely different set of requirements from those of existing systems. The model
in this latter case must, of necessity, be based on experience and
judgment rather than a real-life counterpart. Research, in many respects, is concerned with systems which do not exist today. Therefore, a method examining a multitude of possible systems in a test-
tube-like fashion is needed. Computer simulation appears to meet
this requirement.

Suboptimization as a Result of Component Control

Optimizing components or parts of a system may lead to suboptimization in the total system. Thus, for example, costs which are
incurred in purchasing, storing, processing, and shipping should be
combined rather than treated separately. As another example,[3]
rather than compute order quantities without considering other factors, they should be dependent upon inventory status, machining costs,
scheduling requirements, financial status, marketing position, etc. It
is apparent that the simultaneous consideration of many factors poses
a tremendous strain on any information-processing system and would
undoubtedly require computer assistance. However, once these interdependencies have been established, it may be possible to employ a
simplified control mechanism.

Formalizing Objectives

Probably one of the most difficult aspects of establishing controls
is the lack of formalized objectives in business. The old cliché of
profit being the objective of a business enterprise is gradually disappearing.[4] From the system view, there should be a number of con-

commitant objectives. Not all objectives are alike, however, since they
are a function of the willingness of management to take action in the
face of uncertainty and with inadequate information. Presumably, computers can provide information in a form useful for analysis and evaluation of a number of alternatives which can serve as the basis for
establishing realistic objectives. For example, management might
state as an objective an increased share of the available market for a
given product. An economic analysis of the factors involved might
prove this objective unrealistic. It is possible that for a given capacity, capital structure, distribution system, etc., the costs far exceed
the value gained from obtaining a greater share of the market. The
difficulty in formalizing such objectives arises from the fact that
there is no simple method for evaluating the impact of objectives on
a complex system. Without this evaluation, the objectives may be
meaningless. For this reason, simulation seems like a suitable approach to the problem of specifying "meaningful" objectives. This
same argument can be extended to the design of the system itself.
Alternative designs should be compared and evaluated prior to actual
implementation of a system. In business systems, the computer can
provide the necessary vehicle for this experimentation and evaluation.

Measurement of System Performance

Measurement of system performance should be an integral part of
management controls. However, conventional bases for measurement,
in many instances, do not truly reflect performance nor provide control. For example, high inventory turnover may lead to stock short-
ages. Therefore, turnover may be an inadequate measure to insure
desired system performance. The majority of present methods of
measuring performance can be traced to the lack of large-scale data-
processing media. With increased storage capacity in computers, the
processing and summarization of operating data will prove less
formidable than in the past. This should permit the development of
measures of performance which are based on actual operations. Control information can then be a by-product of normal transactions
based on integrated data processing.

Design Considerations in Management Controls

An important consideration in the design of management controls
is that the controls do not become ends in themselves. Budgeting is
an excellent example of the situation where funds are often spent,
not because they are needed, but to prevent a cut at a later date.
Costing is another example of requiring system performance to con-

form to arbitrary controls. Thus, the management control problem is further confounded by the fact that given properly designed systems and correctly established objectives, the controls may lead to poor system performance. This has been demonstrated by Forrester[5] in his treatment of induced fluctuations in inventory and production as a result of poor controls.

A number of considerations should be taken into account in the design of management controls, such as:

- What are the limits or deviation from standard which provide the basis for action?

- How is the system aspect included?

- How can decision rules be used for control?

- Can feedback be treated as a sampled data problem?

- What controls are sensitive to transient problems?

- Can general principles such as the exception principle be developed?

In addition to the above, management controls will depend on the system design, although there are control principles which are independent of the particular system. Optimization procedures or decision rules are also controls since they assure specified system performance.

Relationship of Decision Rules to Control

Unless formalized decision rules are available, the computer merely acts in the role of a data processor. On-line computer control, in reality, implies a form of automated decision making. On the other hand, the computer can also be used to present information to managers as an aid in decision making. The majority of decision rules developed in business to date, however, give no consideration to the system aspect of the problem. Rules for optimal safety stocks, for example, do not consider the cash position of the company at the time an order is placed. As an alternative to formalized decision rules, computer simulation can be applied in a heuristic approach to problem solving. Thus, if the cash position were low, a simulation run could be made to predict the effect of alternative solutions to the problem.

A problem in the use of decision rules for management controls is that the solution of a problem having a large number of variables is formidable. Although the outcome of a particular combination of variables is difficult to predict, the results often form a stable distribution. Thus, for example, when jobs are processed in a factory,

the completion of any specific one cannot be predicted, nor the sequence in which other jobs will be completed. However, it is possible
to predict the over-all distribution of job completions. This can be
depicted graphically as shown in Figure VI-B-1. Thus, rather than

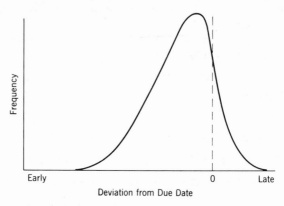

Figure VI-B-1. Distribution of Job Completions.

treat this as a permutation problem, it is considered a stochastic
process having a definite distribution. In a like manner, problems involving a large number of variables in management controls can be
treated from the statistical viewpoint.

The use of a combination of formalized decision rules and computer
simulation for management controls opens up interesting new vistas.
In effect, it would be possible to have detail planning for problems
which extends further out in time than it currently does. Thus, rather
than daily or weekly labor forecasting, it would be possible to have
realistic monthly or quarterly forecasts. Also, the problem of annual
budgeting could be handled on a more refined basis. Thus, rather than
wait until year's end to find out that a budget was over or under the
predicted amount, the business could respond to changes as they
occurred. This of course presumes that flexibility has been designed
into the system to permit rapid response to the changing environment.
Research in management controls should have as one of its objectives
the study of real-time problems such as these.

A RESEARCH APPROACH IN BUSINESS MANAGEMENT CONTROLS

A basic question to be answered in management controls research
is the scope of the problem to be considered. The majority of control
research in industry today can be classed as component or subsystem

control. There is a lack of concentrated effort, from the system viewpoint, on the business as a whole. Thus, our approach is to study the entire business as a logical system.

As in any research program, the starting point should be a survey of the field to establish the state of the art. These findings should prove helpful in providing guidance in the research. In addition, a research plan should include the following:

- A well-formulated model of the elements, characteristics, and structure of management control systems.

- A general-purpose computer model for simulation.

- Design of decision rules for management controls.

- A study of the behavior of the computer model to gain insight into the problem and validate experimental conclusions.

Developing a Model for Management Controls

In order to study these problems in management controls, the programming of a general-purpose simulation model appears appropriate. This model would be designed for use on a large, high-speed computer and, when programmed, would provide both a research and a training tool. An important factor favoring a general-purpose model is that this would serve as a basis or focal point for discussions with persons concerned with management control applications. It would also permit the research to be of a broad and fundamental nature rather than the solution of specific problems.

An important characteristic which the model should have is the ability to examine the effect of changes in management controls on system performance. For example, how would a change in decision points affect information flow rates, time lags, or queuing in a given system? Similarly, how can decision rules, which provide systematic response to variable inputs, permit optimization in a system? To permit study of component interactions the program should also contain decision rules which have a conditional response based on given decision criteria.

A Computer Model

To model the organizational structure of a business, a network of decision points, information channels, and authority relations can be used. The interactions and interdependencies of a typical business should be taken into account; as well as, formalizing inputs and outputs, and system transfer functions. Objectives would be formulated in quantitative terms. The information flow, feedback loops, and decision points would be used in the model to establish the organization structure for decision making.

One means of indicating information flow or relationships among decision makers is the use of a matrix notation. Conditional decision responses can be represented by a special logical notation. These decision responses serve as transfer functions which describe the behavior of the system under varying conditions. Measures of system performance would be an integral part of the model with the computer summarizing various kinds of data. Alternative methods of summarizing these data would be useful for studying information flow and evaluation of system design. In addition, the model would be capable of handling stochastic behavior of the system elements.

Design of Decision Rules in Management Controls

Quoting from Drucker's[6] article on long-range planning, we can clearly see the need for formalized decision making in management:

> "It is not within the decision of the entrepreneur whether he wants to make risk-taking decisions with long futurity; he makes them by definition. All that is within his power is to decide whether he wants to make them responsibly or irresponsibly, with a rational chance of effectiveness and success, or as a blind gamble against all odds. And both, because the process is essentially a rational process, and because the effectiveness of the entrepreneurial decisions depends on the understanding and voluntary efforts of others, the process will be the more responsible and the more likely to be effective, the more it is a rational, organized process based on knowledge."

Although there are many ramifications to management decision making, from the point of view of management control research, the following aspects of decision making can be considered:

- The bases or criteria for making decisions.

- The information required to make decisions.

- Where decisions are made and by whom.

- The number and type of decisions made at various organizational levels.

- The response rate required for decisions after information is received.

- The time taken to actually make the decisions.

- The induced lags or delays in information flow due to decision making.

- The noise or errors in the decision-making process.

- The relation of organizational structure to decision making.

- The bases for automating decisions.

Although this list is not exhaustive, it indicates the kind of problems confronting research in management controls. Behavioral and motivational characteristics of decision making will be considered, where these can be quantified or modeled.

Testing the Model

In order to have assurance that a model responds to inputs in a manner comparable to actual system behavior, it is necessary to validate the outputs. Using actual data, or suitable approximations, the results obtained by running the model should be comparable to known behavior. Following the validation, experimentation is necessary to test hypotheses on system design and decision rules. Both types of testing are difficult and require designed experiments. In view of the fact that simulation is a synthetic means of generating experimental data (often referred to as the Monte Carlo Method[7]) and that computer time is expensive, unlimited sampling would not be justified. Special sampling techniques are necessary to have assurance that a given decision function is applicable as a basis for action with a minimum expectation of risk.

The research approach, then, is to start with a well-formulated statement of the elements, characteristics, and structure of management control systems. This would serve as the input for an initial model in which only the critical variables have been included. A sensitivity analysis would be used to determine which are the important variables as well as to determine the significant range of parameters. One method for determining which factors are important, and for assuring realism, is to discuss the initial model with various business managers. The formalizing or modeling of the problem is a difficult, yet critical, task. The model should be designed for ease of modification or adaptation to suit specific variations in order to cover a wide range of research problems in management controls.

DESCRIPTION OF A GENERAL MANAGEMENT CONTROL MODEL

Many problems must be surmounted to adequately model a business system for studying management control problems. The purpose here is to explore in some detail the means whereby this modeling can be achieved. The problems discussed are not intended to be all-inclusive; rather, the effort is directed towards demonstrating that many aspects of business system behavior can be formalized and stated in quantitative terms.

By starting with a simplified hypothetical organization as an example, an approach to modeling can best be explored. Figure VI-B-2

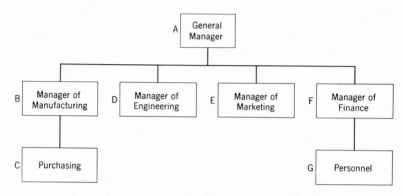

Figure VI-B-2. Hypothetical Organization Chart.

represents some of the typical functions found in a business enterprise. Department heads B, D, E, and F report directly to the manager A. Purchasing C reports to B and Personnel G reports to Finance F. These are similar to conventional authority channels; however, they do not represent the dynamic interrelationship of these functions. A simulation model, on the other hand, can portray various alternative relations as a function of time, urgency, or decision criteria. For the present, let us represent this conventional organization chart in the form of a matrix, as shown in Figure VI-B-3. Thus, as was shown in Figure VI-B-2, B, D, E, and F report to A, and C reports to B. Note the ease of showing where all the persons report by merely placing x's in the matrix, and also the possibilities of modifying these relationships. Informal or secondary channels can be represented by other letters such as y. Thus, for example, the fact that purchasing may report informally to the engineering manager is shown by the "y".

In a similar manner, matrix format can be used to indicate information flow, material flow, etc. For example, a formal information flow pattern might be as shown in Figure VI-B-4. The numbers shown inside this matrix indicate the sequence of flow through the organization, as well as the originator of the document. The letters correspond to the organization chart in Figure VI-B-2. Special codes such

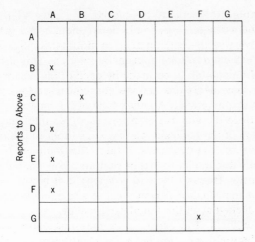

Figure VI-B-3. Organization Matrix.

Decision Makers

	A	B	C	D	E	F	G
D_1	1	2		2	2	2	
D_2		1		2	3	4	
D_3		1	2				
D_4	0				1		
D_5		0					1
.							
.							
.							
D_n			1				2

Directives, Documents, Data, Information

Figure VI-B-4. Information Flow Matrix.

as zero can be used to indicate that the document or data originated outside of the system.

The letters alongside the matrix, $\underline{D}_1$ . . . $\underline{D}_n$, are the cording to identify specific information. This may be a telephone call, a sales report, a customer order, an absenteeism report, etc. In this way, the communications network can be formalized. In addition, informal information flow can also be incorporated into the matrix.

This matrix arrangement can also be used to represent raw data or system status. Referring to the matrix in Figure VI-B-4, the manager may issue a directive $\underline{D}_1$ to his department heads (who are all presumed to receive the communication simultaneously) and they, in turn, may be expected to take appropriate action. This directive, in effect, causes a decision to be made by each of the department heads. The basis for their decisions and the consequent actions would all be part of the computer model. Another type of information flow is shown opposite $\underline{D}_4$. Here the general manager receives information on the market position of the company and forwards this to the marketing manager. However, the dynamics of this situation must be represented within the computer model to attain realism. For example, how soon is the information transmitted and how long is it before the marketing manager takes appropriate action? These are some typical questions which can be looked at in the simulation model.

Still another form of information is shown opposite $\underline{D}_5$. The manager of manufacturing notifies personnel that there is a shortage in a given skill category and that hiring should proceed. The zero in the box opposite $\underline{D}_5$ is now used to indicate that this information is a result of the system performance. Thus, as data are summarized and made available at various points they become inputs to the information flow. The kind of data, manner of summarization, and frequency of reporting would all be part of the simulation program. By providing for variation in the pattern of information flow, it should be possible to examine the effect of reporting on system performance.

The Model of Decision Making

Decision making and information flow are both critical aspects of a business simulation model. For our purpose, we can conceive of the decision-making process as consisting of the following elements:

- A triggering or forcing function which initiates the decision process.

- Decision criteria which provide the basis for response to given stimuli.

- Decision rules which provide formalized response as a function of variable input.

- Action taken as a result of the decision process.

- Outcome or result of the actions on system performance (including latent effects).

- Feedback to correct decision criteria or decision rules.

One aspect of human behavior is the problem of predicting exact response for a given stimulus. Therefore, certain behavioral or motivational aspects of the problem can be subsumed by variability in the above elements of decision making. However, it is possible to construct formalized organizational relations which directly alter or affect the decision-making process. Where these can be explicitly modeled, they would be included in the program.

It is possible to establish logical relationships which use the state of events as the basis for decisions to be made. Thus, as systems change, certain events become critical and trigger information flow to decision makers. Suppose, for example, a part completes its processing in the factory and is ready for assembly. When it reaches this state of completion, the information could be transmitted immediately to various decision points. Or, the information processing system may be such that at the end of each day Production Control is the only department notified as to which parts have been completed. They, in turn, might take certain action depending on the state of completion of mating parts. Thus, a logical comparison as a basis for decision making might be made as follows:

- Is part A complete? Yes.

- Is part B complete? Yes.

- Is part C complete? No.

If the assembly requires all three parts, then the answer—yes, yes, no—would lead to a different decision than three yeses. This can be represented as follows:

- Part A has been completed. What decision should now be made?

- Determine completion status of mating parts.

- If all three are completed, proceed to assembly.

- If any component is not completed, place parts into an accumulation area.

- Repeat the check on status of mating parts after a suitable time interval.

The various specific decisions, or classes of decisions, to be made at decision points can be represented in tabular form. In the computer model, a search would be made to determine where the decisions are carried out. This search technique can be simplified by using the logical characteristic of computer operation. Thus, for example, the following table shows two triggering functions which initiate the decision process. The first function is a result of a change in the system status, whereas the second function is the result of a formal document requesting the purchase of some raw material. The logical considerations and action to be taken are shown in Table VI-B-1.

Table VI-B-1

Decisions Normally Made at this Point— Trigger Function	Logical Considerations or Decision Criteria	Action to Be Taken or Decision Rules
1. Part reaches completion status	1. Review all mating parts to be completed.	1. If all mating parts are completed, send to assembly. 2. If one or more parts have not been completed, send this part to accumulation area.
2. Request for raw material.	1. Review order point.	1. If order point has been reached, check forecast usage: a. If forecast usage is the same, compute the economic order quantity and send order to purchasing. 2. b. If usage has changed, send a request to engineering for further information.

It is obvious from Table VI-B-1 that a logical comparison implies a yes-no type of response. An important advantage of this method of comparison is that computers operate in a binary or yes-no mode so that this approach simplifies the computer programming as well as formalizing responses to avoid ambiguity.

This logical format for representing the decision-making process is especially useful in studying problems involving a number of interacting elements. For instance, the disposition of a part for assembly was made contingent on the status of the mating parts. It is the computer's ability to update and store consideration information which permits the exploration of these considerations in such detail.

Time Lags in Information Flow

A significant aspect of the control problem is the time phasing for contingent decisions. The flow of information can introduce time lags into a system as a result of queuing effects.[8] In a sense, information flowing through a number of decision makers is comparable to jobs flowing in a factory or cars flowing on the highways. For example, if the decision maker is viewed as a processing center, the rate of arrival of decisions and the time taken to make each decision will determine the average delay or queuing effect. Where priorities are assigned the various decisions to be made, it is possible both to improve effectiveness and reduce delay times.[9] Another means of reducing delays is to have alternative channels for the given decisions. Filtering or screening decisions is still another means of reducing the flow time through the system. However, this latter manner of treating decision making might lead to radical changes in organization structure and could hardly be tested initially in a real-life environment. These and related questions can readily be examined by computer simulation.

The formal and informal information channels in an organization, and the points at which decisions are made, directly affect system performance. Graphically, the system effectiveness as a function of speed of response might appear as in Figure VI-B-5. That is, for a

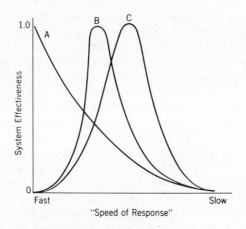

Figure VI-B-5. Relationship of Information Flow to System Effectiveness.

given type of decision and given organization structure and given cost there are alternative response rates which are optimal. For Case A, shown in Figure VI-B-5, the faster the response, the greater the system effectiveness. Any time lags would seriously hamper performance. On the other hand, rapid responses in cases B and C are not nearly so critical. Thus, the information flow rate is a key parameter in system design.

Of course, speed of information flow is not a sufficient criterion of usefulness. The right information, in an understandable form, and free from errors, is also a significant factor. For example, the exception principle of management is concerned with minimizing the quantity of information necessary for decision making. In a like manner, system performance information can be summarized or aggregated into more meaningful form for decision making. An important problem is determining what information is required, and in what form and with what speed in order to make effective decisions and provide feedback for control. A more thorough analysis of the kinds of decisions made should yield insight as to where the computer can aid the decision maker. Routine decisions involving a large quantity of data can most easily be automated. Complex decisions involving judgment and analysis could use computers to digest information, evaluate alternatives, and test key parameters as aids in decision making.

Organizational Considerations

A problem related to decision making is supervisory control. Decentralized organizations require increased supervision of people. In addition, as the number of levels of organization increase, there is a greater possibility of distortion and error in information transmission. A cost function relating decentralization or numbers of levels of supervision and centralization or completely automated information processing would provide a quantitative basis for comparing alternative organization structures.

Another aspect of organization which could be explored by computer simulation is the span of supervisory control. If the elements of a supervisor's job are analyzed, it is soon apparent that a certain percentage of his time is spent in direct contact with subordinates. The time spent during a contact with the subordinates would follow some distribution such as shown in Figure VI-B-6. The shape of the curve and spread or variation would depend on the characteristics of the particular supervisor, the level of persons being supervised, and the type of work performed. Thus, rather than a specific number of persons that can be supervised, the arrangement of work content and number and kind of decisions will have a direct bearing on the

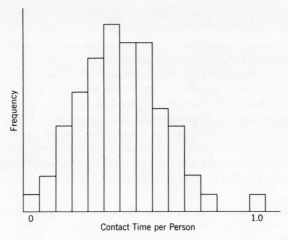

Figure VI-B-6. Distribution of Time Supervisor Spent with Personnel.

problem. Since the supervisor is a decision processor, an economic
span of control could be determined as in Figure VI-B-7. If the supervisor were always available (no subordinates), there would be a

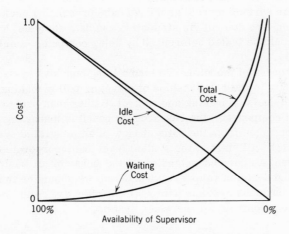

Figure VI-B-7. Economic Span of Control.

high idle cost; however, if there were too many subordinates, decisions
could be held up due to the supervisor being unavailable. This would
lead to a high waiting cost. Taking the systems viewpoint, the correct span of control would consider the cost of delays in decisions
on the entire business. Since the waiting or queuing effect increases

exponentially, it appears that there is an optimum availability of the supervisor which can be related to the span of control.

Thus, detail considerations of business systems behavior are necessary adjuncts to studying management controls. This becomes especially important where control is considered the means of assuring compliance with desired system behavior. Rather than establishing arbitrary bases for component control such as fixed budgets, turnover ratios, return on investment, etc., optimum total system performance should be the objective. Optimum system performance can be defined in terms of the resources available, specified goals, allowable risks, and environmental factors. In essence, the systems approach results in a joint optimization of the many facets of a business.

CONCLUSION

Research in management controls poses many challenging problems and offers many promising rewards. Decision rules which formalize the actions to be taken for specified conditions should improve control through predictability of response. The computer, rather than serving merely as a huge data-processing device, can be used for on-line control via simulation and data analysis. New system designs could be tested beforehand by using computer simulation as the vehicle.

The process of modeling and formalizing business systems should bring clarity to the relationships of planning, policy making, and objectives to decision making and control. Rather than study control of system components, the research proposed in management controls will be conducted from the point of view of an integrated system. Thus, the research will start at the system level and incorporate components as required. As our understanding of the behavior of business improves, and decision rules are formalized, we should be in a position to design business systems with realistic objectives and improved management controls for the whole system.

REFERENCES

1. H. A. Simon, On the Application of Servomechanism Theory in the Study of Production Control, P-234, The RAND Corporation, August 15, 1951.
2. M. E. Salveson, "Organization Planning for Integrated Decision Making," Management Report No. 1, Center for Advanced Management, New Canaan, Connecticut, 1957.
3. George J. Feeney, "A Basis for Strategic Decisions on Inventory Control Operations," Management Science, Vol. 2, pp. 69-82 (October, 1955).

4. Peter F. Drucker, The Practice of Management (Harper and Brothers, New York, 1954, p. 7.
5. Jay W. Forrester, "Industrial Dynamics; a Major Breakthrough for Decision Makers," Harvard Business Review, Vol. 36, pp. 37-66 (July-August, 1958).
6. Peter F. Drucker, "Long-Range Planning," Management Science, Vol. 5, pp. 238-249 (April, 1959).
7. George W. Brown, "Monte Carlo Methods," Chapter 12 in Modern Mathematics for the Engineer, edited by Edwin F. Beckenbach, McGraw-Hill Book Co., New York, 1956.
8. D. G. Malcolm, "Queueing Theory in Organization Design," Journal of Industrial Engineering, Vol. 6, pp. 19-26 (November-December, 1955).
9. A. J. Rowe, "Toward a Theory of Scheduling," to be published in The Proceedings of the Western Data Processing Center Dedication Symposium, University of California Press, 1960.

DISCUSSION (Following Dr. Rowe's presentation of his paper)

A. R. BROWN: I hope that in your model building you will be thinking of the ignorance factor (or noise), which is a very difficult thing to assess at times.

A. J. ROWE: One could test the sensitivity of the system to noise. One way would be to start with exact information and see how the system responds, then superimpose various kinds of noise and see what happens to the system.

J. F. LUBIN: It might better be called "silence."

A. J. ROWE: There are two characteristics of system response in the modeling. One is innovation, and the other is malfunctioning. We ask: "Is it possible to predict response, even where there are formalized decision criteria? Can you tell what a decision maker will do?" This research should permit sampling from many distributions of possible responses.

C. K. SIMON: In your talk you inquired about how the rule of exception is limited by the manager. I wonder if the procedure of only dealing with the exception causes the reduction in the time needed for the routine job of management? Will there be time left over for reviewing data from the system, from normal reports, and from senior supervisors? The system itself will solve this problem. You don't have to worry about the manager limiting himself solely to the exception. If he does, he should not be a manager.

A. J. ROWE: That is a good point. I meant only to imply that in some instances exceptions are just as bad as too much information. These are two extremes.

C. K. SIMON: Not if you eliminate the inferior supervisor and let a more competent one have more responsibility.

A. J. ROWE: Under certain circumstances it is not enough to know that everything is all right. You may want to know details of an activity. For example, it might not be sufficient to know that people are working. You may have to supplement this with other information such as skill categories that are available.

C. K. SIMON: Which is done first? Probably, the exception first, and then we apply the balance of our time to other important management problems.

A. J. ROWE: It is dependent upon what information is appropriate, and that should be based on decision criteria. There are times when you have to have detailed information. For example, at budget time you might want information you don't need at other times. Well, the exception principle just wouldn't apply in that case. The exception principle is a good general rule. However, we need rules that respond and change with time.

C. K. SIMON: I think you have proven that we still have to describe the rule of exception a lot better than any of us has done to date.

W. E. ALBERTS: In the research program, you might consider simulating the exchange of information between engineering and sales in any company, regardless of what they are making. This is a universal language even though the words are different.

A. J. ROWE: When studying a real organization this information should be readily available.

J. F. LUBIN: A problem that is often discussed is the inadequate theoretical foundation on which the technique of simulation is built. Also, it is usually not certain whether the results of a particular simulation represent the transient or steady state. Will these difficulties hinder your research?

A. J. ROWE: I do not think so. One of the things we can bring to bear on this problem is considerable simulation experience. Certainly, SDC has had a lot of this kind of experience.

A. SCHULTZ: I can point to a number of simulations that have been run, in our opinion, a hundred times as long as they needed to be run, because the people didn't understand the technique and didn't have at their command the mathematics and statistics and the abilities that are needed in order to properly design their experiments.

W. E. ALBERTS: I think this is a question of distribution of available information and know-how.

A. SCHULTZ: You have distributed your results, and have indicated satisfaction because the final result of your simulation is in agreement with the real world. Perhaps your simulation was one hundred times as complete as it needed to be.

M. O. KAPPLER: From my viewpoint, I am sure I would agree that tools for simulation are not in as good shape as we would hope; but I am not terribly pessimistic about this. We do have a reasonable representation of the necessary skills available here at SDC. Our experience with simulation for design and for training in military situations taught us that it is vitally necessary to have people that can make professional judgments about the adequacy of the simulation. Mathematical tools are needed to show how complete the simulation has to be or how many runs must be made; however, to determine utility, the best tool we have is professional judgment, and we are pretty well equipped with that here.

R. H. GREGORY: I wonder what was meant by "effectiveness" as used in one of your illustrations. I have struggled with the notion of effectiveness for a number of years and have concluded that we probably need to divide it into two components: the cost of processing data and the value of information produced. I would like to know with what success you have been able to measure and combine the two components.

A. J. ROWE: I tried to represent a means of evaluating the effect of speed of response on the system performance using a scale of effectiveness. It undoubtedly is a combination of cost, timeliness, utility, and other factors. What I was suggesting was that we need a quantifiable base on which to compare alternate systems.

R. H. GREGORY: First, I am disturbed that you have used net effectiveness because the behavior of the cost of processing and the value of results can be quite different. For instance, if you cut the reporting interval in half, processing costs may nearly double. Furthermore, you can easily overload the decision-making capacity of management. People can not effectively use an excessive volume of reports. On the other hand, reducing the delay in preparing reports reduces the time period in which any mistakes are continued without being corrected. Within limits, shortening the reporting interval may help, but shortening the interval too much may make the net effect worse. Shortening the reporting delay is generally beneficial. But considered together, the value of results may go up slightly while costs increase phenomenally to reduce the net effectiveness.

A. J. ROWE: You may have noticed on the chart* that effectiveness decreased after speed of system response increased beyond a given point. It may be necessary, therefore, to express value in terms of a cost function so that where one cost decreases and the other increases an optimal cost can be found.

R. H. GREGORY: The other point that has disturbed me a long while is the interchangeable use of "data" and "information." Do you differentiate between the two? Would you care to define them?

A. J. ROWE: I may be able to clarify the difference by referring to an example. Knowing that part number XYZ is in some stage of completion, I would consider information rather than data.

R. H. GREGORY: I will describe my thoughts in a workable definition. "Data" means raw facts, all the observations you care to make, the whole file. From the data available, those parts that meet certain criteria, such as timeliness, unusualness, and relevance (and relevance hasn't been touched upon here), we select a set of data which I prefer to call "information." Perhaps you prefer merely to call it a subset of the data that is timely, has worthiness, or is relevant to a situation.

A. J. ROWE: I would like to characterize information in relationship to the action to be taken, and I think that is how you have characterized it. In some cases it might be the raw data itself. In other cases it might be summarization of data, but the criterion is that it be the basis for action. Isn't that what you would say?

R. H. GREGORY: I am tempted to consider the element of further usage, but one encounters the definitional problem similar to the physicist's question: Can there be noise in the desert but no sound because no one heard it? You say information exists only if the data are used.

A. J. ROWE: I am not saying one actually has to take action, but I am saying information is what is needed to take action.

R. H. GREGORY: Your definitions are quite particular to the environment; there is information to the extent there is a decision maker that could make use of it. What if that decision maker does not exist?

A. J. ROWE: Well then, I would not call it information.

---

*Figure VI-B-5.

R. H. GREGORY: I concede, definitions are not right and wrong; they are just useful in a context. Another point: little has been said about accuracy and precision. I think you slighted these aspects by calling the lack of something noise, and John Lubin put it nicely that it may be silence. This may be the best situation; just tell the recipient nothing.

A. J. ROWE: One way of treating this problem is to establish the number of levels through which the information must pass. The more levels you have, the more people the information or data would have to flow through. I think it is a well-known fact that distortion enters as information is transmitted further and further. What we have to do is to look at information in relation to the number of channels it has to flow through (the number of decision makers and decision points, etc.). This is the kind of consideration we would hope to take into account. As a matter of fact, it is this kind of consideration which leads me to believe that we cannot do this research in a closet. We will have to go out and talk to people. Then, we may be able to work on the problem for a while. Then we should go out and talk to some more people.

R. L. SISSON: It seems that one of the key things in systems analysis is how to define what the system is. The usual method consists of setting arbitrary boundaries, and assuming that outside of these we will assume certain things exist and we will only work on the problems inside. What is your system? Your topic is business management control systems, and yet the impression you give from this talk is that you are going to model and experiment with the whole business. For instance, if you study a manufacturing business, I have the impression that you will not model the process of cutting a metal, but just take the data from that process and feed that into the system. On the other hand, an insurance company only processes information. It is not as clear where to make the distinction between that part of the system which is a "management control system" and that part which is the operations or the activities. It is all an information process. Part of the job is to define the area of study. Rather than trying to solve all business problems, it appears preferable to study "management control system" or "management information system" problems.

A. J. ROWE: This is a perfectly valid observation. One could easily get swamped. This is one of the reasons why it makes good sense to keep reviewing plans with other people to make sure research doesn't get off on tangents.

D. G. MALCOLM: A general question involved here is: How much detail is it necessary to have in order to get an adequate simulation? This will be a fundamental part of the research, for it is essential that the model be realistic and adequate if any valid inferences are to be made. On the question of optimization, I have never seen any operations research study that optimized anything. They are all sub-optimal, in one sense, if you go to a high enough frame of reference. The kind of approach that Warren Alberts was talking about in his simulation activities was merely to provide a method of expressing the "operating characteristics" of the system. This dodges the question of building the optimizing criteria into the model. In a simulation model one hopes to arrive at the best balance of these operating characteristics to achieve many different kinds of objectives, only some of which will be direct dollar cost. We have only begun to appreciate the possibilities of such types of system modeling and experimentation. Since there will be a heavy sociological flavor in all of this, I suspect we will never design a truly optimal system with only a mathematical view. Design will have to be adjudicated by some broader standards. How you bring the broader judgments to bear in regard to the simulation effort is going to be an interesting thing in itself. We will probably have to make some assumptions initially and then have it reviewed.

A. J. ROWE: Essentially, this is the way I view research in this area. To start with, an initial model which might be quite aggregate could be used to explore how best to elaborate the model and proceed. The initial model would not include all possible aspects of a business that could be conceived or designed.

W. R. FAIR: The point that Don Malcolm made about everything being suboptimized and the one that Bob Gregory raised about a measure of effectiveness raises a significant question. It is the drum that has been beaten rather hard by Herbert Simon, namely the place of multi-dimensional utility measures as something that we are forced to, and the fact that it is now about time that we gave up the notion of a single dimension. To me, this is probably the most significant idea recently proposed, be it right or wrong. It is not yet clear that it is right. I personally think it is because I spent several months going up a blind alley on the opposite presumption. But this whole question of values is beneath much of what we have had to say. This is worthy of some consideration, and it has had none.

A. J. ROWE: I was confronted with precisely this problem in a job shop scheduling simulation study. There were four measures that we used for evaluating the simulation. One measure was the distribution of job completions, rather than a single value such as percentage of promises met. We used the cost of work-in-process inventory. We had the percentage of utilized capacity and the percentage of idle man hours. We didn't attempt to arrive at a single combination of this multi-dimensional value. Whether this is possible, desirable, or achievable I don't really know; but I think to some extent the fact that you can demonstrate that it is multi-dimensional rather than a single dimension is at least a step forward. It is an extremely difficult problem to combine these into some new single dimension which is a combination of all the factors.

W. R. FAIR: My point goes one step beyond the establishing of multi-dimensional measures. If Simon is right, and I think he is, there is an enormous obstacle to be overcome before we are going to get anywhere; and simply because this notion is so far from the current thinking of 99 per cent of all people in the business world. This implies a total re-educational process and one that won't occur in a short time. The number of factors tied to profit in a most loose, inconsistent, and contradictory way is staggering.

A. J. ROWE: I agree with you that there is a real educational problem.

C. K. SIMON: There is no model of a business corporation today simply because we have never created a model. I believe a model can be created if we are willing to standardize. While standardization can be a media for creating the model, a tremendous amount of work is involved in standardization. Consider labor control. You would think that building a model to include the control of labor in all business firms would be a difficult task. But if you take a basic book on the subject of Methods-Time-Measurement your model need not use the more vague and common terms, but rather can deal with labor control only in terms of MTM. This could resolve the problem of labor control in your model. If you then convert this labor data into workable digital data, labor control via the computer becomes practical. I haven't seen the details of what General Electric has done but I feel it must be along this line. If we can discover how to standardize each of the other factors of management, we may end up with a model, even though doing so now appears to be a difficult task.

H. O. DAVIDSON: If you are willing to make this degree of abstraction, certainly you can build a model.

C. K. SIMON: The model would possibly have a more limited application than an ideal model.

H. O. DAVIDSON: I think characterizing all of labor just in terms of Methods-Time-Measurement is not suitable for modeling.

C. K. SIMON: I have used MTM only as an example and because it is generally understood. The MTM basic element can be understood and built into labor control. Therefore, if we can develop appropriate elements for management, we can then choose those elements and summarize them, and we may have a solution to the problem of building a model.

M. O. KAPPLER: I want to defend this approach, based on what happened in the weapons assignment function of SAGE. The criterion function initially written for machine assistance was not really adequate, but it started a lot of people thinking about the problem, especially the people who had to use the method. As time went on they thought of other things that could be quantified or stated in a different way, which has led to more sophisticated weapon assignment aids furnished by the computer. The lesson one can learn is to use whatever is available and work with it until a better method is found.

R. H. GREGORY: In spite of all the experience in management controls with the military, there still seems to be a problem as to how best to conduct research in this field. Furthermore, I am not certain that all managerial systems will be more efficient because they are better organized and involve more equipment. There may be more economical methods. It is possible that model building itself may not be done most efficiently by large-scale, highly organized methods.

W. E. ALBERTS: You mean that there must be a simpler way?

R. H. GREGORY: There is possibly a simpler way. We seem to rely on the presumption that more mechanistic ways are always much more economical. Possibly they aren't.

A. J. ROWE: It is more than just economics; feasibility is also involved.

M. O. KAPPLER: Our initial efforts in air defense were based on a manual system; then, we went to SAGE. Even though SAGE may not be more economical for the job, the manual system never could do the job that the SAGE system is designed to do. Therefore, a valuable comparison can't be made. Also, if you tried to expand the manual system to do the greater volume job that SAGE does, it would probably mean having an Air Force five times as large as the one we have, which would make the cost prohibitive.

R. H. GREGORY: Is it fair to extrapolate from this that the highly mechanistic system would be generally superior.

A. W. RATHE: I think this is one of the possibilities, not that the conclusion has already been reached.

D. G. MALCOLM: I thought we just agreed with Bill Fair that there were other values involved besides the mechanistic efficiency. The value of time, for example, in obtaining the information necessary in the control function is something to be considered.

*M*anagement control simulation

CHAPTER **C** by JOEL M. KIBBEE

INTRODUCTION

Simulation is one technique for the study of management control systems, whether of their design and evaluation or in the search for fundamental principles. That aspect of the general research approach with which we shall be concerned here is the simulation model. We shall begin with some comments on the type of simulation to be undertaken, shall describe certain "business games" which are related to such simulation, and conclude with a proposal for a preliminary model.

The term "simulation" has been applied to a variety of situations: a model of an airplane in a wind tunnel, a pilot in a Link Trainer, the simulated environment and inputs used in the SAGE System Training Program, research into the design of a bus terminal by the Port of New York Authority. Some authors have used the word "simulation" as a synonym for the Monte Carlo method. In its broadest sense any construction of a model, physical or symbolic, might be called simulation. Let us introduce the term "symbolic system simulation" for the type of experimentation to be discussed here. This has also been referred to as "analytic simulation," "computer simulation," and just "simulation."

SYMBOLIC SYSTEM SIMULATION

Symbolic System Simulation can be best illustrated by an example. Consider a retail store which handles one product, sells it daily to customers, and carries an inventory which may be replenished by orders placed at a factory. At the beginning of any day there is a particular quantity of stock on hand; during the day this is increased by deliveries from the factory and decreased by sales. When the stock is not sufficient to meet the customer demand there are stockouts, and the sales are less than the demand.

We may build a mathematical model of the above system: the inputs are the customer demand and the deliveries from the factory, the output is the number of sales, and the state of the system at the end of any day is the quantity of stock on hand. Suppose we are given the state of the system on day 1, i.e., the stock on hand, as well as the customer demand and the factory deliveries for each day for one month and that we want to know the total sales, the total stockouts, and the state of the system on day 30. If we knew that the inventory had always been sufficiently large to meet demand, and thus that there were no stockouts, the stock on hand on day 30 would be simply the stock on hand on day 1 plus the total deliveries minus the total demand. But in general there is no simple analytic expression relating the state of the system on day 30 to the state on day 1, nor for computing the total sales, and it is necessary to perform thirty computations, albeit simple ones, representing a day by day stepping through of the model.

Symbol System Simulation is thus characterized by the construction of a mathematical model of a real system—mathematical, meaning to include both logical and algebraic operations—and the "running" of it through a sequence of time intervals. Building mathematical models of real systems is a fairly common technique, and the behavior of such models is often investigated by analytic techniques. It becomes simulation, at least in our sense here, when the current state can be computed from the initial state only by stepping through all intermediate states.

Symbolic System Simulation is exemplified by such studies as United Air Lines Airport Model, the Port of New York Authority's Bus Terminal Model, and General Electric's Job Shop Scheduling Model. The mathematical model is nearly always programmed for a computer, the usual reason being that computations are generally too lengthy to be done by hand. However, worthwhile simulations have been performed without using a computer. Most real systems which one is likely to study will contain stochastic elements but stochastic elements are not necessarily a part of every simulation. In job shop scheduling if one begins with a known set of orders, rather than a sequence of random ones, there still may be difficult combinatorial problems, and such problems have been attacked through simulation.

Symbolic System Simulation has a variety of applications. As a research tool to search for optimal procedures, simulation of petroleum refineries has been particularly successful, and this is now a generally accepted technique. Other applications have been in such areas as production planning and control, distribution, transportation, and more recently in marketing and finance. It can be used as a management aid, helping a manager to select among several alternative decisions. When computers are placed "on-line" one can imagine operating decisions being quickly tried out, through simulation, before their implementation.

Symbolic System Simulation can be used in the design and evaluation of systems. It can be used for testing out a system before implementation, with the mildly paradoxical situation of modeling a "real" system before it exists. It can also be used as a research tool for discovering general principles of system design.

It is conceptually useful to think of a Symbolic System Simulation as a black box with certain dials and meters. For the moment let us place a man in front of the box. (Figure VI-C-1.) He sets the dials,

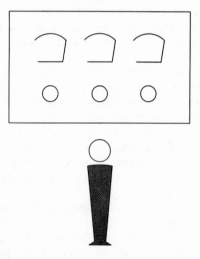

Figure VI-C-1. A Man and a Model.

the box purrs, and results appear on the meters. He observes the results, perhaps records them, sets the dials to new positions, and the cycle repeats. Normally the procedure would be carried out by a

separate program within the computer, instead of by the man. This
program would cause the model to be stepped through a sequence of
time intervals, with relevant data being printed out, and then certain
changes would be made in the parameters, and the model would again
be stepped through a sequence of time intervals, etc.

Let us return to the man in front of the black box; perhaps a research worker is interested in studying the man's behavior. The human subject moves the dials, reads the meters, etc., and the research
worker observes this through the usual one-way glass windows. For
the research worker the model is no longer just the black box, it is
the man and black box. When humans are included in the model we
shall use the term "Human System Simulation." With several human subjects and several black boxes we have the type of simulation
of the SAGE System Training Program, and also of the RAND Logistics Simulation Laboratory, though this is an oversimplified description: the black box is a bit more fuzzy, beginning to surround the man,
and there are questions about simulating the environment.

Let us now assume that we construct some sort of mathematical
model of the human subject himself. The model of the man is added to
the other model inside of the black box, and the research worker is
now twisting the dials on this new box attempting to learn something
about the man-machine behavior without using a real man. Let us
ignore for now the question as to whether we can usefully construct
an adequate model to the man. What we have done is return to a Symbolic System Simulation. Most models used in Symbolic System Simulation do contain factors associated with human behavior. For
example, in studying business problems one may introduce price-
demand curves, as an aggregate model of customer behavior, instead
of using human subjects who, provided with the various prices, feed
back to the model their decisions to buy or not.

Let us turn now to Figure VI-C-2. In (a) we have one man experi-

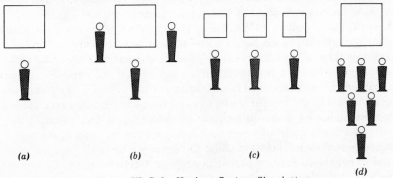

(a)   (b)   (c)

                                                          (d)

Figure VI-C-2. Various System Simulation

menting with a model. In (b) we have several men experimenting with the same model and in competitive interaction with one another. This is perhaps a model of several salesmen competing for a common customer. In (c) we also have a competitive situation, but without interaction between the men. This would be a case in which the men faced identical tasks and compared their performance. The first type of competition, characterized by interaction, is analogous to tennis; the second type is analogous to golf. Instead of one man, we might have a group of men, as in (d), each with their own dials to set, but working towards a common goal. And of course in (b) and (c) we could also replace each man by a team of men. In order to study management control systems one would be most interested in the situation represented by (d). To study a business management situation it would be necessary to include the concept of intercompany competition, but most likely one would do this through mathematical models within the box rather than by adding additional teams.

BUSINESS GAMES

Simulation has extensive use today as a training technique, and in particular there has been considerable publicity about its use in what are usually called "business games" or "management games," or, in order to avoid certain unfavorable misinterpretations of the word "game," are frequently called "simulation exercises." A business game involves humans using Symbolic System Simulation, in one of the forms illustrated in Figure VI-C-2; the model is of a business, or some part of a business, and the objective is training.

The first business game was introduced by the American Management Association, being initially demonstrated in December, 1956, in Los Angeles. This game is usually referred to as the AMA Game, though it would be more properly called the AMA Executive Decision Making Simulation, as AMA has since constructed, and has in use, several other games. UCLA, IBM, The Pillsbury Company, and many other organizations are using quite similar games. This particular set of games is characterized by several companies competing in a common market, each manufacturing and selling one product, and with decisions being concerned mainly with selling price, advertising, production level, and the purchase of capital equipment. However games, like automobiles, undergo frequent model changes, and a variety of other business elements such as credit, dividends, stocks, the ability to purchase information about the economy or one's competitors and to engage in market research are now fairly common. Games may be modeled after a complete business, or after some particular component such as production planning and control. They also may be specialized to a particular type of organization such as banking, public utilities, supermarkets, or the detergent industry. We have recently seen such specialized games as SMART, for systems and procedures management, and STEPS, for computer programmer management.

The pedagogical intent of the various games may differ greatly: practicing decision making, improving analytic ability, learning to learn from experience, gaining an appreciation for particular business problems. Of more importance to our present discussion is their use in exemplifying certain general management principles in the areas of organization theory, planning, communications, control, and human relations. It is possible that certain management principles could be evidenced by having the participants play football. Perhaps going out for the team should be a requisite in business administration colleges: as English leaders are developed on the playing fields of Eton, corporation presidents would be developed on the playing fields of Harvard Business School. There are, however, some fairly obvious advantages in providing a business model for business executives.

There are some important relationships between business games and Symbolic System Simulation. Executives playing a business game provide a ready-made laboratory for studying management problems, though very little work has so far been done along this line. Existing games can, at least, offer guidance to the research worker. Modeling techniques are quite similar whether one is interested in training or research. Furthermore, a few Symbolic System Simulations undertaken for problem-solving purposes have been models of a complete business organization, and certain business games now existing can serve as a preliminary step—one is tempted to speak of a model of a model.

Any business game could be used for some form of research; the obverse of the coin is that any simulation could be used for training. This has actually been done in several cases, such as in job shop scheduling, where, though the model was primarily designed to search for and evaluate decision rules, it can also provide training for operating production people. A simulation, used as a game, can serve as an orientation device. One can perhaps more easily evoke critical feedback by allowing someone to play with the model than by having him listen to an exposition about it.

USE OF SIMULATION FOR RESEARCH

In order to do research on management control systems one would want a simulation represented by item (d) in Figure VI-C-2. Until recently, most business games, while perhaps complex in concept, were at least simple in the playing details; optimum size teams were usually five or less. One could obviously have allowed ten people to work as a sort of executive committee—such large teams have been used—but this represented a type of cooperative decision making and the individuals did not each have detailed tasks to perform. If one is interested in a management system, as distinct from the behavior of one manager, then one must provide for quite a few tasks and quite a few decisions, so that an organization structure is a necessity, and so that information networks must be established, authority delegated, and so forth. In most organizations it is not a question of whether the chief executive wants to make all of the decisions, or whether he is capable of making the best decisions, but that it is impossible for him to make all of the decisions that have to be made.

There are games today which do have an increased complexity—complexity from the standpoint of the number of details that have to be considered by the participants rather than by the extent of the sophistication of any one element. We shall consider three of these games here: The TASK Manufacturing Corporation, a new game under development at UCLA, and reported on in this book* by Clay Sprowls and Morris Asimow; the Carnegie Tech Management Game, for which complete details have been published; and the AMA General Management Simulation, which will be discussed more fully below.

The new UCLA game is an extremely ambitious project. The model will comprise a great amount of detail, but also considerable flexibility. One type of flexibility is the possibility of having certain operations controlled by computerized decision rules or policies, or, instead, the possibility of breaking into the system, as it were, and allowing human beings to take various managerial roles. The model is being designed as a tool for both research and training. The model will certainly be able to accommodate quite a few human managers and as such can be used for studies on management control system problems. In addition, because of its modular structure, control system research can be performed completely within the computer through changes in interconnections between the modules, changes in decision rules, and so forth.

The Carnegie Tech Management Game was also an ambitious undertaking. It was designed to allow participants to exercise habits of thought and analysis rather than to give practice in rapid decision making. It is very complex and can accommodate, typically, a team of say nine participants, and each would be kept adequately busy. The

---

*Section VI, Chapter D.

model is patterned after the detergent industry, has extensive submodels of the production, marketing, and financial functions, allows
for introduction of new products and for removing them from the
market if they prove unsuccessful. The model is designed so that it
can accommodate either several teams acting as separate companies and competing in a common market, or one team, still in a
competitive market, but with competitors programmed in the computer. Part of the research plan is to attempt to replicate—i.e.,
mathematically model—some of the decision processes of the participants. One would expect research results in the general area of management control systems as well as in other areas.

THE USE OF SIMULATION FOR TRAINING

The General Management Simulation, henceforth referred to as
GMS, is currently being used as the basis of the fourth week—called
"Management in Action"—of the four-week management course conducted by the American Management Association. This particular
unit of the course was introduced in January, 1959, and since then has
been given a little more often than once a month, with, on the average
about sixty business executives participating. The unit is held at the
AMA Academy at Saranac Lake, New York, and the IBM 650 installed
there is utilized for the computations. GMS was expressly designed to
exemplify certain general principles in the areas of organization theory, communications, control, and human relations. It was designed
to teach management principles rather than business principles. Considerable design effort was directed, in fact, towards the de-emphasis
of such things as the relationship between price and demand, and other
quantitative factors. The task is one of running a business represented
by the mathematical model within the computer, but the emphasis is
not on the task as such, not on the profit attained, but on the management problems associated with the task, and on the human interrelations that result.

The simulation takes place in quarters, with decisions being made
at the beginning of quarters, and operating reports, prepared by the
computer, distributed at the end of quarters. A history of the company is provided to the participants before they arrive at the Academy, together with the most current quarterly reports. A typical
history states how the company started—in a Circleville, Ohio, gar-
age in 1935—and how it grew, expanded to new areas, improved its
products, and so forth. Today the hypothetical company manufactures
and markets a "Gopher" and a "Midgit," and may develop additional
products. Some reality is given to these products with regard to their

general nature, but they are not identified with any particular industry.

The model is somewhat intermediate in size between the first generation aggregated games and the more complex UCLA and Carnegie Tech games. The simulated company has plants, sales regions, and a home office. It markets several products, some of which may be developed during the play through a research and development program. There are the usual problems of production scheduling, marketing policies (i.e., pricing, advertising, the number of salesmen to employ and what to pay them), purchasing, shipping, finance, and so forth. Altogether there are about seventy decisions which can be made for each quarter.

USE OF THE GMS IN ORGANIZATIONAL TRAINING

The accounting system has been specially designed to allow for a flexibility in the management organization structure. An average costing system of inventory evaluation is used, and all manufacturing costs, raw material costs, and corporate overhead costs find their way out to the sales regions so that individual profit and loss statements can be prepared for any product or any region. As such it permits a company to organize by product line, or by geographic location, or by function, or by any combination.

The GMS requires about fifteen participants to adequately operate one company—the complexity of the model and the pace of the decision periods were designed for about this level of participation. Many companies can be in operation simultaneously, each facing similar problems. There is no interaction between them. On the average, one year is simulated in a couple of hours, many "years" of operations taking place during the week. A method of job rotation has been introduced and each participant gets the opportunity to fill various positions.

It would be pleasant to discourse at length on the various noncomputer aspects of the week at AMA; however, from the standpoint of training, the mathematical model (which was the author's primary responsibility when with the American Management Association) is of somewhat minor importance. The model without its environment is like an outboard motor without a boat. Briefings, planning sessions, critiques, and so forth are all of considerable importance, and the manner in which they are being handled is most impressive. There are also many projects or incidents completely unassociated with the profit and loss aspects of the model. The emphasis is always on humans, not on mathematics.

In order to allow additional feedback on less quantifiable aspects of performance, an "observer" role has been created. The physical setup includes one-way glass observation booths with earphones connected to microphones in the various company offices. In addition to verbal reporting at critique sessions, the observers could influence the profit and loss directly by feeding their judgments to the computer, based on the observation of non-quantifiable elements of company performance such as stated personnel policy, which in turn can directly affect, within the computer, such items as worker or salesman effectiveness.

The GMS model seems well suited to its needs. Discussions in critique sessions, which are usually not directed by the staff, center more often around management problems and management principles than around pricing or production policies. GMS is being used solely as an aid in management training. It does provide an example of the type of laboratory that one could use for studying management control systems. A footnote to this is that GMS has been used in the AMA Systems and Procedures Course, where the participants operate the company for a few years, then engage in a project session where procedures and controls are designed, and are then implemented in an additional few years of company operations.

Most business games are run in a somewhat similar manner. The participants represent new management taking over a going concern. The first problems they face are ones of organization, planning, and setting of policies. They have to decide on particular organization structure, assign individuals to specific positions, and designate the lines of authority. This is not just a question of drawing an organization chart—there are decisions to be made and individuals have to be designated to make them. There is a need for coordination, for controls, for communications. It is gratifying that in most games disorganization leads to poor performance, even to chaos. The pedagogical objective is to give practice in the application of organization principles, not to try to demonstrate the efficiency of a particular organizational scheme.

The organization chart that does emerge will usually be of some conventional hierarchical form. There will usually be a president and vice presidents, sales manager and plant manager, manager of research and development, of personnel and purchasing, controller, and so forth. One of the principles soon apparent is that the particular organization established must be suited to the task to be performed, and not merely something that looks good when drawn up by the company's art department. There is not much use in having a manager of research and development if the model does not include research and development. This is not a failing in the model, but a reinforcement of the realization that people organize to do something, not just to be organized. Thus an executive leaves his real-life company, replete with traditions, and its own way of doing things, and is faced with a new real-life-like situation. It is an exercise in the design of a management control system.

We should note again that the majority of games being used do not require very large teams and are not as useful for demonstrating organization principles as the second generation games discussed. All games do, however, produce a variety of problems in coordination and control, an example being the conflict between sales and production. There are problems of pricing, of scheduling, etc. There is a need to coordinate the hiring and training of manpower with company long-range objectives. There is the ever-present problem of cash flow. In every decision that is made there is a need for coordination and control.

Most games produce a large quantity of information in the form of reports and there are questions as to who gets what reports. In the newer games the information content can be as perplexing as in real life, and thus can be used to exercise the participants' system design abilities. Furthermore the games are dynamic, with new situations arising, perhaps the introduction of new products; and from time to time—just as in real life—management may decide to reorganize, or to overhaul the system.

We have then, in present-day business games, laboratories which could be used for research into management control principles. A great amount of data has been generated; however, nearly all games are being used almost exclusively for training purposes, and no research has been published. This situation will no doubt be altered for the Carnegie Tech and UCLA games.

MANAGEMENT CONTROL SYSTEM SIMULATION

Using business games as a laboratory for research into management control principles would be an example of what has previously been called Human System Simulation. This is also related to the type of work that has been done, or is being done, by such people as Bavelas, Guetzkow, Christie, Ackoff, and others through the observation of small task performing groups. In such work the groups are usually small, the tasks simple, and the experimental conditions well controlled—even here experimental design is a severe challenge. Controlled experimentation using business games with ten to twenty participants poses formidable problems. The amount of data to be collected and analyzed is in itself staggering.

The advantages and disadvantages of using human beings in the study of human behavior have often been discussed. An alternate approach is the construction of a completely computerized model. Experimenting with numbers inside a computer rather than human subjects inside a room offers many inducements, such as ease of control, reproducibility of results, and above all, the immense increase in speed. In the AMA GMS, a typical decision cycle would be about thirty minutes, with about twenty minutes spent on making decisions, and about ten minutes spent on processing them. Of this ten minutes only about two minutes are devoted to internal processing within the computer, the total ten minutes representing the interval from collection of decisions to distribution of reports. Thus, even with the comparatively slow speed of an IBM 650, the computer could run through several simulated years of operations while the humans are planning their decisions for just one quarter.

The primary challenge to a Symbolic System Simulation is the inclusion into the computer of certain aspects of human behavior. However, to study organization, communications, and control problems, one is not interested in individual behavior in its idiosyncratic sense, but in over-all sociological behavior. Certain individual characteristics can be included—e.g., the rate at which decisions can be made—and one might even develop managerial types, analogous to social types; but one would ignore the particular image—syndromes, neurotic or otherwise—and the myriad of interpersonal relationships which we know greatly affect real-life situations. It is hoped that there are fundamental management principles which are independent, except in unusual circumstances, of the particular personalities involved.

The social sciences offer a sufficient number of abstractions and generalizations that have been drawn in spite of the variety of the individual man. The search for general principles to guide the design of management control systems is too important to be put aside simply because of the difficulty of computerizing those aspects of the system that arise from human behavior. Furthermore, as machines continue their invasion into the field of decision making, the value of such an approach will increase.

A PRELIMINARY MODEL

As a first approach to the design of a Symbolic System Simulation to be used for research on management control systems it is helpful to make some arbitrary separations within the over-all model. We begin (see Figure VI-C-3) by assuming that within the total black box there are three smaller black boxes, which we shall label "control," "operations," and "environment." Each of these is a subsystem of the total system.

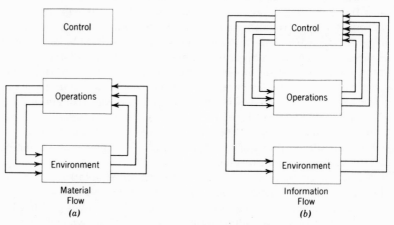

Figure VI-C-3. Separations within the Total Model.

The operations subsystem is essentially a physical mechanism for performing a task. It could consist of business, military, or government organizations. As an example, let us think of a manufacturing organization. The operations subsystem would represent the flow of material, men, and money, which we might generalize here by the single term "material flow." The task is to take raw material, capital equipment, men, and money and to produce products and distribute them to the customers. It would be something similar to the UCLA, Carnegie Tech and AMA second generation game models already discussed.

The control subsystem is the management control function, being made up primarily of decision making and information flow. We shall describe this subsystem in more detail in the next section. The environment represents those items external to the manufacturing company, such as the vendors of raw material, the customers, and the competitors, as well as the government, the over-all economy, the sources of funds, and so forth.

In Figure VI-C-3, we show first of all the separation of the over-all model into its three subsystems. We have further separated the material flow and the information flow. In item (a) we see the material—using the term in a very general sense to include such non-material items as financial credit and purchasing by consumers as well as such obvious items as raw material and labor supply—

originating within the environment, being processed by the operations subsystem, and returned as products, as well, perhaps, as several less obvious items, to the environment. In item (b) we see information originating in the environment, such as raw material costs and general economic indices, together with information originating in the operations, such as stock reports and production costs; these are communicated to the management control subsystem, which in turn uses this information to arrive at certain decisions such as level of production, as well as certain information which may be thought of as being supplied to the environment, such as the sales price, which are communicated to the operations subsystem.

Before examining the inside structure of the various boxes shown in Figure VI-C-3 it is necessary to point out that in any model there can be various levels of detail, or of aggregation. As an example, consider customer demand. For certain questions it is adequate to provide, as input, random customer demands generated within the computer. In other cases one might wish to tie the demand to the company policies through somewhat aggregated functions, such as a price-demand curve, an advertising-demand curve, and so forth; this is essentially the method used in the AMA's General Management Simulation. In certain competitive-type business games an individual company's demands are dependent on the behavior of the other competing companies. In the UCLA TASK Manufacturing Company, detailed models—such as the "customer image"—have been constructed. If one is mainly interested in marketing problems then perhaps one has need for more details in the models of customers and competitors. If one is interested in inventory control, a simple aggregated demand function should prove adequate. The most desirable procedure is a modular one, where at the outset certain aggregated submodels are used, but when the need arises, they can be replaced by more detailed models.

In looking at management control systems, at least in those aspects which are mainly associated with the internal flow of information, and with internal controls, one would want the control subsystem to be quite detailed, the operations subsystem only moderately detailed, and the environment least detailed. This suggestion is predicated on certain types of research questions. If the main problem in the control system is one of coordinating the needs of the marketing and production functions, in such things as setting and implementing an inventory control policy, then a quite aggregated model of the national economy is adequate. If the control system is mainly concerned with pricing, long-range capital investment, or research and development, the model of the national economy would have to be more detailed. The same is true of the operations subsystem. It needs to be sufficiently complex to provide the control subsystem with realistic control problems, but it need not be so detailed as would be necessary, for instance, if one were studying job shop scheduling problems.

In a preliminary model the environment would provide merely some over-all economic factor which, coupled with a set of curves for price, advertising, and perhaps research and development, would yield a customer demand for each product. A price-demand curve implies both the behavior of the consumers and the existence of competitors; the curve can also change with time, representing, for example, price changes on the part of the competitors. The environment would also supply such items as the cost of raw material, the size of the labor market, etc.

An adequate operations subsystem might be that shown in Figure VI-C-4. This represents a manufacturing organization which pro-

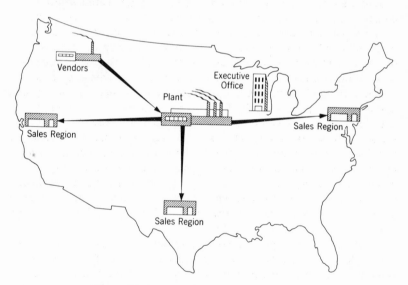

Figure VI-C-4. An Operations Subsystem.

duces and markets several products. In the particular model there would be one plant, and several sales regions. The products would require several raw materials, some of them shared by more than one product. The vendors would be represented by a very aggregated model (not shown in Figure VI-C-4) which would give merely the cost of the raw material, the maximum possible supply, and the time from placing an order to delivery of the material. This delivery time would be represented by a probability distribution.

The plant would have a raw material warehouse, a finished goods warehouse, and possibly, depending on the production mechanism used, one or more in-process warehouses. There is considerable variety in the type of production process that could be modeled. A simple scheme would have several production lines, each capable of handling only one product at a time, and each with its own flow rates, and so forth. Including a limited capacity, and production set-up time, the management control system would be faced with production scheduling problem. The plant would also have a work force, but perhaps only one class of workers. However, for costing purposes there could be provision for both direct and indirect labor costs, as well as supervision and management costs. Again we have an analogy here with several business games; on the other hand, the new UCLA game permits a distinct image for each individual worker, not only his capabilities, but also his desires.

Finished goods would be shipped directly from the finished goods warehouse at the plant to the warehouses in the sales regions. One would provide for perhaps a normal and expedited method of shipment; otherwise the transportation aspects of the model would be kept simple. Even the most simple model engenders adequate problems for the control system, there being the fundamental problem of inventory control as affected by warehouse costs, expected demand, and so forth.

In the sales regions one would have a certain number of salesmen, perhaps problems about the level of compensation, together with the usual marketing questions of price and advertising. There could be both local and national advertising; there could be local or national pricing. These are the types of problems that the management control system would face—there is not only a question of what price to set, which of course is very much tied to the environment model, but also the question of who is to set the price, when, on what basis, and how it is to be implemented.

THE MANAGEMENT CONTROL SUBSYSTEM

In Figure VI-C-5 we take a look inside the management control subsystem. The operations and environment subsystems are shown as black boxes, the remaining structure in the figure represents the inside of the box previously shown as the control subsystem. At the outset it is necessary to distinguish between the experimental variables, which represent those inputs provided by the staff research worker, and those inputs which are outputs from the other subsystems. The variables which are to be manipulated are primarily the

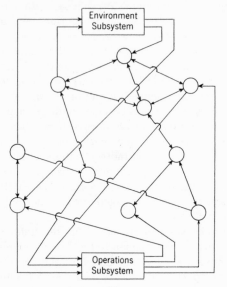

The Management Control Subsystem and a Typical Information Flow

Figure VI-C-5.

organizational structure, the information flow network, and the decision rules. Figure VI-C-5 illustrates one possible information network with a particular set of rules. The management control subsystem takes information from the other subsystems, such as customer demands, stock status, and costs, and by means of decision rules provides the operations subsystem with such information as a production schedule, shipping orders, and sales price.

Within the other subsystems, there are also parameters which can be varied, such as costs, general economic condition, etc. The experimental plan is to study a particular management control system, observe its effect on over-all system performance, of which there are many measures in addition to the most common one of profit and loss, and to also test the sensitivity of the management control system to variations in the parameters within the other subsystems. One can then experiment with some other management control system. The schematic plan shown in Figure VI-C-5 is then merely one experimental setup. The model would allow complete flexibility in the choice of an information network.

For want of a better word, the circles shown in Figure VI-C-5 will be called "nodes." A node is any point at which information is received, processed, and transmitted. A node may be a man, a machine, or it could be a group of men acting as a committee. Although many straightforward data-processing tasks are now performed by computers, it is helpful in discussing this model to take an anthropomorphic view and assume that each node represents one human being.

From the internal structure of the model, as it would be programmed on a computer, there is a great similarity between what might be called data processing on the one hand and decision making on the other. We may, at least in this preliminary model, think of a decision maker as a man who takes certain information, such as customer demands and stock on hand, and, by the use of a decision rule, arrives at what might be called new information—such as the production level—it is information to the person who is informed of the decision. Structurally this is the same as a clerk or a computer adding up a column of numbers and arriving at a total. There are, of course, some important differences between decision making and data processing; two of these, as pointed out by Roger Sisson, are the difficulty of formulating the decision rules and the search for optimum ones. But if one is provided with a set of decision rules, then, within the model, the node acts like a data processor. This is obviously true for such decision rules as an inventory reordering rule; it becomes more questionable as one looks at what might be called higher order decisions.

DECISION MAKING AND INFORMATION FLOW

In a preliminary model one might provide the management control subsystem with only those decisions which are necessary for the operations subsystem directly, such as how many units of raw material to purchase, what production level to set, and so forth. One might call these, "operations decisions." At the next higher level of complication one might allow the management ctonrol system to make decisions affecting its own operations directly, such as the decision rule at one node changing the decision rule at another node, or automatically changing the information flow network: we might call these, "procedural decisions." As one examines the types of decisions made in the real world it is obvious that the operations decisions are only a small subset of all possible ones.

If one is interested in the decision maker qua decision maker a great amount of research and effort would have to go into the attempt to model him. However, certain questions about the management control system might be investigated with even a quite simplified model of the decision-making process. For this preliminary model let us

assume that only operations decisions will be made by the management control subsystem.

Each node will have a certain amount of internal structure. A node
will have several tasks to perform, be they simple data processing or
decision making. Each of these tasks will take time and certain queuing
problems will arise. In addition there will be various random tasks
facing each node. The node will be able to communicate with other
nodes, receiving and sending information, either in the form of reports, or as specific requests. In any particular scheme the nodes will
take on the names of typical blocks in the organizational structure,
as the plant manager, the president, the shipping clerk, the controller,
the regional sales manager. The experimental scheme will consist in
the assignment of tasks—just where do shipping orders originate and
how are they implemented: perhaps the regional sales manager, based
on his information as to stock status and past sales, sends an order
directly to the shipping clerk, who immediately fills the order; perhaps the orders have to be cleared through a materials manager;
perhaps the market research manager first supplies the regional
manager with a sales forecast, or vice versa. The myriad problems
of coordination, planning, and control are fairly obvious.

Associated with every information channel there would be time
delays, costs, and random noise. There would be a choice of sending
a report by a slower and cheaper medium, or a faster but more
costly medium. The number of messages sent on a particular channel could be counted. As mentioned previously, the computer plays
two roles: one part of the program is the model itself; another part
monitors the operations and prints out that information which the
staff wishes to analyze.

SOME MODELING CONSIDERATIONS

It should be noted that the simplified picture of the management
control subsystem is a generalized one. In computer terminology it
is somewhat analogous to a program compiler. Given a particular
management organization—real or hypothetical—with its decision
rules and information pattern, one manipulates the various parameters so as to achieve the applicable model.

Simplicity is not a too-well-defined word: an algebraic expression might be simple to look at, but complex to solve, and vice versa.
A simulation model may be conceptually complex, but, as most people
who have worked in the field continually stress, simplicity in the details is essential. Computers work fast, but not instantaneously. In
designing models one is constantly faced with the problem: what to

leave in and what to leave out. If the model is ever to be successfully programmed and run on a computer it is essential that it be kept simple. Fortunately, quite complicated behavior can result from the interaction of many simple elements.

There is no a priori reason to assume that complicated questions can only be answered using a complicated model, as is evidenced by much research that has been done in the physical sciences. There are a variety of techniques for combining initial simplicity with flexibility for expansion. For example, one can program for a polynomial function but begin by using only the linear terms, later, as part of sensitivity studies, introducing quadratic and higher order terms. A business game that used a linear price-demand curve exhibited quite real behavior. Thus one need not be delayed because of difficulties, such as the precise shape of a demand curve, in representing reality. One might expect to find certain management control principles which are independent of the shape of a particular curve; one might also be able to at least demonstrate those situations in which more precise knowledge is necessary.

Similar remarks can be made about random factors. While some stochastic elements are certainly essential, this does not mean that every factor in the model need be randomized. In one business game all random effects were eliminated, but, as one participant said, "Sales still seem damn random to me." Jigsaw puzzles can be tough even when one has all of the pieces at the outset. Since computer capacity and speed are always limited one should only introduce random factors when there is a clear understanding of their relationship to the activity being studied.

Symbolic System Simulation always requires the use of some basic time interval. The choice of that time interval presents problems: if it is small it might require too much computer time to cover an adequate total period and if it is large it might mask certain of the factors in which one is interested. Consider a manufacturing organization: Does one want to use simulated hours, days, weeks, months, or years? The answer of course depends on the questions to be asked. The same model cannot be used for all problems. In the preliminary model discussed here it seems fruitful to allow the operations subsystem to run in days—that is, all sales for a particular day are aggregated—and to allow the management control system, by means of a clock arrangement attached to each node, to proceed in minutes. In this latter case it does not mean that one would cycle through several hundred minutes each day, but that task times would be given in minutes, and that the clock would then indicate whether a particular node was free for its next task.

If the operations subsystem is carried forward in days then it is obvious that certain types of problems cannot be examined with this model, problems relating to long-range planning, to capital investment, to financing. The preliminary model would then be used to examine day-to-day type problems associated mainly with the flow of material through the system. One would use a different model, in which certain quantities were now aggregated, to examine the behavior of the control system under conditions of new product introduction, long-range economic factors, and so forth. One could use one over-all model in which, through parameter changes, certain components would be aggregated or not, though this is conceptually similar to having two models. A somewhat different approach would be to allow for two types of time intervals, a short and a long, and to use the short one to perform a sort of sampling experiment for the latter. That is, the model would proceed in detail for one month, then extrapolate the results for the remainder of the year. The next year conditions may have changed—perhaps a new product has been introduced—and again a month of operations is sampled. In the approach first mentioned, one has to supply the program with separate functions, those for short time intervals and those for long; in the second approach the computer, through simulation, arrives at its own functions for the larger time interval run.

CONCLUSION

Management control problems can be studied by means of simulation, either of the Human System type, which is similar to doing research on executives playing business games, or of the Symbolic System type, for which a preliminary model has been discussed here. The Symbolic model presents many design problems, but it does avoid the complications inherent in experimentation with human subjects, and, above all, it offers the speed of modern computers.

Some scientific advances are made by starting with a particular hypothesis and designing an experiment to test it, but this is not the only approach. The existence of an adequate simulation model will help formulate the problems to be investigated, and the modeling process itself can lead to new insights. We can best conclude with a quotation from an article by Chapman, Kennedy, Newell, and Biel in the April, 1959, issue of Management Science: "A scientific investigation is not the cold-blooded, straight-forward, logical process that texts proclaim. It's an adventure. Sheer scientific excitement arises from the unexpected event, from the obvious assumption that's very wrong, from the hunch that pans out, from the sudden insight, and from the invention that covers the unanticipated procedural gap. The fact is that as organizations took form before our eyes, their struggle determined ours."

A computer simulated business firm[*]

CHAPTER **D** by R. CLAY SPROWLS and MORRIS ASIMOW [†]

The objective of developing an idealized representation of a business firm which can be programmed for a computer and then manipulated on a greatly contracted time scale is to provide the capability to simulate the real operation of the firm. The most immediate use of such a simulation is as a laboratory for teaching the elements of management and business operations in industry. The whole spectrum of business operations is treated in the simulated firm—financial controls, cost accounting, scheduling, customer relations, personnel relations, equipment maintenance and replacement, new product development, etc. The simulation can involve decision-making situations and other situations requiring operations research type of analyses. In fact, virtually all of the problems which arise in business firms can be generated in the simulated business firm. We will consider the effort expended in developing the business simulation as a worthwhile project itself even if nothing else is accomplished. We are hopeful, however, that this type of simulation will also be a powerful research tool.

_____

[*]The research reported in this chapter is supported in part by a grant from the Division of Research, The Graduate School of Business Administration, The University of California, Los Angeles.

[†]Professor of Engineering and Director of the Engineering Executive Program, The College of Engineering, The University of California, Los Angeles, California.

The simulation of the real operations of a firm may uncover information which will allow for better design, prediction of performance,
and improvement of the operations. If so, it will be a powerful tool
for pretesting some of the major decisions, policy changes, and plans
of the business firm. At best we live in a world of uncertain future.
The aim of science has always been toward lessening this uncertainty,
and if a business simulation can discriminate between good and bad
decisions, good and bad policies, or good and bad plans, it will indeed
lessen uncertainty. If it can do these things for conditions that are too
complex for direct analytical techniques, it will prove to be an inval-
uable tool.

The TASK Manufacturing Corporation is a computer-simulated
firm which utilizes the 709 data-processing machine located in the
Western Data Processing Center at UCLA. It is designed to explore
research and educational possibilities of business operations. The
name originally grew out of the initials of the two principals and their
research assistants (Tauchi, Asimow, Sprowls, and Krafts). It now
still seems most appropriate both because it implies tasks for many
students and researchers in the future and TMC may well become a
giant among simulated firms.

GENERAL CHARACTERISTICS OF TMC

The TASK Manufacturing Corporation is a small business firm. It
employs about four hundred people, two hundred engaged in direct
labor in the manufacturing process and two hundred in indirect labor.
It manufactures and sells a line of five related products with total
annual sales between 3 and 3.5 million dollars. Although the products
are not specifically named, they are thought of as building hardware-
type items which sell for around one dollar each. The sales of these
items are influenced by the seasonality of building activity and the
economists' "building cycle." In addition, each item has a life cycle
which implies a research and development function for its replacement in the product line.

The five items in the product line are manufactured in some combination of seven different manufacturing departments. Four of these
are in a machine shop—drill press, punch press, screw machine,
and spot weld—and the other three are finishing, assembly, and packaging. Only the packaging department treats all five products and no
one product uses all seven manufacturing operations. The product
flow continuously through the departments with the outputs from some
stages the inputs to others. Production is in anticipation of sales so
that items are stocked in inventory from which sales orders are

filled. This characteristic of the manufacturing process is assumed intentionally in order to avoid job shop, special order, or large and expensive equipment-type products.

Sales are made from the home office in Los Angeles, California, to customers scattered geographically over the whole United States. In each of the major cities of the Midwest, East, and South, at least one large customer is to be found who distributes the products to other sales outlets. These are customarily either wholesalers or large building supply houses. In the Western United States, customers are more numerous and vary more in size. In the Pacific Southwest, and especially in the Los Angeles Metropolitan Area, customers may range in size all the way from large wholesalers and building supply houses to small, independent retailers. At any one time between 100 and 150 customers are in the market for the product of this firm.

The raw materials from which these products are made are castings, steel strip, and steel bars. Foundries in the Los Angeles area are the vendors of the castings. Local steel mills and distributors are the primary vendors of the strip and bars, although Midwestern steel mills are also possible sources of supply.

The organization chart of Figure VI-D-1 is intended to place the firm in perspective with respect to size and complexity. It implies neither the number of people who may actually run this firm in a laboratory or experimental situation nor a final organization structure under which the firm must operate. Similarly, the short financial reports of Figures VI-D-2, VI-D-3, and VI-D-4 are first approximations to the relevant financial data on the operating characteristics of the firm. From these one may get an additional feel for the magnitude of the simulation being taken.

Subsystems of the TMC Simulation

The simulation of the operations of a complete business firm imposes the task of developing idealized representations or models of a number of component subsystems. These include a work force, production facilities, customers, products, raw materials, inventories, accounting systems, credit sources, and so on. The subsystems which comprise TMC are shown in Figure VI-D-5. At the present, only the following models have been programmed, tested, and run: control, sales forecast, production schedule, machines, employees, and production. The remainder of the models are in either the formulation or programming stage. Each of these subsystems is sufficiently general, self-contained, and complete that it can be dealt with as an entity. In a sense, each model of a subsystem is analogous

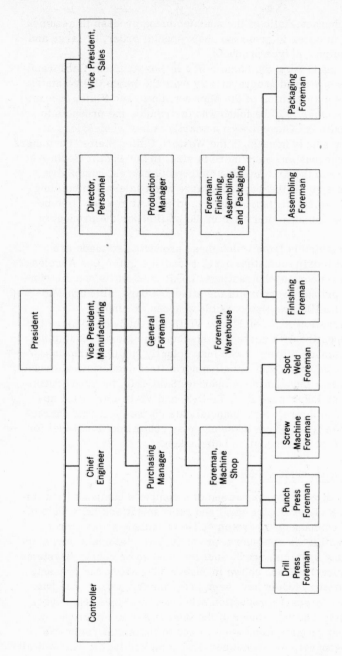

Figure VI-D-1. Organization Chart.

Figure VI-D-2.—Quarterly Balance Sheet

Assets

Current Assets

Cash	100,000	
Marketable Securities	88,000	
Net Receivables	233,094	
Inventories	495,400	
Total Current Assets		916,494

Fixed Assets

Land	36,000	
Buildings and Improvements (depreciated value)	231,900	
Machinery and Equipment (depreciated value) .	359,140	
Office Furniture and Fixtures (depreciated value)	20,000	
Total Fixed Assets		647,040

Deferred Charges

Prepaid Insurance		3,000
Total Assets		1,566,534

Liabilities

Current Liabilities

Notes Payable	0000	
Accounts Payable	94,700	
Accruals	57,318	
Provision for Income Taxes	15,027	
Total Current Liabilities		167,045

Funded Debt

Mortgages (less current year's payments to principal)	175,770	
Total Funded Debt		175,770
Total Liabilities		342,815

Owner's Equities

Capital Stock, common 55,000 shares at $10 par	550,000	
Paid-in Surplus	300,000	
Earned Surplus	373,719	
Total Liabilities and Equities	1,566,534	

Figure VI-D-3. Quarterly Profit and Loss Statement

Gross Sales 623,200
    Deduct Returns and Allowances   5,000
    Discounts on Sales, etc.   12,000
Net Sales 606,200
Cost of Goods Sold 421,918
Gross Profits 184,282

Selling and General Expenses
Selling Expenses   63,925
General and Administrative   71,205
Engineering and Development   16,595
Total Selling and General Expenses   151,725
Net Profit from Operations   32,557
Miscellaneous Expenses   2,503
Net Profit before Extraordinary Charges   30,054
Reserve for Federal and State Income Tax
  @ 50%   15,027
Net Profit to Surplus   15,027

Figure VI-D-4. Quarterly Manufacturing Statement

Primary Materials Consumed
    Beginning Inventory, Primary Materials. . . .   180,000
    Purchases   221,720
    Total Materials   401,720
    Less Ending Inventory.   218,600
Primary Materials Consumed   183,120
Direct Labor   200,018
Total Manufacturing Expense   187,530
Manufacturing Charges for the Quarter   570,668

    Beginning Inventory, Goods in Process   76,000
    Total Goods in Process Handled   646,668
    Less Ending Inventory, Goods in Process   75,000
    Cost of Goods Manufactured   571,668

Add Beginning Inventory, Finished Goods   51,750
Total Finished Goods Available for Sale   623,418
Less Ending Inventory, Finished Goods 201,500
Cost of Goods Sold   421,918

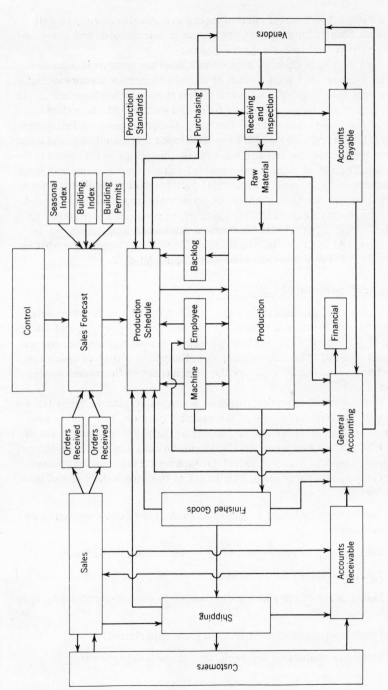

Figure VI-D-5. Subsystems of TMC.

to a "black box" and if certain inputs are specified, outputs will
appear. Some of the outputs are uniquely determined, and some are
determined only in a stochastic sense.

Just as a collection of subsystems does not comprise a business
firm, neither does a collection of models comprise a representation
of a business firm. The subsystems must be coupled together to permit inputs and outputs to come from and exit to both the external
world and other subsystems. Formal policies, managerial decisions,
and informal policies which have developed from customs and traditions determine the ways in which these couplings are allowed to
occur. The set of human and material subsystems and the couplings
conditioned by formal and informal policies comprise the business
firm. Correspondingly, the set of separately programmable models
of subsystems coupled by interconnecting programs comprises a
representation of a business firm—a simulated firm which can be
manipulated on a computer. Some of these interconnections—but by
no means all of them—are shown in Figure VI-D-5.

Present Operation of TMC

There are two definite phases in the operation of the simulating
system. The first corresponds to the function of <u>planning</u> and the second to <u>operation</u>. Both of these phases are dealt with in the earliest
model of TMC. The forecasting model supplies a plan of operation;
the production model supplies the counterpart of the actual operations.

The forecasting model prepares a suggested plan of operation for
each of the thirteen weeks of the ensuing quarter. The plan is prepared on the computer and is subject to the physical constraints of
such things as number of available employees, number of machines,
and cash, and to policy constraints such as hiring, new equipment
purchases, and borrowing. The output of the forecasting model includes:

- Total standard hours required in each of the seven operating departments.

- Number of new employees to be hired in each department.

- Total overtime hours required.

- The number of standard hours needed in each department by type
  of product.

- Total production of each item in each department.

- Total raw materials for each item in each department.

The plan is prepared in the middle of the prior quarter to allow for lead time in ordering raw materials and hiring new employees. The plan comes out in the form of two reports: a departmental breakdown and a product breakdown of all summary data for the week.

The production model consists only of employees and machines at each stage in its development. Employees and machines are in each department, with an employee assigned to operate a specific machine which is assigned to work on one of the five specified products. As of the end of a given operating period, say, a week, each department has a given state with respect to employee-machine-product-operating hours assignments. If none of these is changed, the department operates with the same assignments during the next operating period.

The forecasting model may suggest a different plan of operation for a department than its current state. Putting this plan of operation into effect may involve a change in the machine product assignment, a change in scheduled overtime, the hiring of new employees and their assignments, etc. Such changes are now made by people. The interconnecting link between the forecast plan and the actual production operation—the production schedule—is a human link outside the simulated system. This is done on purpose for two reasons: (1) it provides a means to involve students (the word is used loosely here) in the simulation of the firm from a very early date, (2) it avoids the need for writing a set of complex rules to connect the plan to the actual production operation. In other words, it lessens the task of getting the simulation going by leaving out the hard job of computer programming a complex production scheduling operation.

Students who take the roles of, say, the foremen of the seven operating departments must follow certain policies in making changes. For example, a set of personnel policies is given below. Some of these policies are also constraints on the forecasting model, e.g., G2 and G3.

Example of Personnel Policies

Policy G: Recruitment of New Employees

1. The work force may not be shifted from one department to another. (Exception: individuals may transfer to another department through normal channels.)

2. The work force may not be increased by more than 5 per cent per week in any department.

3. A new employee is to be reckoned as working at 70 per cent of standard productivity for the first four weeks for purposes of planning and budgeting.

4. A new employee is not to be worked overtime for the first four weeks.

Policy H: Overtime Work

1. The maximum overtime that a worker may be employed during a regular weekday is two hours.

2. The pay for overtime shall be one and a half times the pay for the classification.

3. The maximum time a worker may be employed on Saturday is ten hours.

4. The pay for Saturday work shall be one and a half times the pay for the classification.

5. The maximum overtime allowable for a worker is twenty hours per week.

Policy I: Starting a Night Shift

1. Every second shift in a department must be manned by at least three scheduled people. This is to comply with safety rule XXX, which requires at least two workers in any operating department.

2. Three must be scheduled so that in case of absence, two are left. In case of two absences in a three-man crew, the third man is paid for one-half shift and sent home.

3. No new employees are to be placed on the second shift.

4. Premium pay for second shift is 10 per cent of regular pay.

The production schedule suggested by the student operators need not follow the plan suggested by the forecasting model. The plan may call for hiring two new employees without working any overtime. The actual schedule suggested may deviate from this and substitute overtime work as an alternative to the hiring of new employees. One pays a price for either method of operation. New employees are less productive in their early weeks on the job; the overtime pay rate is higher than the regular time rate.

Changes in the schedule of employees and machines are accomplished by a file maintenance on the employee and machine master files. Actual production data simulating the operation of the firm come from running the employee and machine models together with their assignments. The outcomes depend not only on the actual operating plan used, but also on the initial state of the system. At the end of one operating period, a summarizing of the inputs and outputs and the new internal state of the firm influence the planning and operation of the next period. During the operating period, the record files of the firm are updated and at suitable times these files are interrogated for reports which the management desires in order to operate the firm.

An Example of a Subsystem Model

The machine model is an example of one of the subsystems presently in TMC. It is described here in general terms without giving any specific mathematical equations. The term "machine" is used loosely to mean the physical production process in any one of the seven operating departments. In the drill press department, the machine is obviously meant to be a drill press. In the finishing, assembly, and packaging departments, "machine" means only a production process.

A machine is in one of two operating states as of any given time period: broken down or in operating order. If the machine is in operating order, its productive capability is an exponential function, decreasing with time, the parameters of which reflect the following characteristics:

1. Age since purchase.

2. Capabilities when new.

3. Recency of overhaul.

4. Level of production.

5. Immediate mechanical state, which includes:

   • How recently overhauled.

   • Breakdown record.

   • Level of maintenance service.

An overhaul policy governs when a machine which is in operating order is pulled off the production line for an overhaul.

The probability that the machine is not in operating order but is broken down, is a function of:

1. The number of overhauls.

2. The time since last overhaul.

3. Its breakdown history.

The latter is included on the assumption that if a machine initially exhibits frequent breakdowns, this implies some inherent fault in its design or construction which predisposes it to more frequent failures.

All of the machines in the seven operating departments have the same general characteristics. Each is described by a different set of parameter values to distinguish it from other machines with respect to the characteristics listed above. The ease with which these parameters can be changed gives one great flexibility in changing production model characteristics for experimental and educational purposes.

THE FUTURE OF TMC

These first efforts at the simulation of a complete business firm have pointed out the difficulties and obstacles to simulation procedures. However, they have proved reasonably successful and TMC is undergoing a major overhaul in those models already completed. Initially, the amount of detail included was too great. The production process was run daily with the machine model run hourly and the employee model daily. Even for the limited number of models in the simulation, computer time rapidly approaches an upper limit. The first change will be designed to make models run for either one week or one thirteen-week quarter. It appears that this can be accomplished with only parameter changes.

As additional models are added TMC will simulate a complete business firm. All of the subsystems listed earlier will be added.

As efforts in simulating the complete firm continue, we envision many models of component subsystems. Eventually there would be a library of such models available to serve as the building blocks from which a particular system simulating a particular firm may be synthesized. Some of these models may reflect in great detail a theory about the behavior of their real-life counterparts and be useful for testing hypotheses about this behavior. Others may be merely the sampling from distribution functions which appear to reflect real-life data and behavior without any attempt at modeling a theory behind the phenomenon being simulated. Further effort and experience is needed to test an original premise that the simulation of the operations of a complete business firm is a fruitful educational and research undertaking.

Management, engineering, and scientific functions

CHAPTER **E** by HAROLD O. DAVIDSON

In view of the interest in management control systems, it seems appropriate to offer some views on the nature of the management function which the control systems are to support. In my opinion it is essential that we look at the control problem in this context in order to guide research along productive lines. To most of us the simulation and synthesis of management control systems is a fascinating challenge. It is but a slightly explored area insofar as the techniques now coming to hand are concerned. But there have been earlier explorers and quite a few have left their bones on the field. In fact, there have been organized parties in or near this field continuously for the past eighty years, and most of them have perished.

There are only a few survivors left of the "Scientific Management" party, which came upon hard times because it understood too little of science. If misfortune comes upon the presently active "Management Science" group it will be, I predict, because it understood too little of management. Among some members of this group, the "executive" has already slipped away into a dim abstraction—a little black box concept called "decision maker." The object of their activities is a "decision model" that will make the little black box work better; or, in more general terms, it is the replacement of a tottering subjective decision-making process with a scientific hypothesis testing type of process.

To reach this point we must make the implicit assumption, which is both naive and conceitful, that the particular form of rationality

333

that has proven effective in scientific endeavor is also the most appropriate for other human endeavors. Moreover, to account for the present state of affairs we would seem to need a further assumption that executives have not been sufficiently intelligent to appreciate this and must therefore be helped.

I find it more plausible to consider that a good deal of superior intelligence has been at work in the executive function. Perhaps it is a different kind of intelligence than "scientific" intelligence, but I doubt this. It has, however, been directed to different purposes and it has, I am convinced, developed rational concepts of operation that are particularly effective for these purposes.

Thus, what executives want of science is not an instruction in the virtues of scientific methodology but the applied results of scientific inquiry. To transfer this benefit, an appreciation of the management function and its rationality is required. It is also necessary to restore discarded details in translating back from scientific generalizations in order that they may have suitable correspondence to a specific reality. This is precisely the function of engineering. To put it another way: the scientist who wants to be directly helpful to executives had better learn to "act like" an engineer. I use the phrase "act like" for the particular reason that it leads into the main line of my argument.

It is elementary to suggest that inquiry into the nature of the management function begins properly with observing the behavior of people who perform this function. If we also observe behavior in engineering and scientific activities and seek to identify the ways in which they differ, I believe we will be on the way to useful understanding. I propose that when we do this sort of thing we will find some of the commonly presumed characteristics to be useless as differentiating variables. The subjectivity-objectivity contrast that is sometimes supposed to exist between executives and scientists appears unsupportable. Subjective judgments are found to be dominant in the creative phase of scientific activity. And if we discount the influence of exterior discipline imposed by international criticism of published work, it appears that scientists as a group are probably not more objective than executives.

Some interesting and significant differentiations are possible, however, if we consider characteristics that I have called the environment coupling of behavior and the time coupling (see Figure VI-E-1). When we look at what a scientist does we find that the activity is directed toward abstraction from the specific environmental data of his research to the highest possible degree of generalization; and so we would say that in science there is a low degree of environment coupling. The broader the generalization, the

greater its scientific importance will be, and the lower the environment coupling. We would find also that the connection of the scientist's activities to deadlines is highly elastic. Perhaps the simplest
definition we can give of pure science (a partial one, of course) is:
no deadlines. So we would characterize scientific activity in the
lower left of the "coupling" space.

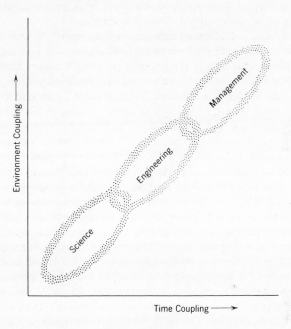

Figure VI-E-1.

If we then look at engineering activities we find a higher degree of
environment coupling. An engineer is not interested in thermodynamic
theory as an abstraction. He is concerned with its particularization to
the design of a specific power plant at a specific site to meet a peak
power demand of so many kilowatts. He is also time coupled to a
much higher degree than the scientist. He must have his plans ready
on a certain date to go out for bid. Within that period he has some
flexibility in the use of his time from day to day, but he must schedule
toward the deadline.

The executive is highly environment coupled. He is concerned with
influencing the crucial vote on his board to win approval for investment in the new plant that his engineering staff is designing. In general, he takes the economic and physical particularizations worked
out by his staff and adds to them the political, social, and individual

specifics. He sets the engineer's plans into the action context. His appointment calendar suggests the high time coupling of the management function.

The apparently high degree of correlation between environment and time coupling suggests that I have merely chosen two somewhat different ways of saying the same thing. In trying to find out what that "thing" is my introspection leads me back to the fundamental objectives of these functions. What are they?

I find a quite satisfactory answer for "science" by tracing the word back to its Latin root—Scientia, "Knowing." It is very interesting, I think, that this is the present participle rather than the noun. It is a simple, elegant statement of a noble objective. It seems shameful that it should have been contaminated by so much sloppy usage in recent years. ("Applied Science" sounds a bit vacuous if one translates back to "Applied Knowing.")

There are, of course, some special requirements for knowing as science, as against knowing in the usual sense. I mentioned previously the importance of subjective judgment in science. The whole progress of science depends, in fact, upon the willingness of men with great insight to announce conjectures on the basis of subjective validity. However, the rules of science prohibit the acceptance of any structure erected on conjectures until the formal objective processes have converted the conjecture into a scientific conclusion. In the case of some famous mathematical theorems it has taken hundreds of years for the formal processes to establish the validity of the original insight in an acceptable fashion. To make matters worse, mathematicians occasionally decide to "tighten up" the rules and then some theorems have to be proven all over again. I make this remark to bring out the point that the formal objectivity of scientific activity is not an absolute concept but is defined by rules agreed upon by scientists in the field as being appropriate. Since rules are simply a means of sorting "good" ideas from "bad" ones, and since "good" ideas foster development of a field whereas "bad" ones inhibit it, we may conclude that appropriate rules are those which at any given time tend to maximize the progress of a science.

The obvious implication of this is that different fields of science may have different rules. And we can see clearly that the rules are in fact different on comparing the broad fields of mathematical, physical, biological, and behavioral sciences. There should be a very strong expectation, then, that other kinds of activities, such as engineering, have still different rules appropriate to their operations. And this also turns out to be true.

The function of engineering is the design or planning for solutions of particular problems. The rules which prescribe appropriate engineering behavior are markedly different from those of science. The difference is much greater than it seems to be in the popular, but erroneous, conception of engineering following along in the footsteps of scientific advances. In reality, the reverse is more often true. The accomplished engineering fact provides a powerful stimulus to scientific inquiry. James Watt's engines were already a commercial product and their designer was dead when Carnot formulated the beginnings of heat engine theory.

Engineering does not defer its progress until the ground ahead has been fully prepared by scientific inquiry. It moves whenever there is a practical need and when technical insight suggests that the chance of success is sufficiently good. And this insight, like scientific conjecture, typically surges ahead of the formal scientific development. Here, then, is another reason for saying that "applied science" is an inadequate as well as inappropriate term for engineering. This is not to deny the dependence of engineering on formal science. There is a limit to this "forward reaching" such that until scientific inquiry has built a foundation under the steps already taken, further engineering progress is increasingly inhibited.

The terminal product of a scientific inquiry is generally the published communication of results to the scientific community at large. The terminal product of engineering on the other hand is an implemented plan or design. We can imagine, then, that the mutual interactions between engineering and the management function must be equally important and far more personal than those with scientific activities. The mutuality of the interactions needs some special emphasis, for there seems to be a tendency toward the one-way flow conception. The dependence of engineering on science, for example, is quite widely accepted (if not understood); whereas the suggestion of a reverse flow of stimulus is often received as a novel idea (though it is not really obscure). I feel that there is a similar tendency among technical people to undervalue the usefulness of mutual interaction with management in enabling the engineering function to perform effectively. I sense something of this conception when I hear operations research people speaking of "problem solving _for_ executives," but rarely mentioning how much of the total problem the executive had to solve. I wonder then whether there was effective interaction and, if not, how much more difficult was the executive's task for lack of it.

If problem solution is defined as the accomplishment of a change in operating results the joint nature of the endeavor is inescapable. Technical knowledge must be joined to operational insights and appreciation of policy and other constraints. The executive role is again significant in the evaluation of alternatives because of the inability of formal methodology to get at the multi-dimensionality of "value".

This, at least, is my present judgment, for I have yet to see convincing evidence in the operations research literature or elsewhere that any of the formalistic devices for operating on lower-order subjective judgments led to better results than a subjective synthesis at the executive level.

This subjective synthesis is one of the crucial roles of management and I think it would help us a great deal in the development of management control systems if we could learn more about it. I am persuaded that these endeavors will be successful to the extent of helping executives to increase effectiveness of the process. An infinite optimism would be required, however, to support anticipation of its replacement by a formalized methodology. I base this conviction on several considerations.

There is first to be taken into account the power of intuitive processes. By these processes and with an algebraic notation that was clumsy in comparison to what was later available, Fermat arrived at some remarkable mathematical theorems. To reconstruct these theorems by formal processes so that they could be considered rigorously proved required a much greater volume of effort by some of the world's most skillful mathematicians. It is certainly true that the initial insights were not rigorously supported. For the purposes of mathematical science it was probably worth the expenditure of effort and passage of time (several hundred years) for some of these theorems to be proved. But the engineering and management functions have different purposes, and there are other ways of buying the kind of practical validity that is required. If a certain yet-to-be-proved theory should appear useful for the design of, say, a missile, the engineer uses it to design, build, and test one. A successful flight might or might not be rigorous proof for correctness of the theory, but it would provide practical assurance that a missile designed and constructed in that particular way could fly.

The point has been made that formal methodology can buy rigor. It should be mentioned that this rigor is internal only. If the assumptions are wrong, the answer is wrong even though rigorously derived. The mathematician himself is haunted by this problem, for he has been unable to establish, except by faith, a number of primitive assumptions on which all of mathematics hangs. Perhaps to make the faith easier these assumptions are called axioms.

The formalist has learned to keep himself happy by living within his axioms, and finding aesthetic pleasure in the pursuit of internal rigor. The engineer and executive must live with results. Competitive pressure to improve results works against the hope of raising assurance out of the subjective realm and, in fact, puts a premium on the sensitive feel for trade-off of assurance against time and effort.

All experience indicates that there is a trade-off as indicated by the heuristic equation:

$$\underline{R} = \underline{T}\underline{E}$$

where $\underline{R}$ is rigor, $\underline{T}$ is time, and $\underline{E}$ is effort (perhaps roughly measured in dollars). It is impossible to make a decision without playing the trade-off. The scientist plays conservatively. The engineer will take less primary assurance, but usually buys some secondary assurance with a "safety factor," which is often cheaper. The executive must play aggressively without a safety factor. But he has in many instances the unique advantage that the effect of decision quality on the ultimate payoff is considerably modified by other factors.

The executive who mischances to make only a fair decision but implements it skillfully and vigorously may still best the competitor who makes a superior decision but defaults on implementation. In fact, skill in selecting the superior alternative is probably of lesser importance than organization skill, a sense of decision timing, and an ability for vigorous implementation. A man with these talents can apply the resources of many more intellects than his own in accomplishing the selective act of decision making. He can, in other words, create a decision process to which he mainly contributes the timing and the "maintenance" effort to keep the process operating effectively.

The suggestion is before us then that management is not a simple function, but is perhaps better described as a complex of functions requiring some rather impressive executive talents. The end objective of management is, of course, not simply the making of decisions nor even the making of good decisions, but the achievement of practical results. Managements are not judged on the number of decisions made, or on the quality distribution of decisions. Managements that get results are not called upon to justify their decisions, while managements that do not produce are not given the opportunity to explain. Evaluation by results is the only sound principle, even though in the actual application the tendency is to emphasize present results with insufficient allowance for the expectation of future results arising from present actions and long-range planning.

The importance of long-range planning is intensified by technological change and associated economic factors and this is reflected, I think, in corporate organization changes and allocations of resources. While the general subject of long-range planning is beyond our present interest, it is here that the interrelationships of scientific, engineering, and management functions can be seen in a useful perspective. It is a perspective from which we may wish to view our own activities as they contribute to the process of change that presents management with its planning problem.

I shall refer to another heuristic diagram, Figure VI-E-2, which

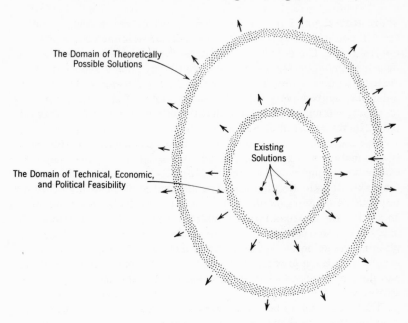

The Domain of Theoretically Possible Solutions

Existing Solutions

The Domain of Technical, Economic, and Political Feasibility

Figure VI-E-2.

may help in visualizing the important relationships. I conceive of management in its operating role directing attention to maximizing the output of "existing solutions." Since I am not now concerned with current operating problems I show the existing solutions as static points. They are static in the "System Configuration" sense. The near-future possibilities for improvement of results lie within what I call the domain of technical, economic, and political feasibility. (I am using "political" in a broad sense to include basic corporate policy as well as external feasibility constraints such as tax law, etc.) The boundary of the feasibility domain is shifting and never precisely defined. In military weapons development, for example, we are pressing against this uncertain boundary—forcing it to yield. In industrial development it is rarely economic to expend the resources and energy necessary to force it, though we generally want to work close to it.

This means that we want to locate the boundary as well as possible and attempt to predict how it will shift so that the near-future solu-

tions will have "growth potential." Accordingly, we must look beyond the feasibility domain to the domain of theoretically possible solutions. The mapping of this domain is possible because of scientific
activity. The actual formulation of possible solutions to specified
practical problems is an engineering type of activity because the
statements of scientific results do not appear in this form. (We are
speaking here of a creative engineering activity that lies at the "near
science" end of the engineering spectrum, and which in actuality is
probably occupied by more science trained than engineering trained
people. Perhaps this is why many prefer to call it "applied science.")

The concern of science is with pushing out the boundary of this
domain, which it does by conjecturing something beyond it and devising ways of testing the conjecture. It would appear then that long-
range planning operates in the region of possibility beyond current
feasibility, and that one of its special tasks is to take note of scientific advances and interpret their significance to the enterprise. Long-
range planning must surely do this, but it will be inefficient if it does
only this, for the feasibility boundary is crucial to the long-range
planning. Every long-range plan must become a near-future plan
(i.e., come within the feasibility boundary) or there is no use having
it. It is part of the planning job to clearly identify the engineering,
economic, and political barriers to feasibility; to estimate the time
and cost of removing them; and to develop specific strategies for
attaining feasibility.

In military research and development this has typically been the
least adequately performed phase of planning. Underestimates of time
and effort to reduce feasibility barriers have been a predominant
characteristic. In some instances the "new solution" came too late to
be of much operational value. A failure to consider feasibility barriers other than technical can have much the same result. It is worth
noting, therefore, that there are some problems for which much better solutions than those currently employed are both technically and
economically feasible but as yet politically unfeasible. Population
control is such a problem. There are many others. Operations research must also be cognizant of the "feasibility boundary." A major
problem is to demonstrate effective methods for reducing these barriers. In my opinion, the reduction of many feasibility barriers depends upon the application of executive skills and energies; I use
this in further support for my emphasis on engineering-management
interaction, and for the proposition that "problem solving" is a joint
activity.

It has not seemed necessary to point these remarks in the specific
direction of our immediate interest in management control systems.
Most of the implications are quite readily derived. There is, however,

one speculative suggestion of possible things to come that does not emerge from the preceding discussion. The computer simulation technique, while not unique to control system research, will undoubtedly be a major research tool in this field. It will also be a control system design tool. And it will also be used by executives in increasing understanding of operations and their control, and in studying future alternatives. Heretofore, each of these functions has employed widely differing kinds of techniques. May the scientist now find it easier to explain his research to an executive because his technique is one that the executive has himself employed? Might it be that common use of the simulation technique for the various uses of each function will be a point of contact through which manager, engineer, and scientist will each gain a better understanding of the others' functions?

DISCUSSION   (Following Dr. Davidson's presentation of his paper)

M. O. KAPPLER: Do you see any reason not to do both the scientific and engineering activities? At SDC we have people oriented in both areas.

H. O. DAVIDSON: No. There may, in fact, be an advantage. If you have the capability for both scientific research and engineering design on control systems, and can keep the distinction clearly in mind, I believe there is an advantage in carrying out both functions in a single organization. The engineering activity produces results that stimulate further research.
I believe Roger Sisson pointed out that it would be regrettable to direct all effort in the engineering activity and neglect the scientific research.

D. G. MALCOLM: I took some of your earlier remarks to indicate that we aren't really prepared to build a model of management. Perhaps we have to operate in the engineering realm on something that can be observed—on subsystems—before we can tackle the modeling job.

H. O. DAVIDSON: Scientific study of management can be done now— but one really has to go out and study management, not sit back and say: "Let's write some equations about management." We need to observe the real phenomena much better than we have. The building of "models" in an observational vacuum may lead to some interesting and worthwhile mathematics but it has no necessary connection with management.

R. L. SISSON: However, you have to retain scientific detachment and truly observe what occurs and not be swayed because you happen to know that the manager that you are observing can talk back.

A. J. ROWE: Rather than proposing to work in either the science or engineering areas, I think management controls research at SDC will straddle the fence. We will be doing abstraction and will certainly not be trying to solve specific problems. We are trying to learn more about the behavior of business systems. To this extent we may be acting as scientists. But, on the other hand, we probably will be looking at real systems; in this case, we may be doing more of a design function.

H. F. DICKIE: I would like to see a symbol connecting management to that common area between engineering and science from which we might expect to receive these new ideas.

A. W. RATHE: Does this sort of reasoning indicate that there is no such person as a management scientist?

H. O. DAVIDSON: A "scientific manager" is probably nonsense, but there could be a "management scientist"—a man who attempts to know about management.

W. E. ALBERTS: This management scientist may still be in the embryo stage.

J. D. GALLAGHER: According to John Lubin many managers are designing in that sense.

A. SCHULTZ: I would like to reinforce several ideas and perhaps refute something which I feel is being conceded here. I am concerned about the discussion of constructing a model. I cannot conceive of a management control systems model any more than I can conceive of an electronics control systems model which has anything more than the grossest conceptual value. I am trying to be rather precise in making suggestions; therefore, one of the first steps that appears appropriate in management control research is to study the organism and its structure. We may be dealing with a series of structures, if you will. We keep coming back to the personnel organization itself. We are also very much concerned with certain aspects of the informational flow in an organization. This is now assuming a structure far more concrete than it had ever had before; however, of much more importance is that one is still clearly allied to the other. We are also concerned with what I have often called the physical structure of the organization or business, which is of course directly related to the primary function or reasons for the organizations's existence.

Companies such as SDC operating in air defense have objectives and inputs which are very clearly defined; and, I might add, relatively deterministic. In the business systems which Roger Sisson described the objectives are much more loose and relaxed. We might even consider a whole series of industrial and business examples—some of these have been mentioned (the difficulty of contrasting an insurance corporation with a manufacturing business or with an airline—these are all quite different).

For almost a generation many of us have been verbally beating around the systems design concept. Whether we speak of electronic systems designers or industrial designers, we use the same words, and in the qualitative sense these people are reproducing what one might term the enlightened industrial engineering designs of the recent past.

On the other hand, it seems that there really is some significant asset in the ability to take complex information systems and operate on these with mathematical or other devices of the electronic engineer. Implicit in this is a method of analysis that to date has been applied to relatively simple information systems, not the complex ones. It seems to me that this method in alliance with the knowledge of the computer and the simulation methods are extremely important assets. It is wonderful to find the possibility of a significant effort putting these assets together on this problem.

I would like to support what Alan Mann said. We can see what is happening to our economy, what foreign countries are doing. Studies made in technological development abroad reveal some interesting facts. There is evidence of this development in Russia, but the whole world is involved in this progress. If we are to maintain some relative degree of leadership in the area of technological development, some major breakthroughs are required. I think SDC's research project is most important in providing this leadership.

J. BECKER: Returning to our earlier discussions, more than any other, the word "information" has threaded its way through. There seems little doubt that information is the key ingredient for better management control.

In handling information for the military, SDC has acquired a rich and rather unique experience. Information has been used in conventional ways as well as in real time, bringing the best of both to bear in the solution of a specific problem. The application of computers in the military area has been wise—considering them extensions of human skills rather than as cure-alls designed to usurp management's responsibility.

Information, in all of its aspects, needs to be carefully and deeply examined in the business environment. Information theory, information handling, and the identification of the information variables which contribute to the decision-making process all deserve formal treatment and additional fundamental research in the field of management control.

A. J. ROWE: I agree that the study of information flow is important, but unfortunately this can't be studied in a vacuum. If you talk about information for decision making, you have to know something about decision making. If you are going to talk about information for operating procedures, you have to know something about operating procedures. Thus, rather than abstract information from the body of a business system, it should be treated as an integral part.

M. G. HOLMEN: As Warren Alberts indicated, half of what we are talking about is management information systems. "Management controls" has been used in the sense that implies some sort of levers of management as opposed to getting information. Maybe Warren can give us a word for that half of the job, too. There is considerable semantic difficulty in discussions and in doing research on these problems.

D. G. MALCOLM: One of the important contributions of research in this area is that new concepts and new languages will be developed. Concerning the direction research should take, I would say this: There has been a tremendous amount of guidance from qualified experts. The job now is to distill the essence from these discussions and proceed with the research.

A SCHULTZ: A number of people have questioned industrial cooperation. It would appear desirable to state that we as a group were heartily in favor of this research and would pledge ourselves to cooperate in this venture, and would recommend that others do this as well because of the long-range benefits to the community of a program of this nature.

D. G. MALCOLM: I think we have felt from time to time from every person here that there was a serious interest in this kind of research.

R. L. SISSON: Two problems seem to arise frequently:

1. Management oriented people think the scientifically oriented people are impersonal in their approach.

2. There is a feeling that the researcher might usurp the manager's responsibility by creating his own management control system.

I believe Hal Davidson's diagram* provides answers to both of these related topics.

There is confusion on the first point because managers think of actual management situations which are far from impersonal. The scientists on the other hand consider a subject of study—like a thermodynamic system—only in this case it happens to be a management system. The fact that there are people in the latter system and not in the former is trivial; the scientist must act as if he can quantify and measure his subject matter to the extent it influences his area of interest; even when the subject matter includes humans. The scientist, then, does look at management systems as impersonal entities, not only because he is unaware of the complexity of humans, but because it is only in this way that he can create models useful in his studies. (As we note below, managers do not have to sue the scientist's results, if they think too many human factors are left out.)

The difference of point of view just discussed stems from the confusion of the role of the scientist and the engineer. This confusion also results in the second problem. A manager is responsible for his system. On the other hand, a scientist should not care whether his results are useful or not (to a manager or anyone else). The fact that a scientist is working on describable systems which are couched in management terms should not lead one to feel he is necessarily solving management problems. He is solving interesting puzzles—interesting in themselves, but perhaps more so than other puzzles because they do come from the real world. The scientist's duty is only to explain and disseminate his results—not to implement them.

It is management's job to implement a system. To do this he wishes (or should wish) to use the results of any applicable research. A manager often employs an engineer as a staff assistant to translate research (and also rule-of-thumb experience) into the needs of his specific situation. Thus, if a manager does not have a proper tech-

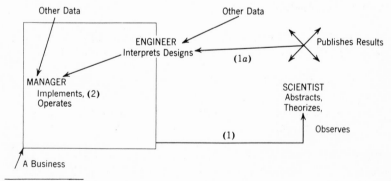

*Figure VI-E-1.

nical understanding he may find the engineer installing systems
which he does not want. The manager still has the responsibility; he
may have used the research wrongly due to his own or his engineer's
bad judgment. But, in no case is the research or the researcher to
blame; he offers generalities; the manager makes his own specifics.
The illustration above summarizes the comments just made. The scientist can observe and impersonalize anything he cares to (1). The
manager does not have to use the results [(1a) is optional]. A manager
looses his authority to design his system only through his own default
(2).

These problems, (1) and (2), remain in practice only because one person can play several of these roles. A few managers are engineers. A
very few are scientists. Many management system engineers also participate in management. Many scientists (e.g., operations researchers) are also often engineers. To avoid confusion, we should all state
which hat we are wearing at a given time.

I hope that research in Management Control Systems will be in scientific research. If from time to time researchers act as engineers
for some agency or activity, these efforts should have an appropriately different objective, which should be clearly stated. Finally, research results should be published without thought as to specific use.

SUMMARY

SECTION **VII**

Research and development in management controls— a discussion

CHAPTER **A** by DONALD G. MALCOLM and ALAN J. ROWE

D. G. MALCOLM: Our objective here is to explore what is involved in developing a new management control approach and what constitutes an effective research program.

M. O. KAPPLER: I would like to say a few words concerning management controls as an area of research. First, we at SDC have speculated about what a reasonable level of support for such research should be. At this point, an expenditure of, say, a quarter of a million dollars during the first year, and then something on the order of a half-million to three-quarters of a million dollars in the ensuing years would seem appropriate. The research in management controls could be continued fairly indefinitely and operate at about the above scale, providing it is worth doing.

W. R. FAIR: How do you review the research and determine whether it is appropriate?

M. O. KAPPLER: I would not be inclined to say, "Let's do research for a year and then switch it off." I think you would agree that any research requires continual monitoring rather than frequent justifying.

N. J. REAM: I thought John Lubin raised a most interesting question when he said that none of us really knows what constitutes management. Peter Drucker touched upon this a few years ago when he said we have never developed a discipline of management. We talk

about the interactions of management; however, we should also give
serious consideration to the outer actions of management. I will define outer actions by saying that we live in a world where we have
(referring to Drucker) a macro-micro economic structure; the
micro-economic unit is the business itself and the macro-economic
structure is the government.

Now, before building a model of a business or getting into detailed
data-processing systems, our first efforts must be to determine all
of the factors that influence management. After all, in developing
management information systems we are trying to furnish information to management to better plan, operate, and control business. If
we don't know all the factors that influence management, I don't think
we can develop a system that will furnish the appropriate information.
Therefore, a great deal of research effort can be devoted both to defining what management does and to defining all the factors that influence management in the decision-making processes.

G. O. PEHRSON: Is this top level in management, or does management run through from top to the bottom?

N. J. REAM: I think, initially, our concern would be the requirements at the top.

R. C. SPROWLS: Simulation has been mentioned as a tool of management controls research. I believe that there is real hope for successful simulation in this research. The point was made earlier that
the manager today is not operating in the real world; he is operating
on an abstraction. Well, if he really is operating on an abstraction,
does it make much difference whether he has real people, machines,
physical plant, and products, or merely simulations of these? I believe that the various subsystems of a business firm can be modeled
with computer programs and that these can be linked together both
with people—which is what we have in the real world—and with other
computer programs reflecting company policies and environment.
The manager of the simulated firm can be put into situations similar
to those he faces in the real world. This is what Professor Asimow
and I are attempting at UCLA.

J. D. GALLAGHER: Concerning the role of the manager, Drucker
refers to disciplines in business—the factors that affect the conduct
of an enterprise. He doesn't refer to a series of restraints that you
have to operate within.

A. W. RATHE: How can management ever achieve the obligations of
a profession if it isn't backed up by one or several disciplines?

I. KESSLER: I would question whether management should be considered a profession. A profession presumes standards; it presumes that someone is qualified to establish the standards, and that the standards qualify the practitioner.

D. G. MALCOLM: It seems to me that, over the long run, if the individual who claims to be a manager doesn't measure up to some sine qua non, he isn't a manager very long after that. These standards may not be easily or generally defined but they must exist. In this sense there are certainly management standards. However, it is more difficult to measure performance in regard to the standards.

J. D. GALLAGHER: If management doesn't establish standards over a given period of time, then isn't it true that someone else will?

D. G. MALCOLM: I am certain that in ten or fifteen years we can expect to have a management profession. The real question is: Are the forces here requiring a profession likely to develop?

R. L. SISSON: It seems reasonable to assume that multi-dimensional objectives come from the owners and that the manager is constrained within those boundaries. Under these conditions it is not unrealistic to represent some part of the manager's activity in a model form.

J. M. KIBBEE: The enunciation of principles of good management will not in itself stifle creativity. Using the analogy of a composer, most great composers did study composition and learn rules and principles from which they could then deviate in a creative manner.

D. G. MALCOLM: As I view it, the model is a means for developing operating characteristics of a business system. It is a diagnostic tool primarily designed to find out what happens if we vary the inputs which can be studied.

A. SCHULTZ: One of the prime functions of top management is the design of the organizational structure, and the planning of its operation.

G. O. PEHRSON: Every manager is in a sense a systems designer, he is a personnel director, he is a budget man. The only reason for classifying these various staff jobs is to provide the manager with some help. In a similar manner, over the years, various specialists have attempted to assist managers to perform more effectively. In the thirties, "Personnel" was a field that attracted many competent people. They were followed by organization and methods people. The budget analysts used to be men who acquired considerable knowledge about programs. Then, there came the accountant in a new staff role. Now, we have electronic data-processing people. Well, these ascending and breaking waves of staff influence are good. Enthusiasm is necessary in these staff fields, but they never are completely out of control of management.

A. O. MANN: I would like to make some observations on the subjects of objectives, implementation, and equipment requirements. It seems to me that we are all deeply concerned with the lag of information handling behind the technological developments and population growth in the world around us. I sincerely think that each of us, down deep within, feels concern for what this worsening lag may mean.

The five system efforts with which I have been associated all failed to achieve integration of the total information handling system within the total organization. This is a must which is not being achieved as yet in the business world, where concern for the short-term dollar gain takes precedence over the long-term conceptual solutions. Thus, I think it is a gift of providence that SDC is taking an initiative at this time with research toward the solution of problems which businesses seem unable really to solve.

It seems essential that we pre-establish with some degree of accuracy what will be the technological capabilities and structure of the electronic equipments in future time, when simulations and research have established a clearer and more ordered concept of the management control system. Of course, the control system research may well disclose new needs for new concepts and developments in the equipment area but we cannot wait for such disclosures exclusively. Otherwise, our simulations might be somewhat misleading, geared as they would be to present capabilities of present hardware on which we run them.

Historically, our prime limitation in the development of data-processing systems has been based on existing concepts and hardware, with the inherent capabilities in the state of the art constantly forging out ahead of our ability to use those capabilities. This trend is getting worse, not better.

It seems to me that the equipment we use in our simulations is characteristically less in capabilities than the true needs of those who perform the simulations.

Roger Sisson predicted yesterday the increase in the percentages of automated management control activities that he thinks will occur as a result of the technological developments in the next ten years, and that this might well occur within five years or less. I lean to the shortened estimate—the "less than five years" part of it.

So not only are we confronted with the simulation of the management control aspects themselves but also with the attempted prediction and simulation of the equipments with which we will be handling our controls some years hence—with the future machine portion of our

future man-machine relationships. We need better conceptual formulation in the equipment field than we have had in the past.

There are strong indications that the equipment portions of future
systems will move over from the free enterprise sale of products to
the publicly regulated rental of facilities and services. I think it ex-
temely important that some initial research be directed toward con-
firming the likelihood of this occurring. If this does occur, it will
make major, perhaps even startling, changes in the economic and
sociological environment in which future management control systems will have to operate. It may also radically increase the scope of
application of the management control system even to include the
smaller businesses, and perhaps even the individual householders or
families—the public at large.

M. O. KAPPLER: Were you thinking of a public utilities service
that one could subscribe to like a telephone?

A. O. MANN: Yes, I sense that, more rapidly than we think, this is
already taking place. But more is needed than just my individual
opinion.

W. E. ALBERTS: There are several companies that have plans for
specific industries. Are you thinking of it in a much broader scale
ultimately?

A. O. MANN: Yes, and with speed. It took only thirteen years for the
American Telephone Company to change the telephone business from
free enterprise to public utility.

A. J. ROWE: As an example of this trend, a computer has been installed in Wall Street, to process transactions for a larger number
of brokers.

D. G. MALCOLM: Roger Sisson talked about total automation as being economically feasible, and said that we are about one-sixth of the
way toward reaching this at present. He didn't say how long it would
take, however. Are you saying that in five to ten years we will be at
the point where it is economically feasible?

A. O. MANN: No. Rather, that the trend line to total automation may
turn up more sharply and sooner than we think.

W. E. ALBERTS: The point concerning specifications for the future
equipment that will provide the nucleus of communication, management control systems simulation is highly significant. Our station
simulation model at United Air Lines now is five years old. At the
time of its installation we indicated a need for a combination of the
digital and analog computer. To my knowledge nothing happened. At

the same time, we asked "Will you please develop input-output devices." We even provided the specifications for two of the stages. The
equipment is just now becoming available.

M. O. KAPPLER: We are planning to have such a device here at SDC.
We will install a computer and build digital-analog input and output.
We are thinking of using it in an experimental facility, where you
could set up an experiment and go through the analog and digital machine and back out. This would provide a general-purpose simulation
facility centered on a digital computer with an integral analog machine.

Concluding remarks

CHAPTER **B** by WILLIAM C. BIEL

Looking into the future, I think that we should emphasize basic research instead of trying to solve the individual and immediate problems of United Air Lines, General Electric, etc. We will certainly not want to ignore the specific problems of one organization or another, but will want to study these in their relation to basic problems of management control.

SDC had its beginnings in a research project; a brief look at the history of our organization will therefore be of interest in light of the present concern with establishing a research project in management control systems.

The RAND Corporation does system studies for the Air Force; these studies assist the Air Force in making long-range planning decisions. In past studies of systems, RAND personnel were confronted frequently with the need for numbers representing human factors in the system. So, in 1951, a small interdisciplinary group was set up for the particular purpose of looking at a system study from a man-machine (human factors) viewpoint. I was a member of that group.

We decided that we couldn't very well study an organization that was operating in real life and exert enough control over the situation to do a proper scientific study. We wanted to control our inputs and vary certain variables as we desired. We decided to limit ourselves to information processing systems because we felt that these were something we could simulate in a laboratory. We also wanted to study a system which had a good criterion of system performance.

We may have been a little "naive" in wanting a single criterion, but as we looked around we found a system with a fairly good one. We knew that the mission of the Aircraft Control and Warning Net of the Air Defense Command was the defense of the continental United States from air attack. So a good criterion was: How many hostile aircraft would get through and bomb their targets? We could also state this in terms of how much damage would be incurred. We had something that was reasonably well packaged.

I could name a whole series of other reasons that led us to select the Aircraft Control and Warning Network as the model to study. We knew we couldn't put the whole Air Defense Command in the laboratory with all its vertical echelons and lateral connections. So we decided to simulate one actual radar site completely, with its operations crew, and to partially simulate three other radar sites that had very close interaction with it. At that time these four sites essentially formed a whole division. We designed a radar console that would give simulated information to the operators. We designed all the rest of the inputs that the crew would normally get and on which they would base their decisions. We simulated peripheral telephone groups like the Civil Aeronautics Authority which called flight plans into the site. We simulated the real geographic area, the airlane traffic, etc. In other words, we built a realistic simulation.

We used a civilian crew to begin with, and were faced with a problem of training this crew before we began to introduce the independent variables that we wished to study. The dependent variables are comparable with many of those that have already been discussed. For instance: What information is transmitted under various load conditions? How do operators change their procedures under changing load conditions?

As part of our experimentation, we deliberately planned to cut telephone lines so things would not operate. We planned to study certain decision-making functions and to put different types of leaders in the system. We tested people for basic capabilities and also observed very carefully how they went through their air defense runs. As a matter of fact, we planned a series of studies with different crews.

In training the first crew, we wanted to get it to a high, stable level of performance before we introduced any experimental changes into the task itself. We found that even with such variables introduced, the level of performance continued to improve in general and reached a level several times higher than that which we had observed in the Air Force field sites which we copied. We thought this was interesting enough to tell the Air Defense Command. Initially, they had not provided us with any personnel or special funding. However, they became

interested and felt that this work had real potential for them in the
area of training. At this point they were willing to send us a crew to
use in the next phase of our research. This was a group of thirty-
nine officers and airmen who had never worked together in an Air
Defense site.

During our experimental periods we obtained some very interesting results about change in communication patterns—about what
things influenced the decisions of the leaders of this small group,
etc. From a training point of view we observed that by providing
appropriate feedback to the leader of the crew and to the crew as a
whole, we obtained significant improvements in operating procedures
and performance.

By that time it was very clear to us and to the Air Defense Command that we ought to do something about adapting our techniques to
their training needs. ADC asked us to see if we couldn't adapt what
we had been doing to make it applicable for training their crews in
the field. We were then asked to start the System Training program
in the manual air defense system. And before long we were involved
in SAGE training and then in SAGE computer programming. At this
point, we were committed to doing an extremely large and complex
job for ADC. Since the nature of this job involved us in helping to
implement an actual system and since the rest of RAND was dedicated
to long-range research, it seemed desirable that we separate from
RAND and become an independent, non-profit corporation. So arrangements were worked out in 1957 for separating SDC from RAND.

In one respect it is unfortunate that the research turned out as
well as it did with its by-product of training, because it led to the
formation of SDC and stopped our original research efforts. In another respect, with the formation of SDC we can now take up some of
the things that we wished to do in 1951.

But the point I want to make is that we have people within the organization who have a background and interest in this whole area of
systems. So, SDC's interest has not just sprung up recently; we were
interested in systems and their organizational problems back in 1951.

One of the concepts which we developed during that time was the
consideration of the organization as an organism. Another was that,
although we talked about research, we also talked about "scientific
search"; we used this term because we weren't convinced that we
were doing research in the traditional textbook form. We didn't have
good control. We didn't have good techniques available to study a
system with people in it.

We tried engineering, mathematical, psychological, and sociological techniques and many others. But we really didn't know what tools
were appropriate to use in studying an organization. We were there-

fore reluctant to call it research and, instead, referred to it as "scientific search" because we were observing the crews in every way we could devise to determine what changes took place. I think we are now back at the point where we can approach the study of systems from several angles. In addition, we will be using several techniques—computer simulation, laboratory simulation with people, etc.

With this background, I think it can be understood why we are interested in management control systems and why we are going to approach them in many different ways. Our research in business management control systems is just one of a number of projects that we hope to have under way in the area of systems.

To assist the conduct of research in these areas, we hope to make a facility available—a computerized simulation laboratory—where we can carry out computer simulation. We might simulate a system and perhaps also simulate the people, so that the non-personal variables can be manipulated, the interactions studied, etc. However, we also hope to make this simulation facility the kind which can be used for a system with either real or simulated gear, and with real crews operating the system. We probably will not always be able to get all of the real gear into the laboratory (for example, a missile). In any case, we could simulate the characteristics, let's say, of the missile, and be able to study effects upon the decisions and inputs to the operators. With real operators in the system we would be studying the man-machine system.

In studying systems in a computerized simulation laboratory, we would have to simulate interactions of the systems with outside environments. In a military system some of these interactions are fully prescribed and we can simulate them very well.

In conclusion, it appears that we have both the background and desire to proceed with research in the area of management control systems.

Index